THE
UNIVERSITY OF WINNIPEG
DISCARDED
WINNIPEG 2 MAN

Ancient Peoples and Places

TARQUINIA AND ETRUSCAN ORIGINS

General Editor

DR GLYN DANIEL

ABOUT THE AUTHOR

Hugh Hencken was educated at Princeton and Cambridge Universities and is Chairman of the American School of Prehistoric Research as well as being Curator of European Archaeology at the Peabody Museum of Harvard University. He has directed excavations in England, Ireland, Morocco and Algeria and has conducted museum research in most of the countries of Europe. In recent years this has been concentrated in Italy and related areas.

Ancient Peoples and Places

TARQUINIA

AND ETRUSCAN ORIGINS

Hugh O'Neill Hencken

173 PHOTOGRAPHS
45 LINE DRAWINGS
5 MAPS

London
THAMES AND HUDSON

THIS IS VOLUME SIXTY-TWO IN THE SERIES
Ancient Peoples and Places
GENERAL EDITOR: DR GLYN DANIEL

FIRST PUBLISHED 1968
PRINTED IN HOLLAND
BY KONINKLIJKE DRUKKERIJ G.J.THIEME N.V., NIJMEGEN

CONTENTS

ILLUSTRATIONS

PLATES

Preface

THIS VOLUME is a brief summary of a larger work in two volumes called *Tarquinia, Villanovans and Early Etruscans* published by the Peabody Museum of Harvard University as Bulletin 23 of the American School of Prehistoric Research. There full details, acknowledgements, illustrations and references will be found, but here I would like to thank the Superintendents of Antiquities in Rome and Florence and their staffs for giving me every facility for a prolonged and exhaustive study of this very important material.

NOTE ON MUSEUMS

The grave groups from the Eastern Cemeteries of Tarquinia are for the most part in the Museo Archeologico, Florence; much smaller amounts are in the museums at Ancona, Este, Siena and the University of Milan. Other material formerly in the Museo L. Pigorini in Rome has been transferred recently to the Palazzo delle Scienze, Rome.

The material referred to in this book from Monterozzi is largely in the Museo di Villa Giulia, Rome, and the Museo Nazionale, Tarquinia, though here the grave groups have not been kept intact as units. The Warrior's Tomb from Monterozzi was, before the Second World War, in Berlin; according to my latest information at least some of the objects are now in the Staatliche Museen zu Berlin but are not readily accessible.

H. H.

CHAPTER I

Tarquinian Landscape

ANCIENT ETRURIA is the land lying between the Tiber, the Arno and the sea, and its oldest and greatest cities in the heyday of Etruscan civilization were those along the coast, among them Caere, Tarquinia, Vulci, Vetulonia, and Populonia. Veii, also an important centre, was a little way inland. Cities further north or further inland tended to be of later foundation and somewhat more provincial. The economic strength of ancient Etruria lay in large measure in her mineral resources, copper, tin, argentiferous lead, and iron. These ores occur in Elba, in the Colline Metallifere, at Follonica, Massa Marittima and Monte Amiata. In addition there are deposits north of the Arno in the Alpi Apuane, while southward in the Tolfa Mountains near Cerveteri there is some copper. Though Populonia and Vetulonia were nearer to the chief ore deposits, the three great southern coastal cities, Caere, Tarquinia and Vulci, always had a special importance: perhaps like Paris, London and New York, they depended less upon the proximity of raw materials but were essentially centres of communication and trade. Furthermore, they may well have commanded the seaways to the Aegean and the Near East. All these coastal cities except Populonia were placed at a cautious distance from the sea and often on defensible heights as a precaution against naval attack, but the chief centres in historical times also had their own ports directly on the shore. In the forefront of these ancient cities stood Tarquinia. *Fig. 1*

The present town, renamed Tarquinia but formerly known as Corneto, stands on the high spur of a plateau overlooking the sea and the Via Aurelia about 75 km. up the coast from Rome. Though it bears the venerable name, this town is not the site of the old city. It is nevertheless a worthy starting point for *Fig. 2* a visit to the locality, being in itself an ancient place, which has yielded various early remains, while a Villanovan cemetery has also been found at Le Rose a short distance below its main gate. The Museo Nazionale in the fine fifteenth-century Palazzo Vitelleschi contains a magnificent collection from Villanovan and Etruscan burials, and the custodian there has the keys which enables one to visit the painted tombs that are among the finest monuments of the Etruscan past.

These tombs are on the long plateau called Monterozzi upon whose western end the present Tarquinia is perched, and the funerary richness of Monterozzi, which covers all the periods from the Villanovan Iron Age down to the Roman occupation, is due to the proximity of the ancient city of Tarquinia whose desolate site lies on a smaller plateau to the north-east across the valley of the San Savino stream. To the Romans this place was Tarquinii, and to their Etruscan predecessors it was Tarchna or Tarchuna, while in 1763 the English traveller Joseph Wilcox referred to the same spot as Civita Turchino where quantities of ancient remains were found.

In its prime, ancient Tarquinia was said to have been the chief city of the Etruscan league and also one of the largest: it has been called the oldest of all the Etruscan cities and even the mother city of Etruria. In Etruscan traditions preserved by much later classical writers it took its name from Tarchon, the kinsman or deputy of Tyrsenos who in the familiar story of Herodotus led the Etruscan settlers from Lydia. It was also at Tarquinia that the shortlived child-seer Tages sprang from the ploughman's furrow to teach the Etruscans the sacred 'discipline' for divining the will of the gods, while even in Roman times Tarquinia was the seat of the Order of the Sixty Haruspices or diviners. Furthermore only 40 km. up the Marta Valley is Lake Bolsena beside which was the sanctuary of Voltumna, the national shrine of the Etruscans. Hence in Etruscan tradition Tarquinia and its vicinity held a venerable place.

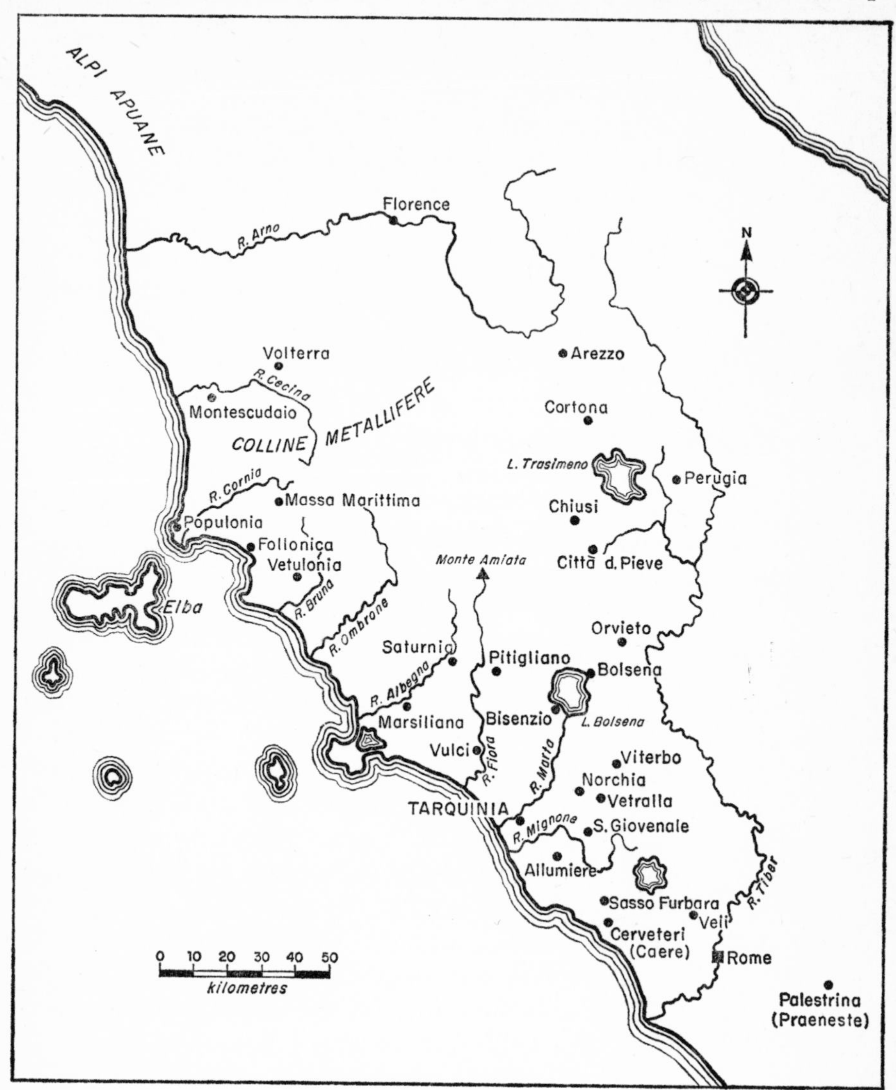

Fig. 1. Map of Etruria

The heart of the ancient city stood on the western part of the plateau, where steep slopes lead up to low cliffs on three sides, and make it a strong defensible position.

Towards the east the plateau narrows to a slim waist, widens again and continues to slope away still further eastwards in an irregular fashion: there on a little knoll are the foundations of an Etruscan temple built in the late fourth or early third century BC.

Also in the fourth or perhaps third Century BC a city wall was added, probably in response to the advancing danger from Rome. This had no towers, but parts of it around the edge of the plateau and also some of its gates are still visible. This wall some 8 km. long embraced not only the city itself but a wide area to the east and even a detached hill some way to the north-east. Its purpose was clearly to take advantage of the hills and slopes to the east of the city where the site was strategically weakest. Since there are few remains in the eastern area, this was presumably given over to orchards, gardens and pastures. In Roman times the city grew eastward, the only direction in which growth was possible, but even the Roman extension occupied only a small part of the area inside the wall. After the coming of Christianity, Tarquinia became the see of a bishop, but the barbarian invasions brought on its decline, and later the Saracens destroyed most of it. In the meantime, Corneto, the modern Tarquinia, was replacing it as the chief town of the region, and the old site was abandoned after a final destruction at the hands of the people of Corneto.

The easiest way down from the ancient Tarquinia is on the eastern side where the slopes are gentler and cliffless, and here beyond the town on a series of knolls and hills were cemeteries of the Villanovan Iron Age. This follows the pattern seen at other Villanovan centres where cemeteries are placed outside the inhabited area on small knolls or hills easily accessible from it. The nearest of the cemeteries to Tarquinia was on the same

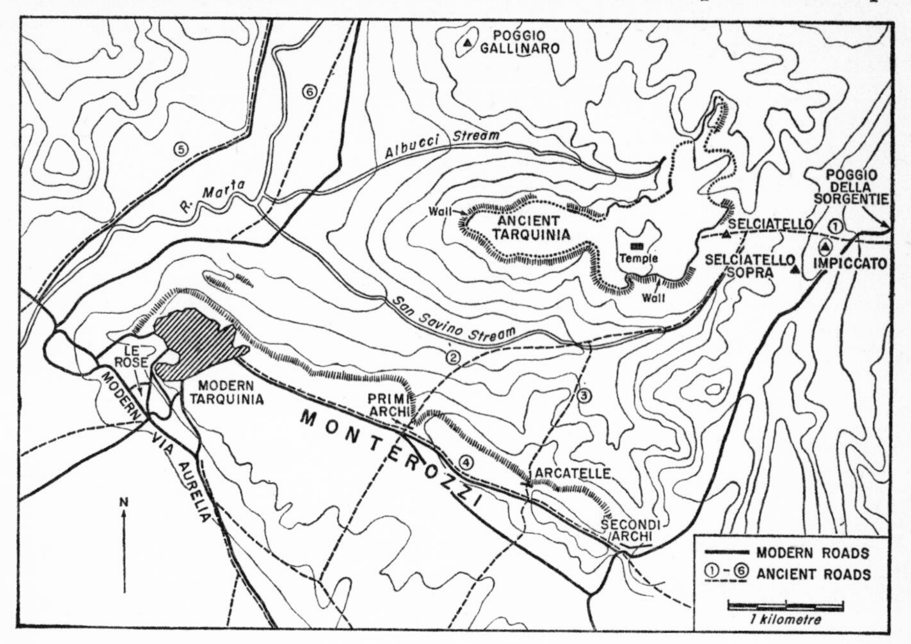

Fig. 2. Map of Tarquinia and vicinity (after Pallottino, Bradford and the Istituto di Geografico Militare)

knoll where the Etruscan temple was later built. This cemetery is only known from broken pottery and debris of graves, and was probably destroyed by the construction of the temple and adjacent Roman buildings.

Still further east and beyond the city wall were other Villanovan cemeteries. Two were on knolls called Selciatello and Selciatello Sopra, and a third lay beyond them on the conspicuous hill called Poggio dell'Impicatto. Selciatello had 78 graves, Selciatello Sopra 204, and Impicatto 110. These three were carefully excavated by Luigi Pernier and form the main basis of this book. During the last war, traces of a fifth cemetery were found still further east when trenches were being dug apparently on the lower slopes of another hill called Poggio della Sorgente. This cemetery has not been further explored. Pernier also excavated a few Villanovan and later graves on the high hill called Poggio Gallinaro north of the ancient city.

Of the three large cemeteries that Pernier excavated, Selciatello, the nearest to the town, was most used early in Villanovan I beginning in the tenth century BC. Selciatello Sopra, further away, was also used early, but its main period was in late Villanovan I ending about 750 BC and also in early Villanovan II, though by the end of Villanovan II about 700 BC it was going out of use. On the other hand the high hill of Impicatto still further away had some graves of all Villanovan phases. But with the end of Villanovan all these cemeteries were virtually abandoned.

Monterozzi, the long plateau with the present Tarquinia on its western tip, has already been mentioned in connection with the painted tombs of the classical Etruscan period. But Monterozzi was also a cemetery from early Villanovan. It may have been the fashionable cemetery from the very beginning, and it certainly became so later, for the tombs of Villanovan II there are richer than any found in the other cemeteries, and in the Orientalizing Period III that followed Villanovan II around 700 BC, almost all burials were concentrated there. Unfortunately the excavations on Monterozzi were far less systematic than those of Pernier, and most of the contents of graves were not kept together. Thus evidence can only be gleaned from old reports and such objects as can still be identified.

Joseph Wilcox in 1763 explains the name of Monterozzi thus. 'This ridge is... almost entirely covered with several hundred artificial hillocks, called by the inhabitants Monti Rossi. About twelve of these hillocks have at different times been opened; and in every one of them have been found several subterraneous apartments cut in the rock.' This account of the former presence of great numbers of tumuli on Monterozzi has

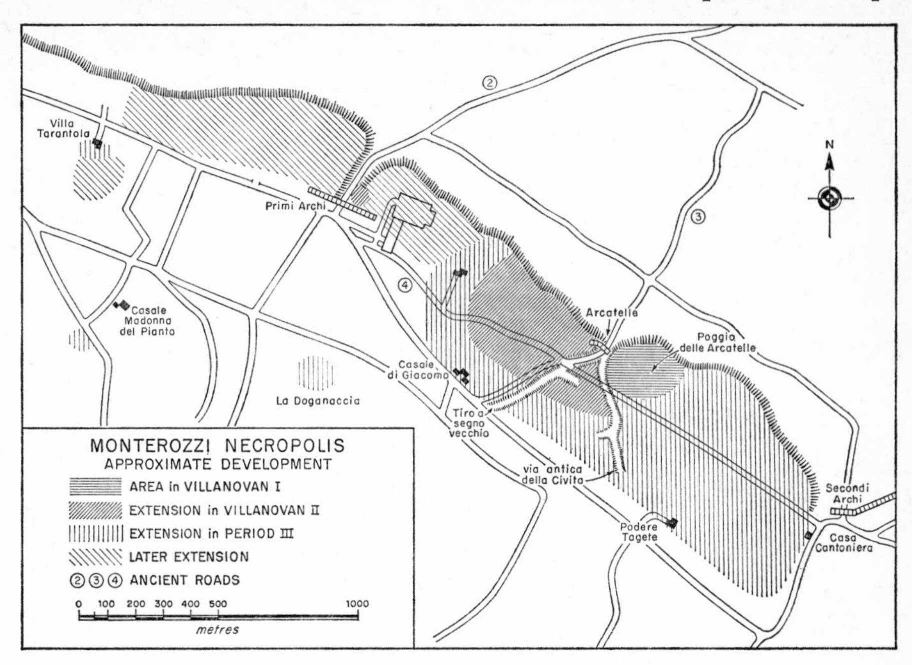

Fig. 3. The necropolis on Monterozzi and its development

since been confirmed by air photography, but only a few are still discernible from the ground.

Other interesting features of the Tarquinian landscape are the traces of ancient roads. The fact that traceable roads lead to Veii, an Etruscan city destroyed by the Romans, shows that the Etruscans were road builders before the Romans. The Via Tarquiniese is a well-attested ancient road that runs eastwards from the ancient Tarquinia to join the Via Clodia, also known to have been in existence in Etruscan times. Indeed, since the Via Tarquiniese went past the eastern cemeteries of Tarquinia, it may well have been the way to them in Villanovan times, though how much further it then continued we cannot be sure.

Fig. 2, 1

The cemetery on Monterozzi was also connected to ancient Tarquinia by roads. The easiest way to leave the city was by the gentle eastern slope, and since Monterozzi is bounded by cliffs on the side facing ancient Tarquinia, the only way to get up to the top of this plateau is through two natural breaks in the cliffs at the Primi Archi and the Arcatelle, called after the arches of a medieval aquaduct that still span them. Further on are the Secondi Archi where the cliff fades away. It is therefore logical to suppose that roads marked 2 and 3 on the maps and now represented by country lanes, led from the eastern slope of ancient Tarquinia to these two gaps in the cliffs.

Figs. 2, 3

From the gap at the Arcatelle, two sunken cemetery roads branch off across the plateau. One is called the *via antica della Civita* and has along it some Etruscan chamber tombs cut in the rock, while the other is called the *tiro a segno vecchio* or old shooting range.

Fig. 3

Excavations beginning in 1881 on a little hill called the Poggio delle Arcatelle beside the Arcatelle gap revealed a large Villanovan cemetery of over 300 graves. As far as one can determine from the old reports, the graves of Villanovan I were on or near this hill, which was the nucleus of the later necropolis. The fact that the cemetery started on the hill nearest to the gap in the cliff at the Arcatelle, suggests that a funeral road came this way from the ancient Tarquinia.

The graves of Villanovan II covered a wider area, and the very important Warrior's Tomb with its associated burials was found beside the Primi Archi, again showing that this route was by then also in use for funerals coming from Tarquinia. This evidence therefore indicates a topographical connection between the ancient city and Villanovan graves on Monterozzi.

By the Orientalizing Period III after 700 BC the cemetery had extended eastward as far as the Secondi Archi, and in the classical Etruscan period it was further enlarged to the west. But this does not, of course, mean that any one area was abandoned when the cemetery spread beyond it, for later graves are found throughout.

Thus we see an unbroken continuity of graves at Tarquinia from Villanovan down to classical Etruscan. This continuity is also evidenced at the site of the ancient city, where Villanovan sherds lie mixed with Etruscan sherds among foundations of Etruscan buildings. We have seen that to the east, where the slope is gentle, lie the eastern Villanovan cemeteries, and that on Monterozzi, also clearly related topographically to the Etruscan city, the Villanovan cemetery was the nucleus of the Etruscan one. Hence at Tarquinia the true Etruscan period is in large measure the continuation of Villanovan.

To return to the roads: nos. 2 and 3 join another called no. 4, that runs the length of Monterozzi and its necropolis as a cemetery road. But in one direction this road no. 4 leads away to Caere and in the other to the modern Tarquinia. From there other roads branched off to the main Roman coastal highway, the Via Aurelia, which in ancient times ran nearer to the coast than its modern counterpart. Two other ancient roads called nos. 5 and 6 ran north on either side of the River Marta towards Lake Bolsena and the sanctuary of Voltumna.

Figs. 2, 3

These roads suggest that, while road no. 1, the Via Tarquiniese, ran directly inland from the ancient city, communication to the coast may have gone over Monterozzi and through the present Tarquinia, which therefore looks like a road junction and strong point set on a height overlooking the sea. But of course we do really not know the age of these roads except that those to the cemeteries must be Villanovan and Etruscan; the Via Tarquiniese is presumably Etruscan, and the Via Aurelia is Roman. Etruscan Tarquinia is also said to have had three ports, though just where they were is not clear, but these ports must have been reached by roads.

Finally the mention of Etruscan origins in the title of this book needs some explanation, and I must admit at this point that the views expressed here are based in the main on the study of Tarquinia alone. Yet such was the importance of this city in ancient Etruria that whatever was true of it might well have a wider application. Also some Villanovan cemeteries in Etruria were excavated long ago before the objects from each grave were kept together as units, and thus their scientific value was greatly reduced. In other cases the material has been inadequately published or is difficult of access. At Tarquinia the excavations on Monterozzi are among the older and unsatisfactory explorations, but the careful work at the eastern cemeteries carried out by Luigi Pernier was a model of precision. The preservation of the material grave by grave at the Museo Archeologico at Florence gives a basis for a detailed study of Villanovan at a major site. The recent excavations at Veii of the British School at Rome, now handsomely published in *Notizie degli Scavi*, provide another large body of material, but here I shall say only that the picture presented at Veii differs from that at Tarquinia in detail but not in fundamentals.

POSTSCRIPT

The following excerpt from the Minutes of the Society of Antiquaries of London for the meeting of Nov. 12, 1761 is of interest with regard to Tarquinia in the eighteenth century. It was published by Mr S. Rowland Pierce in the *Antiquaries Journal*, vol. 45, 1965, p. 211.

> ...Letter from our worthy Member Mr Jenkins, is dated, Rome August 8th. 1761. Herein he informs Mr Hollis that in the month of May last, at the request & expence of Mr Wilcocks, he made a Tour to *Corneto*, which is about ten Miles beyond *Civita Vecchia*. Near Corneto stood once the very ancient *City of Tarquinii*; now called by the present Inhabitants of Corneto, *Civita Turchina*. It is situated on an hill, of an oblong form, the top of which is one continued

Plain; & where this celebrated City flourished, is now one field of corn. This Hill, once *Tarquinii*, is joined to *Corneto* by a ridge of lesser Hills, of about three Miles in circuit; all which Hills are covered with Hillocks called by the Inhabitants Monte Rozzi, in divers of which that have been opened were found various sorts of *Etruscan* Vases, and some other Sepulchral Ornaments; the walls of some of these Sepulchres were adorned with Paintings, & Inscriptions in *Etruscan* Characters. His business there was on purpose to examine into the true state of that vast Subterranean Antiquity; and being furnished with a Licence from the Cardinal Camerlingo, which gave him authority to dig where he thought proper, Mr Jenkins caused three of those Cells to be opened. Although no Moveables were found in them, yet the Paintings & Inscriptions were considerable; copies of which he has brought with him to Rome. The Stile of the Paintings, he says, were well conceived, & prove Talents and those considerable ones, in the Authors of them – Mr Wilcocks, whose whole attention is given to do good to mankind, & to serve Particulars, his motive, he says, for desiring to promote a work of this kind, was in hopes some Countryman of ours, or other of Rank, who might arrive at Rome the ensuing Season, would be pleased at an occasion of being at some Expence, to bring to light one of the greatest Antiquities in Europe, and which hitherto has been so little known, that he apprehends he is the first Englishman, who ever visited it.

CHAPTER II

Villanovan I

VILLANOVAN I, dating in my scheme from the tenth century BC to about 750, was the basic Villanovan. In Villanovan II, which at Tarquinia lasted only about half a century, many of the same forms continued, but one can also see the abandonment of old ways and the strengthening of outside influences. It is really a transition to the Orientalizing Period III when Villanovan elements continued but alongside newly arrived foreign ones.

In my fuller treatment of Villanovan at Tarquinia, I separarated material that I considered certainly Villanovan I from that classed as probably Villanovan I, but here I shall drop this distinction for the sake of simplicity and will treat both together as one unit. Later I shall do the same with Villanovan II. There are also important objects that cannot be assigned with assurance either to Villanovan I or II, but, since these things have much to tell us about the Villanovan culture as a whole, I have included them in this chapter under a separate heading.

BURIAL CUSTOMS

The dead person was cremated, and the charred fragments of his bones were picked out of the ashes of the funeral pyre and put in an urn covered by a bowl. A pozzo or well-shaped grave was dug with a smaller pozzetto beneath it in which the urn was placed, often upon some ashes from the pyre, and the pozzetto was then covered by a stone slab. In the cemeteries these pozzi were sometimes found in groups, perhaps representing family plots.

Fig. 4a

The pozzi were not covered by mounds, but since there are no reports of any of them being intersected by other pozzi, they

Fig. 4. a, Pozzo grave in section; b, stone receptacle in section (both after Ghirardini) b, 1:30

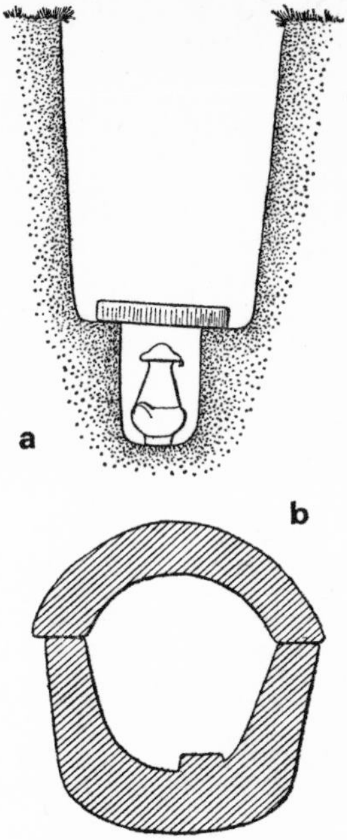

must have had markers of some kind. Among the graves at Selciatello Sopra were found two large carved pieces of stone, one in the shape of the knob of a pottery bell helmet and the other in the shape of the roof of a house-urn, which might have marked graves.

Plates 1, 2

In a minority of graves the pozzetto was replaced by a heavy cylindrical receptacle of tufa sunk below the bottom of the pozzo and covered by a thick dome-shaped lid also of tufa. In the illustrated example the little step was to hold the urn. A still rarer form was a larger rectangular receptacle also of tufa and likewise with a heavy lid. These contained richer burials which could include house-urns instead of the normal urn to hold the cremated remains. The dead person was sometimes cremated in his clothes still fastened by bronze fibulae or safety

Fig. 4b

pins, for these may show signs of having been in the fire. More generally the fibulae had not been in the fire but were found in the urn upon the ashes as though they had fastened the cloth or garment in which the cremated bones had been wrapped after they had been picked out of the ashes. These fibulae often have rings on their pins. In one case a string was still attached to such a ring and perhaps even to the surviving edge of a garment. This suggests that the pins of the fibulae were not always stuck through the fabric but through rings attached to it by strings.

The urn containing the burnt bones was normally covered by a bowl, and poorer graves contained nothing but the urn and cover-bowl. The cover-bowl was often upside down like a lid, but when it was the right way up, it might hold some of the cremated remains. In rare instances in Villanovan I a warrior's urn was covered by his precious bronze helmet, but more often a pottery replica of a helmet was substituted. In a few cases warriors were buried with a sword and spear.

Some graves contained pottery boats, and pairs of pottery wheels and little pottery horses were also found which probably represent chariots and their teams. The case for chariots here is strengthened by the finding of pottery helmets in some of the same graves marking them as warriors' graves, though certainty that these chariots belong to Villanovan I is lacking. It is easy to see here the substitution of pottery ships and chariots for real ones just as in the case of the pottery helmets. An occasional pair of bronze bridle bits also implies a pair of horses, possibly for a chariot.

As a rule small objects were placed in the urn with the ashes. But if spindle whorls were numerous, they might be found around the urn as though they had formed a necklace placed upon it, and they might have been worn so by the living person. Sometimes the graves contained other pots, and in these cases the pozzetto could be hollowed out on one side to accommodate them.

As for separating male and female graves, the use of crema-tion makes the grave offerings an easier guide than the small fragments of burnt bones. Helmets, swords, spears, chariots and razors denote men, while bronze spindles, spindle whorls and pottery spools indicate women. Having gone that far, one can also see that other kinds of objects are found in women's graves but very rarely in men's. These include bronze spirals with un-dulating ends, arc fibulae with glass beads on the bow, and arc fibulae with striated bows, flat bows or twisted bows. Similarly fibulae with multiple bows, commonest in late Villanovan I, were an exclusively male fashion.

One can of course ask how one knows that the things called spindle whorls and razors really were that. One can never prove these things, but when spindle whorls are only found in one or two dubious cases in men's graves but in several graves with spindles or spools, the chances seem good that most of them really were spindle whorls and denote women's graves. As for razors, we cannot say whether they were for shaving in the modern sense or for trimming the beard or hair, but there is only one clear case of a razor in a woman's grave, and that is in Villanovan II. Perhaps, like some Italian women today, she could have used a razor.

While some warriors' graves were among the richest, there were numerous well epuipped women's graves throughout the whole of Villanovan I. One such grave of a woman early in the period even contained a pottery boat, suggesting that like some of the warriors, she had her own ship. Also the bronze animal-bird described below, by far the most remarkable Villanovan object from Tarquinia, came from a woman's grave, and must have been an object of enormous importance. In any case the position of women seems not to have been in-ferior to that of men, though not quite equal to that of the most important warriors.

Plate 86

Fig. 5. House urn of early Villanovan I with white paint as found (after Ghirardini). 1:4

POTTERY

All the pottery of Villanovan I was hand-made without the use of the potter's wheel, and, as in modern communities of this level of development, pottery-making was probably a household task of the women. Most of it was of coarse ware, blackish to dark gray or brown, but for some smaller pots finer black or red wares were used, and these might have a polished surface. Red ware was used especially for spheroid jars.

Decoration took various forms. By far the commonest were lines drawn on the surface of the clay before the pot was fired, and these were usually made with a tool resembling a narrow comb with several teeth. These were supplemented by decoration made with little stamps. Other much rarer forms were little bronze studs stuck into the soft clay before baking, and there were patterns made of small metal strips, perhaps lead, of

Plates 14, 15

which the clearest example belongs to Villanovan II. Even white paint occurs and may have been much commoner than we think, for its preservation is very poor.

Plate 110
Fig. 5

Urns are the dominant feature of Villanovan graves, since they are far larger than the other objects. The shape suggests a water jar suitable for lowering into a spring or well, and the basic form is 'two-storied', a broad body surmounted by a narrower neck with a slight outward bulge. Generally there is a single handle, but rare urns with two handles generally had one of these broken off as though to make the vessel unfit for use by the living.

The ornament drawn with a comb-like tool sometimes includes a pair of figures seated over the handle, and these assume various forms, though not all are found in Villanovan I. They can have their arms upraised or outstretched, be shaking hands, have their hands on their knees in a positive attitude, be bowing to each other or be sitting sullenly back to back. There is even a big one talking to a little one. The more one looks at the ornament on the urns, the more one sees that it is pervaded by these two figures. They can be joined together in plain or complex patterns, but even at the beginning of Villanovan I these patterns often fade away into careless, illogical renderings. Hence these are not a sign of late degeneration. Who these pairs of figures represent is not clear.

Plates 3–7
Fig. 6

Large squares are also found on urns, house urns and pottery helmets especially earlier in Villanovan I, and the commonest ornament in these squares is the swastika sometimes combined with the two seated figures. There are as well numerous step and meander patterns which could be either clearly and neatly drawn or carelessly suggested. But even these careless renderings occur at the very beginning and, as in the case of the patterns of seated figures, are not a sign of late degeneration. A minority of the urns have no decoration at all. These plain urns appear in mid Villanovan I and had their greatest vogue at the end of the

Fig. 7

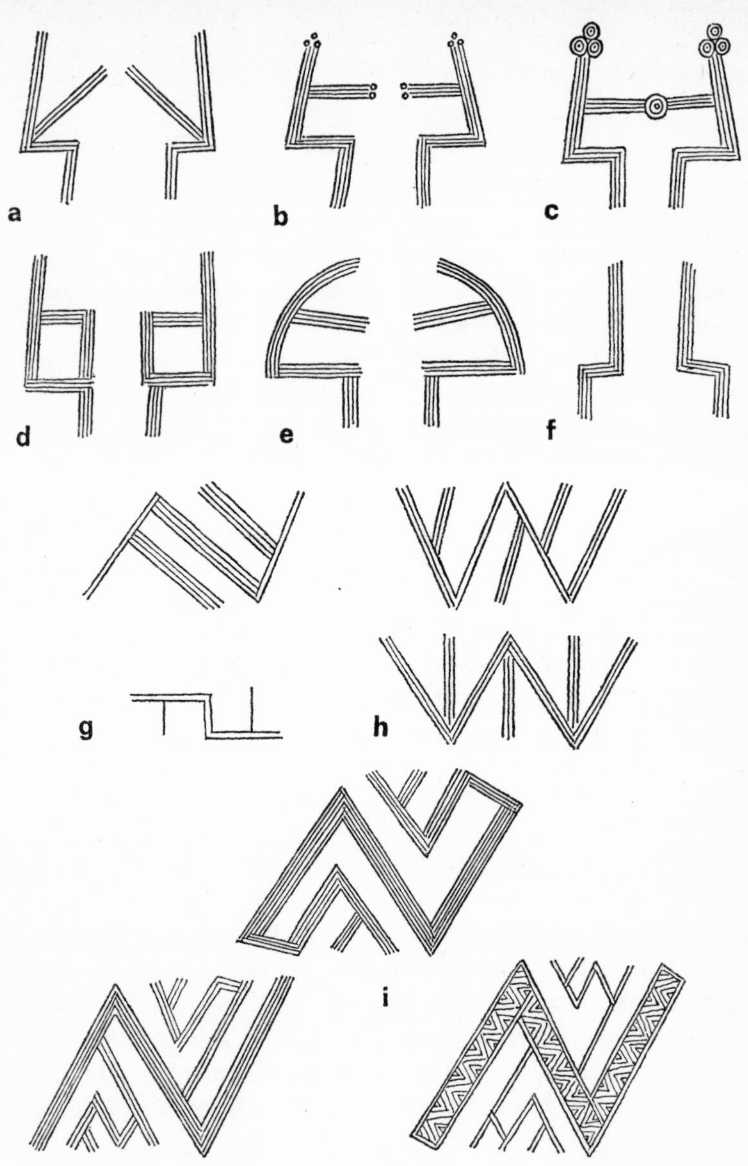

Fig. 6. The two seated figures on Villanovan urns: a, with arms upraised; b, with arms outstretched; c, shaking hands; d, with hands on knees; e, bowing to each other; f, back to back; g, plain patterns of two seated figures; h, careless renderings of plain patterns; i, complex patterns of two seated figures

period, though ornamented ones became more fashionable again in Villanovan II.

Cover-bowls were the lids of urns and assume various closely related shapes. If there is ornament, it generally consists of small bits of the same decoration found on urns. Bowls may have a foot more or less high. High feet were in use from the beginning but were especially favoured late in Villanovan I after which they became fewer. A rare addition is a pair of horns on the handle.

Plates 9–12

Warriors' urns might be covered with a pottery helmet, a substitute for a precious bronze one. The real bronze helmets of Villanovan warriors were of three kinds, crested, bell-shaped or cap-shaped. The bell-shaped type was surmounted by a tubular socket to hold a plume, and the cap-shaped type might or might not have such a socket. Those without sockets belong only to Villanovan II and were never imitated in pottery. In fact the difference between the bell and the cap helmets with sockets is slight and is seldom clearly reflected in the pottery examples, for the potters, unaware of such archaeological distinctions, were merely making lids. But for the sake of simplicity I shall call these pottery ones bell helmets. They often have incised ornament derived from the system of urns, and one of these also has a panel containing little bronze studs. Some knobs that surmount sockets have a hole to hold a plume as in the bronze examples, but others have a knob resembling the roof of a house-urn. This shows a facet of Villanovan mentality that is beyond our grasp. There are also pottery replicas of crested bronze helmets sometimes ornamented with little bronze studs on the crest.

Plates 13–15

Plate 14

Fig. 8

Plate 15

Rare alternatives to the standard urns were house-urns, evidently shrines for the remains of some special class of persons. Only seven of these were found at Tarquinia, and some of the graves containing them were especially rich. The clearly dated examples belonged to the beginning of Villanovan I, and most

Figs. 5, 7

were in heavy rectangular stone receptacles at the bottom of pozzo graves. Out of the seven house-urns, five came from Monterozzi, and suggest the importance of that cemetery from the very beginning of Villanovan.

These house-urns are in the form of a small rectangular or oval structure covered by a gabled roof with overhanging eves, and there are usually smoke-holes under the gable ends in default of chimneys. At one end is a rectangular doorway often provided with a pottery door, and a window is sometimes schematically indicated on the side. Occasionally there are ornaments on the roof in the form of double birds, that is, a bird with a head at either end. There are also ridges running down the roof which may represent the interior beams or alternatively logs laid on the thatch to hold it down in windy weather. One of the house-urns was decorated with white paint when found, but this has now disappeared. Another has especially fine incised swastikas, and in some of the swastikas are seated figures. Pairs of human figures seen frontally also appear on this house-urn, and a similar one in white paint was on the roof of another.

Fig. 5

Jars with binocular handles appear at the beginning of Villanovan I. A wide-bodied form, with feet, and flaring rims, comes from graves of the end of Villanovan I. They can have handles of various shapes and in one case four tall pointed knobs, while the ornament is related to that of the urns.

Plate 16

Plates 17–20

Plate 19

Spheroid jars are generally of red ware and belong late in Villanovan I. Some, including one with a high foot, are sophisticated enough to suggest wheel-turning and foreign origin, but they are really hand-made pots, and I have found no foreign source for them. Indeed the cruder and simpler forms suggest local origin and rapid development toward the end of Villanovan I. These spheroid jars of red ware have a long and involved history in Villanovan II and in the Orientalizing Period III.

Plates 23–26

Fig. 7. House urn of early Villanovan I. Squares over the door and on the back of the urn contain swastikas including seated figures at the ends of the arms (after Pernier). 1:4

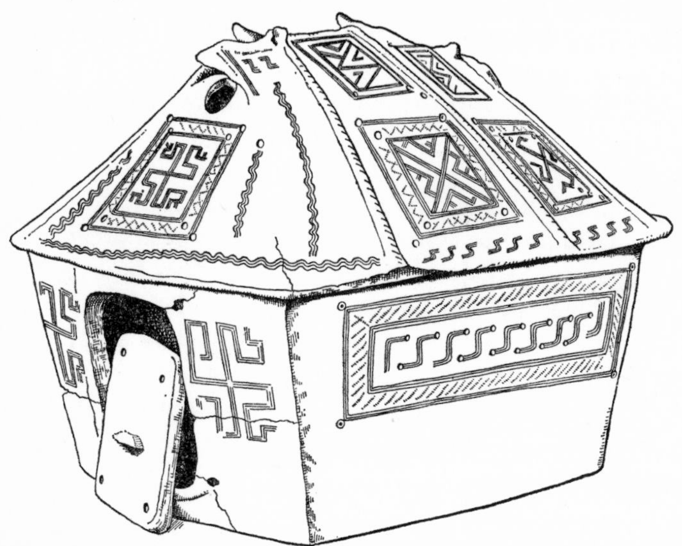

Fig. 8. Pottery bell helmet with a knob resembling the roof of a house-urn, Villanovan I. 1 : 4

Plates 21, 22
Plates 27–34

There is a very great variety of jugs including double jugs. One kind, virtually a miniature urn, appears early in Villanovan I. Two other kinds, which I have called respectively jugs with a neck and one handle and bottle-shaped jugs, begin late in Villanovan I. The handle of one bottle-shaped jug is surmounted by a ram's head, and the handle of another carries a horned animal's head with one horn missing. But more generally the whole top of the handle was broken off, perhaps before it was placed in the grave. There are also numerous jugs that do not fall into any standard types, one of which has a whitish design that may be the remnants of little lead plates.

Plate 28
Plates 35–40

Cups run through the whole of Villanovan I. They often have binocular handles with two openings, and handles may be surmounted by a pair of horns or an animal's head as in the case of the double cup, while the triple cup has a handle that could be animal or even human. The double and triple cups are connected by holes so that liquid could flow between them.

Plate 40
Plate 44

Amphorae are commonest toward the end of Villanovan I, though they first appear a little earlier. The most usual form is not really a Villanovan one but borrowed from the Iron Age people of the Trench Grave Culture of southern Italy, and since the pottery was probably made by women, this could represent the handiwork of wives or slaves from the south.

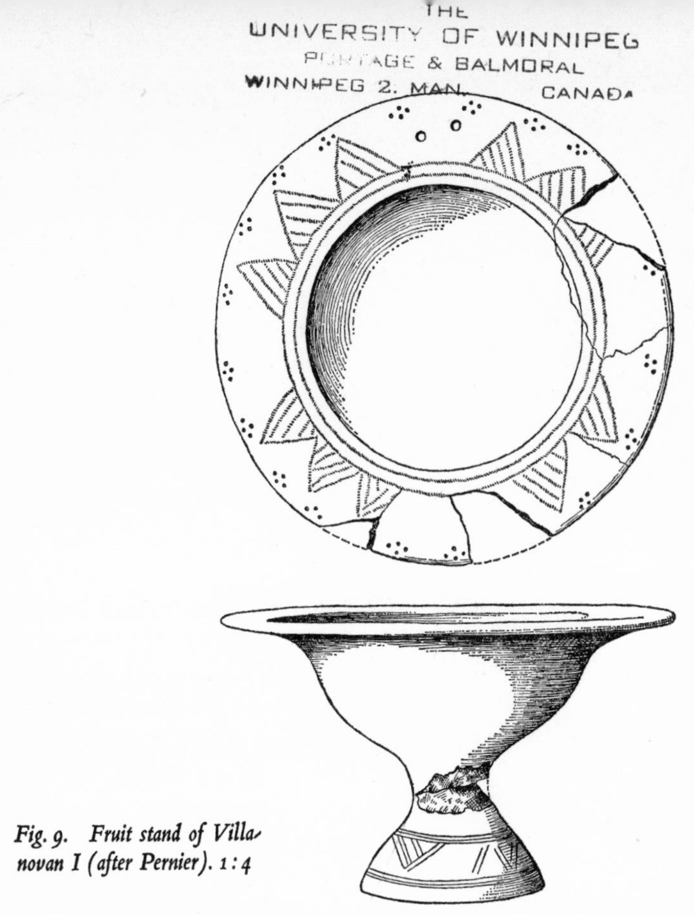

Fig. 9. Fruit stand of Villanovan I (after Pernier). 1 : 4

Stands occur all through Villanovan I, but what stood on them is not clear. They are also sometimes called goblets, but they would be most difficult to drink from. In short, their actual use is uncertain, though possibly they were lamps. They often have two holes in the rim, perhaps for a string by which they could be hung up on a peg on the wall.

Plate 46

The sole example of a fruit-stand belongs early in Villanovan I, but again the name is only an archaeological term, and has nothing to do with actual use. It also has two holes in the rim perhaps for hanging it up, and it looks like an overgrown stand, though the smaller stands may be its stunted relatives.

Fig. 9

Plates 42, 43

As we have seen, spindle-whorls and spools are among the factors determining female graves.

Plate 41

Of the two pottery boats found, one belongs to the beginning of Villanovan I, and it probably had a little cup at one end.

Plate 45

The other has a foot like a stand, and its cup is completely preserved. Possibly these boats served as lamps.

Plates 47–49

The askoi all recall the bird-shaped, ring-shaped and animal-shaped vessels with basket handles from Greece and Cyprus, but though they represent foreign influence, they are made of local pottery and consequently are not imports. The bird-shaped one belongs early in Villanovan I, and the ring-shaped one may too, while the animal vase in the shape of a horned animal-bird belongs to the middle of the period. It can also be classed as a rhyton in terms of Greek archaeology, since the liquid, poured in through a spout on its rump, was poured out again through a hole in its mouth. It had four stumpy legs, but the forelegs are missing and in the photo are represented by a piece of plasticine.

METAL OBJECTS

These are of bronze unless other metals are mentioned.

The usual Villanovan sword of Tarquinia, and indeed the commonest type at this time in central and southern Italy, was a short dagger-like weapon with a T-shaped hilt. The hilt could be flanged or flat but often had a projection on either side

Fig. 10b

of the grip. These swords could be of bronze or iron, and at Tarquinia an iron one might belong to Villanovan I. Also, a

Plate 50

sword of early Villanovan I had iron rivets in the hilt. The

Plate 53

blade of this sword is decorated with fine lines parallel to its edges, but its fellow of late Villanovan I has an ornament of zigzags as well as fine lines. The scabbard of the earlier sword

Fig. 10a, c

has a pattern of zigzags and shaded bands, but on the scabbard of the later one the ornament has become much more developed.

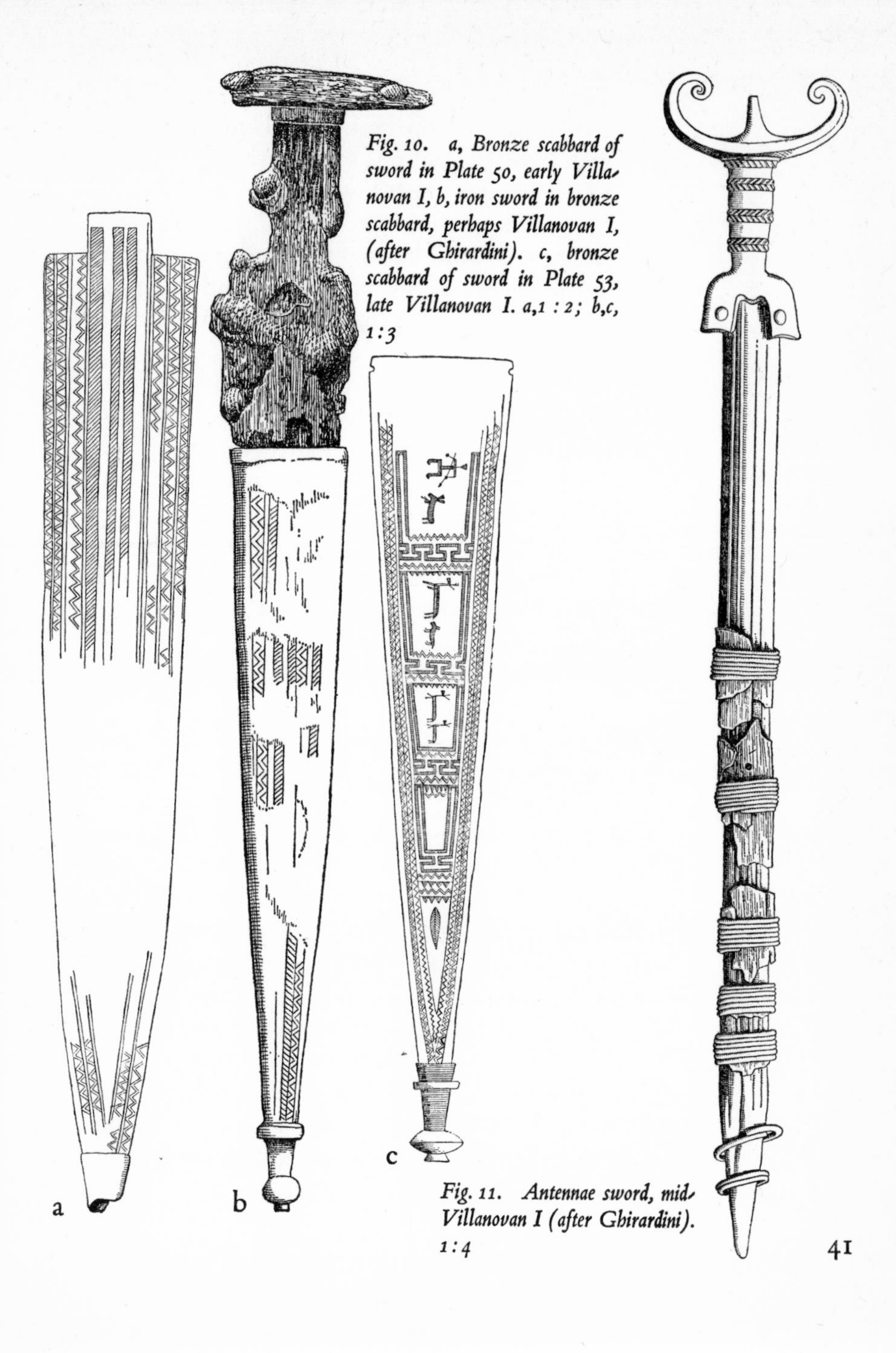

Fig. 10. a, Bronze scabbard of sword in Plate 50, early Villanovan I, b, iron sword in bronze scabbard, perhaps Villanovan I, (after Ghirardini). c, bronze scabbard of sword in Plate 53, late Villanovan I. a,1 : 2; b,c, 1:3

Fig. 11. Antennae sword, mid-Villanovan I (after Ghirardini). 1:4

The zigzags continue but the shaded bands form T-shaped meanders. In the upper panel is a scene evidently representing a boar hunt, while in the one below it is a deer being chased by a hound. Below that again are two deer.

Fig. 11

Another, longer sword belongs to the antennae type, a name which refers to the two curled projections on the pommel. The single example from Tarquinia dates from the middle of Villanovan I.

Plates 51, 52
Fig. 12

Spears can be flame-shaped or plain, and they and their spear-butts sometimes have polygonal sockets.

Plate 54
Plate 15

Two helmets from Villanovan I are of the crested type with three long false rivets under the ends of the crest and ornament of rows of large and small bosses. The three holes at the rim were to attach the cheek-pieces or chinstrap and also the necessary lining of perishable material. Pottery replicas of these helmets, which extend from early Villanovan I to early Period III, indicate that the form had a long life.

Plate 92
Plates 13–14
Fig. 8

Only one bronze bell helmet has been found at Tarquinia, and this can be dated only to Villanovan as a whole, but pottery replicas occur from the beginning of Villanovan I. The bronze example and some of the pottery replicas have sockets for plumes.

Plates 55, 56

A pair of bits and a pair of cheek-pieces came from a grave probably of Villanovan I, and here the cheek-pieces are a form of the central European bird boat with birds' heads either end.

Plates 60, 61
Fig. 13

Razors are of four kinds. The rectangular and elongated lunate ones are found only at the beginning of Villanovan I, while the more curved lunate form appeared in mid Villanovan I, and the sharply curved lunate ones late in the period.

Fig. 14a, b
Plates 62, 63,
Plates 65, 66

Among the many types of fibulae are arc fibulae with various kinds of bows: with herringbone ornament, flat, twisted or striated (with incised lines across the bow). Others have glass beads on the bow. Another form is the leechshaped fibula in which the bow is greatly enlarged. Such enlarged bows may be

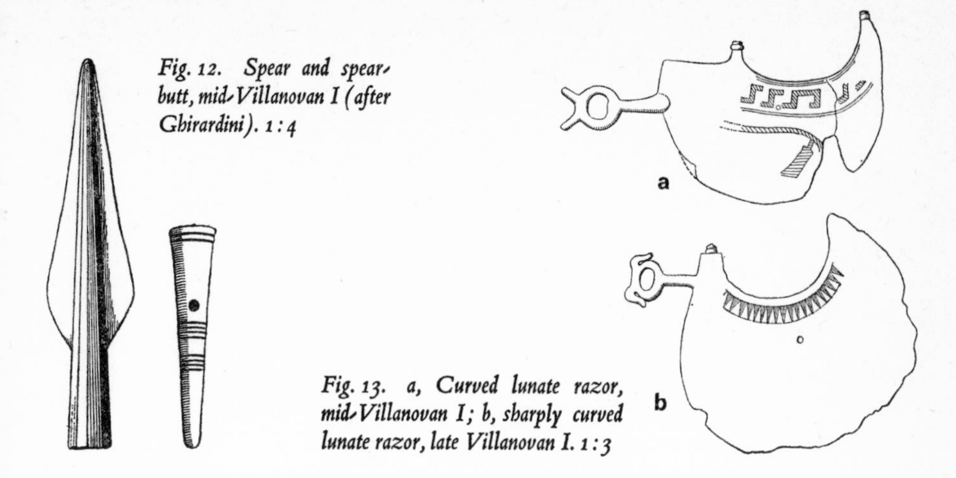

Fig. 12. Spear and spear-butt, mid-Villanovan I (after Ghirardini). 1 : 4

Fig. 13. a, Curved lunate razor, mid-Villanovan I; b, sharply curved lunate razor, late Villanovan I. 1 : 3

made of solid bronze, of amber or bone segments or even of bronze discs.

Plates 64, 67
Fig. 14c, d

There are also serpentine fibulae. One of these has a straight pin and a loop over the catch, while a common kind has a curved pin and either a loop or an elbow over the catch.

Fig. 14e, f
Fig. 36a, b

In the disc fibulae, named from the disc that terminates the catch, the pin is the dominant element, and a cross-bar is sometimes added to hold the pin in place. The disc often has a thin spiral upon it, a reminder that it is really the survivor of the spiral wire coil on the catches of some earlier Italian fibulae. This vestigial spiral disappeared with Villanovan I, but the plain disc with no spiral had a much longer life.

Fig. 14g

Late in Villanovan I there appears another kind of fibula with a curved pin and a straight bow, and here the bow could be double, triple or even quintuple. These fibulae are often made of iron instead of bronze.

Plate 74
Plate 57

One form of vessel found is a tripod consisting of a shallow dish on three legs with a flat decorated rim with small bosses and larger ones surrounded by concentric circles. This first occurs early in Villanovan I. There are also bronze cups with rows of small and larger bosses either on the shoulder or on the body.

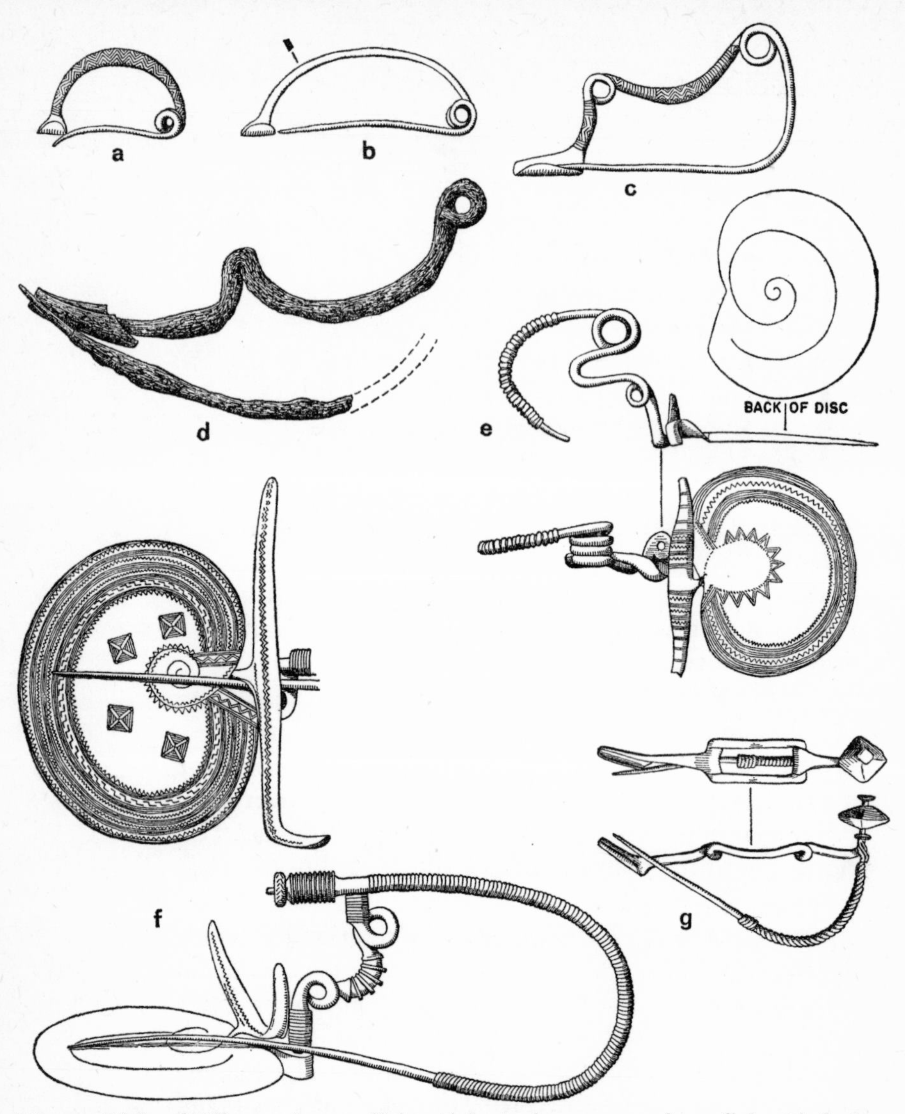

Fig. 14. Fibulae of Villanovan I: a, arc fibula with herring-bone ornament; b, arc fibula with flat bow; c, serpentine fibula with loop over catch; d, iron serpentine fibula with elbow over catch; e, f, disc fibulae with spirals on discs; g, fibula with curved pin and a straight double bow. a-d, f, early Villanovan I; e, mid-Villanovan I; g, late Villanovan I. 1:2. For other fibulae of Villanovan I see plates 62-67

A unique form of the end of Villanovan I is a cylindrical container also with large and small bosses, a double bird on the lid and a long chain.

Plate 58

The most notable of the other articles is the unique mirror descended from Mycenaean mirrors, but this is a local imitation, since the triangular plate with three rivets that holds its handle copies the handle of a contemporary rectangular razor.

Plates 59, 61

Bronze spindles occur from the beginning of Villanovan I, while bronze and even iron bracelets also appear in mid Villanovan I. Hollow bronze objects with one face decorated with rows of bosses also begin in mid Villanovan I, and look as though they were to be attached to a rod. Spirals with undulating ends seem generally too small for bracelets, but in one grave they were attached to the pins of fibulae. Spindleshaped beads, and gold-plated bronze ornaments including swastikas also occur. There are also gold-plated bronze disc pendants of a type represented in Villanovan II in gold.

Plate 70
Plate 68
Plate 73
Plate 69
Plates 71, 72
Plate 133

'EGYPTIAN' OBJECTS

Two graves attributed to a late stage in Villanovan I contained respectively a scarab and a pair of little figurines. These may not really be imports from Egypt, since such things were made in some quantity by the Phoenicians and are also found in Greece. Their presence at Tarquinia and elsewhere in Italy is an indication of the spreading of Phoenician and Greek trade in the central Mediterranean at this time.

Fig. 15

CHRONOLOGY

Colonial Greek contacts at Tarquinia indicate that Villanovan II began about 750 BC, and consequently that date serves as the end of Villanovan I; the beginning of Villanovan I is harder to fix. My inclination is to place it about the tenth century

a

b

c

Fig. 15. 'Egyptian' objects, late Villanovan I: a, scarab; b, c, figurines (after Ghirardini). b, actual size

BC, though here we are in the Dark Age of the Aegean when absolute dates are no better than the vague and scanty evidence on which they are based.

Some of these indications come from fibulae. In Villanovan I there are various kinds of fibulae with parallels in the Pantalica Culture of Sicily where they can be dated to about the eleventh to tenth centuries BC by rather tenuous connections between Sicily, the Aegean and the eastern Mediterranean. These include arc fibulae with flat bows, bows with herringbone ornament or with striated bows. Those with twisted bows are also found in Greece and Crete between about the eleventh and ninth centuries. At the same time it should be noted that the bows of Villanovan fibulae with twisted bows are thicker than their counterparts in the Aegean world. The serpentine fibula of Villanovan I with a straight pin and a loop over the catch is a form also at home in Sicily about the eleventh to tenth centuries. Another kind of arc fibula is that with the leech-shaped bow, and this swollen bow has Greek parallels in about the eleventh to tenth centuries and later, though in Greece the rest of the fibula is somewhat different.

Fig. 14a, b
Plates 62, 63
Fig. 16
Plate 64
Plate 65

The short Villanovan swords also have parallels in Sicily in the Modica hoard dating, like many of the Sicilian parallels to the fibulae, to about the eleventh to tenth centuries.

Plates 50, 53

Fig. 16. Greek arc fibula with twisted bow (after Kraiker and Kübler)

The bronze tripod of early Villanovan I is the metal counterpart of pottery ones from the Roman Forum of about the eleventh to tenth centuries, which in turn are based on a Greek type from Euboea of the eleventh century. The bronze mirror from Tarquinia of early Villanovan I is a local product but is copied from the mirrors of Mycenaean type in use in Sicily about the twelfth to eleventh centuries.

Plate 74
Fig. 35c, d

Plate 59

But Villanovan I also contained from the very beginning other serpentine fibulae with curved pins and either a loop or an elbow over the catch, and these begin in Sicily about the tenth century. Hence Villanovan I is probably no earlier than that, while the numerous analogies to Greece and Sicily in about the eleventh and tenth centuries, and especially the mirror reflecting a Mycenaean-Sicilian type of the twelfth to eleventh centuries, mean that is is not likely to have begun much later.

Plate 67
Fig. 14c, d

UNDATED VILLANOVAN MATERIAL

The following material could be assigned to either Villanovan I or II. In some cases we have insufficient information about the contents of the graves, and in others well reported graves contained nothing distinctive of either period.

POTTERY

Among the helmets there is one where the potter is clearly imitating a bronze bell helmet.

Plate 81

The askoi include a bird askos with the head broken off, and another of a shape common in Sardinia that distantly recalls those of Cyprus and Asia Minor. The latter is very common at

Plates 78, 80

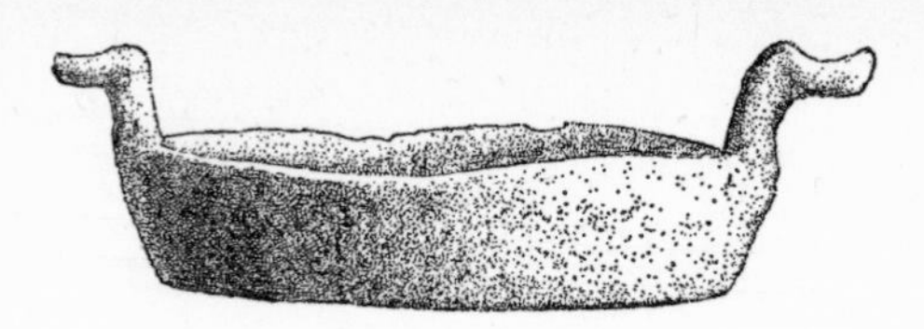

Fig. 17. Villanovan pottery boat with birds' heads fore and aft (after Montelius). 1:4

Fig. 20g Vetulonia further north in Etruria. Also there is a cup with a horned animal facing inward for a handle.

Plates 76, 77 — Boats may have a bird's head at one or both ends, and probably represented the dead man's ship, as the pottery helmet represented his bronze helmet and as the pottery wheels and horses represented his chariot. *Fig. 17*

Plate 82 — Three small pots like little Villanovan urns and characteristic of early Villanovan I are joined together and have a handle in the shape of a woman whose breasts are indicated. Here the three pots are connected by small holes so that liquid could flow between them. Some other undated double and triple pots with human handles also have such holes.

Plates 84, 85 — There are tripods that seem to be humble pottery relatives of the bronze tripods of Villanovan I. They share the same general characteristics, a wide and shallow vessel supported on three legs that approach one another underneath it.

Plate 79 — Another object is that known as a 'candelabrum', though it has no sockets for candles, and its arms end in shallow cups. Also it is topped by a detachable stand like the pottery stands already described.

Plate 75 — A six-mouthed pot is more likely to be early than late in Villanovan, and a dish has around it a band of seated figures like those that appear in pairs on the urns, but most of these are sitting on chairs. Plate 83

Plate 87 — Pairs of pottery wheels and pairs of pottery horses have been reported, but not all have survived. The wheels are solid, but in one case they had painted ornament, possibly indicating spokes. The horses have high manes with a slot for the yoke. The wooden pole and yoke in the illustration are of course modern. The bodies of the model chariots were probably wooden. A burial on Monterozzi had a pair of wheels, a pair of 'animals', and a yoke as well as a bell helmet and a boat, all of pottery. The inclusion of bell helmets in two of these graves shows that they belonged to warriors, and this strengthens the view that the wheels and horses represented chariots. The boat in one of the graves suggests that the dead man was a warlike person at sea as well as on land.

A grave on Monterozzi and another at Le Rose each yielded a single pottery horse, perhaps representing a riding horse.

METAL OBJECTS

The objects described are of bronze unless otherwise stated.

Reproduced among the plates is the finest of the representations of the mythical animal-bird; it shows a quadruped bird with a bovine head mounted on wheels. The hollow body is covered by a lid that is also bird-shaped and has a bovine head of its own. The holes in the muzzles and the loops on the necks were perhaps for chains, reported but not preserved, by which the object was drawn along. It is more likely to be early than late in Villanovan.

Plate 86

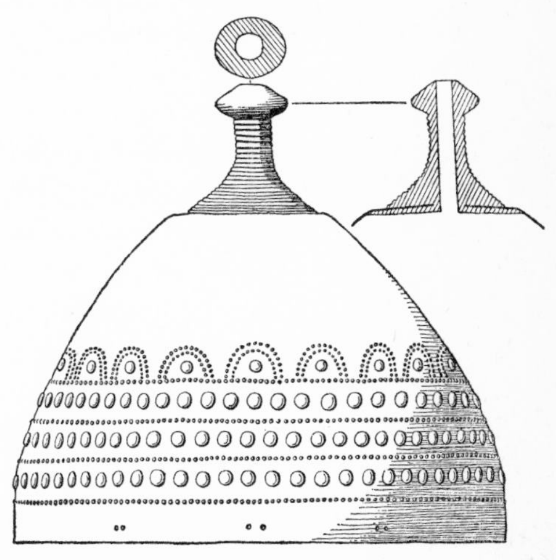

Fig. 18. Bronze bell helmet in Plate 92, Villanovan. 1 : 4

Plate 88 *Fig. 10b* Two iron swords had bronze scabbards ending in round knobs, and such knobs can be an early sign in Villanovan, for they had a tendency to flatten later like that on the more *Fig. 10c* elaborately decorated scabbard of late Villanovan I. One of the scabbards with a round knob had simple geometric *Fig. 10a* ornament like one of early Villanovan I already mentioned.

Plate 89 Iron spears are mentioned occasionally in the accounts of older excavations, but few are preserved.

Fig. 20d The axe (palstave) here reproduced looks like an earlier form of those of Villanovan II.

Plate 92 There is only one bronze example of a bell helmet, and it is more likely to be early than late in Villanovan. It has a tubular *Fig. 18* knob with horizontal ribbing on the shaft which was intended to hold a plume. This knob was cast on; that is, the helmet was held upside down with the mould for the knob fixed in place under it. The molten bronze was then poured into the mould from the inside of the helmet, thus attaching the knob to the helmet. The decoration of the helmet consists of large and small bosses arranged in rows and arcades, and around the rim are pairs of little holes for the attachment of the perishable lining as well as a chin-strap or cheek-pieces.

Plates 90, 91 The cap helmets with knobs differ from the bell helmet only in being rounder and less conical, and they are also more likely to be early than late in Villanovan. Like the bell helmet they have decoration consisting of rows of bosses, and on one example these represent eyes and eyebrows, perhaps a more

Fig. 19. Ornament on the Villanovan crested helmet in Plate 93 in the centre of which is the boat with birds' heads fore and aft and the 'sun disc'. 1 : 3

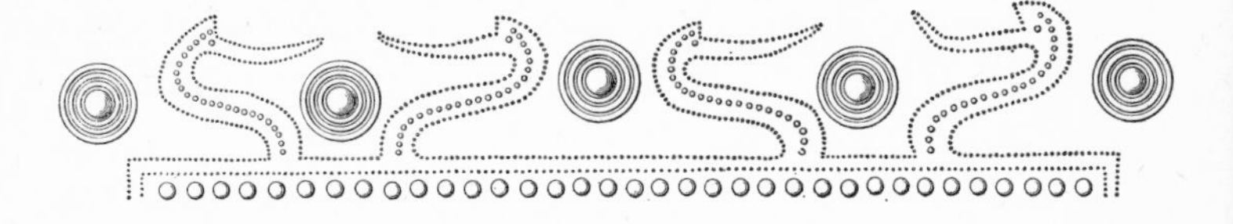

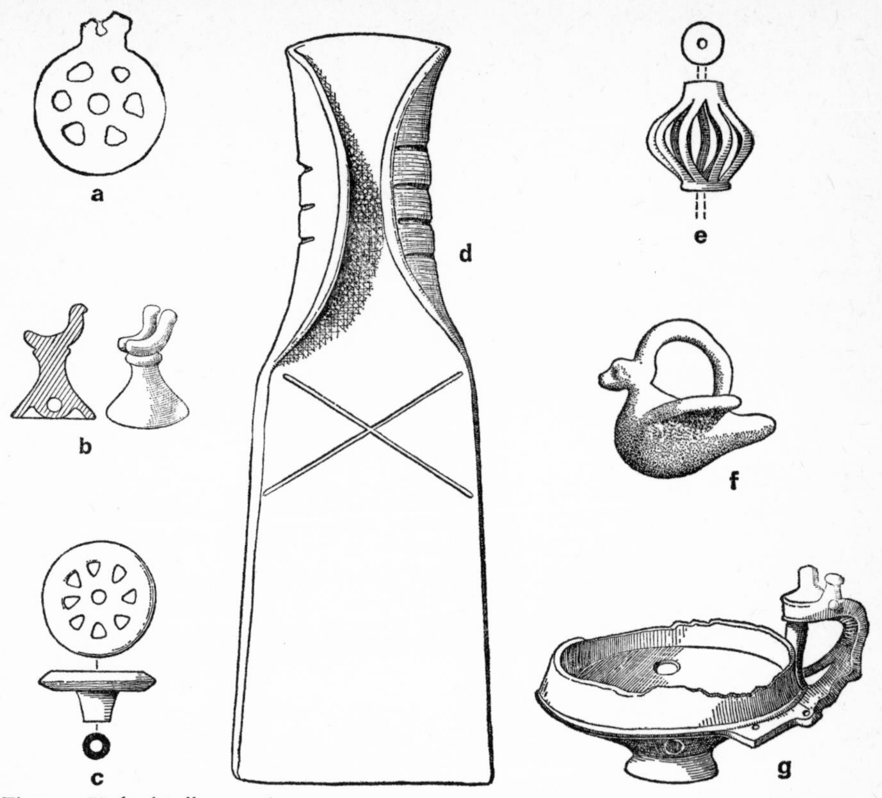

Fig. 20. *Undated Villanovan objects: a, 'sun-disc' pendant; b, bell-shaped pendant surmounted by a pair of birds; c, pin-head; d, axe (palstave); e, openwork object; f, bird pendant; g, cup with horned animal on handle (d, f, g, after Ghirardini). a-f, 1 : 2; g, 1 : 4*

primitive form of the full face shown on a cap helmet of Villanovan II. The broken knob of this helmet was attached in the same way as that of the bell-helmet. The other cap had a similar tubular knob but fastened by rivets.

Plate 122

Plate 103

The exceptionally fine crested helmet may belong to Villanovan I, since it was found with the iron sword already mentioned whose scabbard had simple geometric ornament and a round knob. This helmet has a late version of the central European pattern of the bird boat carrying the 'sun disc'.

Plate 93

Fig. 19

Other objects include 'sun-discs' perhaps connected with Danubian forms and a similar pin-head of Bronze Age derivation. There is also a bell-shaped pendant surmounted by a pair of birds which has eastern connections and may well belong to Villanovan II. A bronze pendant in the form of a bird with raised wings is not Danubian but may reflect the Aegean. An openwork bronze object on the other hand may well be connected with the invaders from the steppe who entered central Europe at the end of the Urnfield Period.

Fig. 20

CHAPTER III
Villanovan II

THIS PERIOD AT TARQUINIA, 750 to 700 BC, is really a transitional stage between the Villanovan proper and the Orientalizing Period III.

BURIAL CUSTOMS

A difficulty in dealing with these is that the great cemetery of Monterozzi, much less completely known than the Eastern Cemeteries, seems to have been in the forefront of change. Apparently Monterozzi had always been the fashionable cemetery, and now it became the centre of innovation in burial customs. At the same time the Eastern Cemeteries show a more faithful adherence to the old ways, though these were observed less completely than before. But the Eastern Cemeteries fell into disuse at the end of Villanovan II, while Monterozzi's importance increased.

The great innovation in Villanovan II was inhumation, the burial of the uncremated corpse, and more than a third of all the graves of this period were inhumations. The great bulk of these inhumations were on Monterozzi, and about a third of the inhumed bodies were simply buried in trenches covered with slabs of stone, while the majority were in sarcophagi cut out of soft stone and covered with a heavy lid. The question, of course, is why this change of burial rite occurred. The peoples of the Aegean and Near East sometimes buried their dead uncremated at this period, but most of the inhabitants of southern Italy had done the same from time immemorial, and indeed at the great Etruscan city of Caere only 40 km. south of Tarquinia the Villanovan cemetery contained inhumations and Villanovan cremations both of which seem equally old. Hence inhumation may simply have spread up to Tarquinia from the south, and intermarriage, suggested by some southern pots in Tarquinian graves, might have been partly responsible.

As for sarcophagi, these were also sometimes used by peoples of the Aegean and the Near East at this time, and Pernier says that most of the inhumations in sarcophagi at Impiccato formed a little group by themselves a short distance from the cremation graves. Hence they might suggest foreign settlers. But the sarcophagi seem to have been like the rectangular receptacles which held some of the richer Villanovan cremation graves, though made longer to hold a body lying at full length. In addition the sarcophagi disappear in Period III when foreign elements became much more pronounced. They reappear much later of course, but that is a quite different story.

At the same time Aegean and Near Eastern elements in Villanovan II were now more pronounced than in Villanovan I. Still there is no special concentration of them in the inhumation graves, which one might expect if the inhumers were foreigners. On the whole it would seem most likely that, while foreign influences were at work, there is no reason to postulate a substantial settlement from overseas. At the same time cremation remained the favoured mode of burial in Villanovan II especially in the Eastern Cemeteries, but even so there were some very rich cremations on Monterozzi.

Indeed the tendency to richer and richer burials as Villanovan I advanced continued to gain ground in II, especially at the end of the period, when there were some remarkably rich graves. The increasing wealth of the graves means that many more different kinds of things were included in them, and some at least of these must have been long in use among the Villanovans. Consequently their appearance now in graves may not mean that they were newly acquired but only that it had not previously been customary to bury them with the dead. From this one might suppose that Villanovan I may have been a richer period than the graves indicate.

The cremations of Villanovan II were in pozzo graves as in Villanovan I, and like them were occasionally in a round or rectangular receptacle of stone. But these were sometimes replaced by an enormous jar often of red ware in which the urn and all the other objects were packed. The ashes were still generally placed in urns of the standard Villanovan type, but change is apparant. Towards the end of Villanovan I, a couple of graves had jars to hold the ashes instead of the usual urn, and this tendency to put the ashes into something other than the regulation urn increased in Villanovan II especially in the latter part of the period. We are not always told which vessel held the ashes in these urnless graves, but one person's remains were placed in a hydria of Late Geometric Greek type, (Plate 118) and one of its handles was broken off as was customary in Villanovan urns with two handles. In other burials a quite new (Plate 97) pear-shaped urn was used, and in some of the richest graves the ashes were put in a bronze amphora, one of which imitates a (Plates 123, 124) Villanovan urn in shape. In any case the standard urn was going out of use in Villanovan II.

The urns might be covered with a pottery bowl as in Villanovan I, (Plates 102, 103) but this could now be replaced by a hemispherical (Plate 125) bronze bowl that, when right way up, might hold part of the ashes or grave goods. Warriors' urns were still sometimes covered with a pottery helmet, either bell-shaped or crested, and in (Plate 110) two cases with bronze cap helmets. Warriors might also be (Plates 121, 122) buried with a spear, axes or sword. Pairs of bridle-bits indicate (*Figs. 22c, e,*) the use of teams of horses. Some women's graves were extremely (*Fig. 30*) rich and were only equalled or surpassed by the graves of the most important warriors.

POTTERY

The traditional urns enjoyed a brief revival of their accustomed (Plates 94–96, 98) ornament as the vogue for plain urns of late Villanovan I passed away, but a new kind of decoration appears on them which I have called the Angular Style. I have already referred to the various patterns involving the two seated figures that often occur on urns and to the fact that in Villanovan I these were often rendered in a very sketchy fashion. But sometimes in Villanovan II these sketchy renderings turned into a mere series of angles in which the two seated figures had entirely disappeared. I have already referred to the new pear-shaped urns.

Plates 96, 98
Plate 97

Cover-bowls do not differ very much from those of Villanovan I, though the high foot in vogue late in Villanovan I was now going out of style. The handle might have two little points recalling the earlier pair of horns, or it might be surmounted by a little cup of the kind already attributed to Villanovan I.

Plates 102, 103

Rounded bowls are confined to Villanovan II, and have handles ending in a pair of horns or a ram's head.

Plates 99, 100

Only bell helmets are found, though a crested pottery one occurred early in Period III. One bell helmet is decorated with patterns of thin metal strips.

Plate 110

Cups with binocular handles now sometimes have a lower hole which is very small by comparison with the upper hole. Some cups have animal-headed handles, and these include a double cup with a binocular handle with a very small *upper* hole. This anomaly is perhaps due to the construction of the handle attached to both the cups. A very strange cup has a pottery tube rising in the middle and a ring of shallow circular depressions around it. Another feature is ribbing or fluting on the underside of cups.

Plate 105
Fig. 21a, b
Plates 106, 107
Plate 108
Plate 107
Plate 105

Jars with wide bodies become rarer but include larger examples with two horizontal handles and also some with a binocular handle which could be surmounted by a pair of horns.

Plates 101, 104

Spheroid jars, usually of red ware, could as before be on a high foot, but now they might have painted ornament or even resemble Greek Geometric kraters in profile.

Plate 117
Fig. 21d

Fig. 21. Pottery of Villanovan II: a, cup; b, cup with animal-headed handle; c, plastic animal vase; d, spheroid jar on a foot (a, b, d after Monumenti dall'Instituto; c after Pasqui). a, c, d, 1:4; b, 1:2

Plates 112–114 There is still a very wide variety of jugs including the bottle-shaped type with a horned handle, while other examples have animal-headed handles.

Plate 115 As before there are some examples of amphorae of the type found further south around Rome and Naples.

Plates 111 One of the askoi is bird-shaped but lacking its head, though it has traces of a basket handle. The other askos in the form of Plate 109 an animal-bird is very like its counterpart in Villanovan I, but its basket handle is flanked by a pair of human figures, though its four stumpy legs have disappeared.

Plates 118–120 The most important of the Late Geometric vases is a large hydria with a pair of water birds. There are also two cups, one of which also has a water bird. These vases may well have been made in Etruria by Greek potters or their apprentices, but they are of kinds found in Greece in the second half of the eighth century BC. They differ markedly from the dark, hand-made Villanovan pottery in being wheel-made, of light-coloured and refined clay and with ornament in reddish paint.

The hydria had served as an urn, for it contained the crema-Plate 116 ted bones. It was covered by a wheel-made bowl of the same clay as the hydria and decorated with reddish lines that recall the ware of Corinth of the second half of the eighth century BC. But the shape is not Greek, and one can only suppose that it is a local product. These vases have a great importance both as evidence of foreign contacts and for chronology. Such contacts began earlier at Veii in southermost Etruria, since the excavators of the British School at Rome begin their Villanovan II at 800 with Greek Geometric vases of 800–750 BC.

Though belonging to a group of very strange vases that are *Fig. 21c* commoner in Period III, there is one plastic animal vase of yellow ware with designs in red paint which may belong to Villanovan II. The handles had vaguely animal shapes and horns, while the lid carried two little men and a horse with

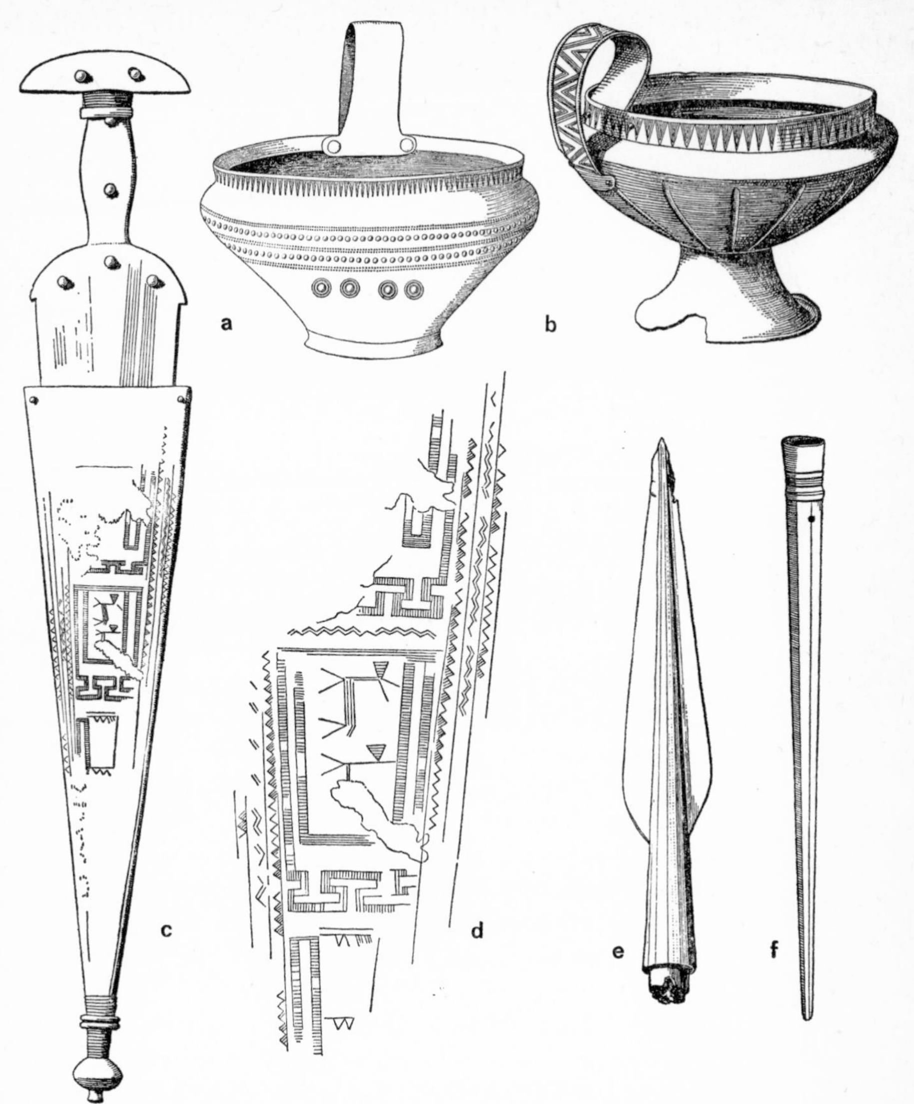

Fig. 22. Bronzes of Villanovan II: a, b, cups; c, d, sword and scabbard; e, f, spear and spear-butt. a, b, 1 : 4; c, 1 : 3; d, 2 : 3; e, f, 1 : 4

red zebra-like stripes. Though there is nothing Greek about its shape or ornament, the yellow ware and the red paint may be due to Greek example.

OTHER OBJECTS

Fig. 22c, d The only example of a sword belongs late in Villanovan II. Its finely decorated scabbard is in exactly the same style as the *Fig. 10c* one of late Villanovan I fifty years earlier, and it must have come from the same workshop if not from the hands of the same craftsman.

Fig. 22e, f Spears are now commoner than before, are as often of iron as *Fig. 29c* of bronze, and sometimes have a butt.

Fig. 27d Axes (palstaves) only occur late in Villanovan II, but they *Fig. 29a, b* are derived from an old Bronze Age type and must have been long known to the Villanovans. Presumably they were not placed in graves until late, but rather strangely they occur in the burials of rich women. Was Villanovan society such that even a great lady needed a handy weapon?

Plates 121, 122 Two urns were covered by cap helmets with no knobs on *Fig. 23* top. Like the bronze axes, they are an old Bronze Age type and must have existed all along but were not placed in earlier graves. One has on each side a panel framed by bosses and containing in the centre the bird boat with 'sun discs'. The most remarkable feature of this helmet is the grotesque face on the front with 'sun discs' for eyes and another in its mouth. Presumably it represented the Villanovan divinity who brought victory to warriors and filled their enemies with terror. The other cap helmet has again the birds' heads and 'sun discs', but Plate 121 here the heads all face the same way.

As before, a warrior might be buried with a pair of horse Plate 128 bits, but now a new kind appears with cheek-pieces in the shape of horses with bird-like beaks, another example of the Villanovan fondness for odd combinations of animal forms.

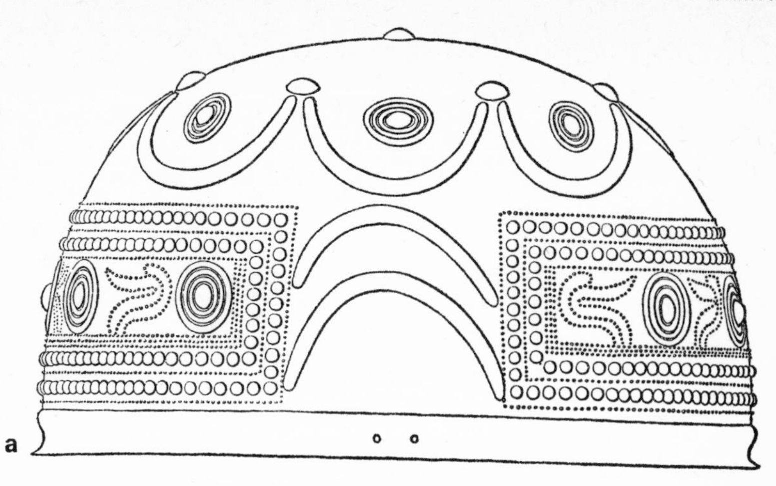

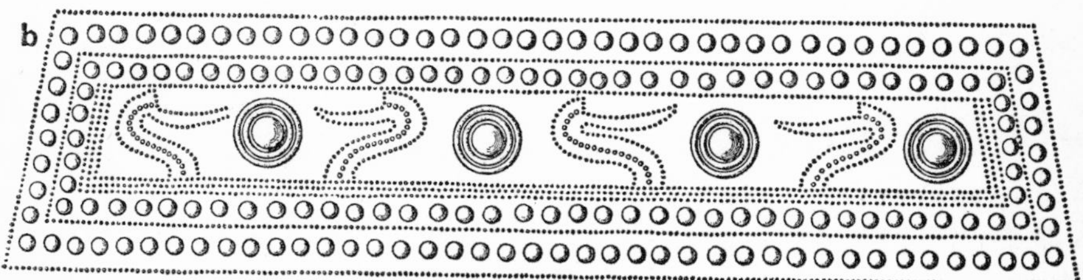

Fig. 23. Cap helmet of Villanovan II: a, back; b, ornament on side in centre of which is the boat with birds heads for and aft and the 'sun-disc'. For front see Plate 122 (a after Pernier). 1 : 3

The old lunate razors of intermediate form lasted to the end of Villanovan II, but were outnumbered by the more sharply curved variety.

One bronze cup in the earlier part of Villanovan II is not very different from the form of late Villanovan I except that it has a low foot. It belongs soon after 750, and in one of the latest pre-Greek graves at Cumae near Naples there is a quite similar cup with a low foot. Since the Greeks occupied Cumae about 750, the dates of the Cumaean cup and the similar one from Tarquinia are close. In the latter part of Villanovan II at Tarquinia, the foot of the bronze cup became much higher.

Fig 22a

Fig. 24. Objects of Villanovan II: a, c, situlae; b, bronze flask with ornament in the ridge-and-boss style; d, wooden vessel (a, c after Monumenti dall'Instituto, b after Montelius, d after Ghirardini). a–c, 1 : 4; d, 1 : 2

The body might be either fluted or ribbed like some of the pottery cups of the same time, and the handle might have an elaborate chevron ornament. A third kind of cup has no foot at all but on its base is so-called pendulum ornament.

Fig. 22b

Plate 127

Bronze amphorae are rare, but they could replace the urn as the container of the cremated ashes. Indeed the best known one resembles a Villanovan urn, and one handle has been broken off before burial as was done with two-handled pottery urns. It is also decorated, like contemporary cap helmets, with 'sun discs', birds' heads and bird boats.

Plate 124

Another kind of amphora had a long neck and resembles in profile the Arnoaldi urns of the northern Villanovans around Bologna, generally dated after Villanovan II at Tarquinia. A third kind of amphora has a form and ornament reminiscent of Europe beyond the Alps.

Plate 123

Figs. 27f, 41

The situlae are really elaborations of central European buckets with swing handles and some have feet like the bronze amphorae and the late bronze cups.

Fig. 24a, c

The flasks represent a curious mixture, for the technique of their manufacture and their ornament are central European, but the basic shape is eastern Mediterranean.

Fig. 24b

Whether the 'censers' were really for burning incense is hard to say. Their form does not have central European parallels, but like the flasks they are an extension of central European bronze work both in their manufacture and ornament.

Plate 126

In Villanovan II there also appear more or less hemispherical bowls and, if parallels for such simple forms are to be sought they are eastern Mediterranean.

Plate 125

No wooden vessels are preserved but some are illustrated in old reports, and they were often decorated with bronze studs.

Fig. 24d

The most frequent form of girdle generally associated with women's graves was a bronze band very wide in the middle. These were long enough to cover only the front of the body, and the rest of the girdle must have been made of leather or cloth.

Figs. 25, 26

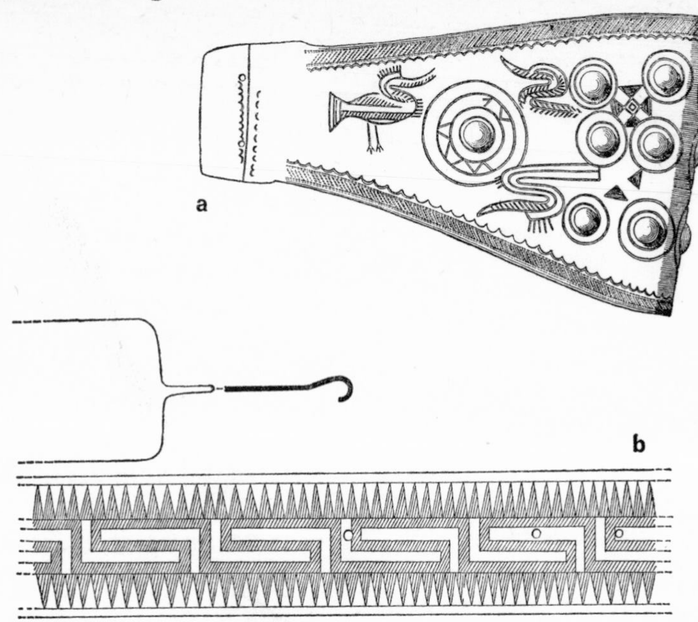

Fig. 25. a, Wide bronze girdle with two birds' heads projecting from a boss, a stylized form of half a double bird boat; b, bronze girdle of uniform width, Villanovan II (a after Montelius). 1:3

They were decorated with birds, 'sun discs', meanders and triangles, and like other kinds of bronzes of this period they reflect central and eastern Europe. A plainer type of uniform width had only meanders and triangles.

Plate 129
Fig. 31f

There is a bronze pectoral which is a plainer version of the much more elaborate one from the Warrior's Tomb of late Villanovan II.

Plate 133

Disc pendants continue as before, and a gold one came from a child's sarcophagus on Monterozzi.

Plate 136
Fig. 27e

Spindle-shaped beads also continue from Villanovan I, and the same child's sarcophagus on Monterozzi contained gold ones. Others were made of spiral wire. Also a new and more elaborate kind of spindle now appears alongside the older form.

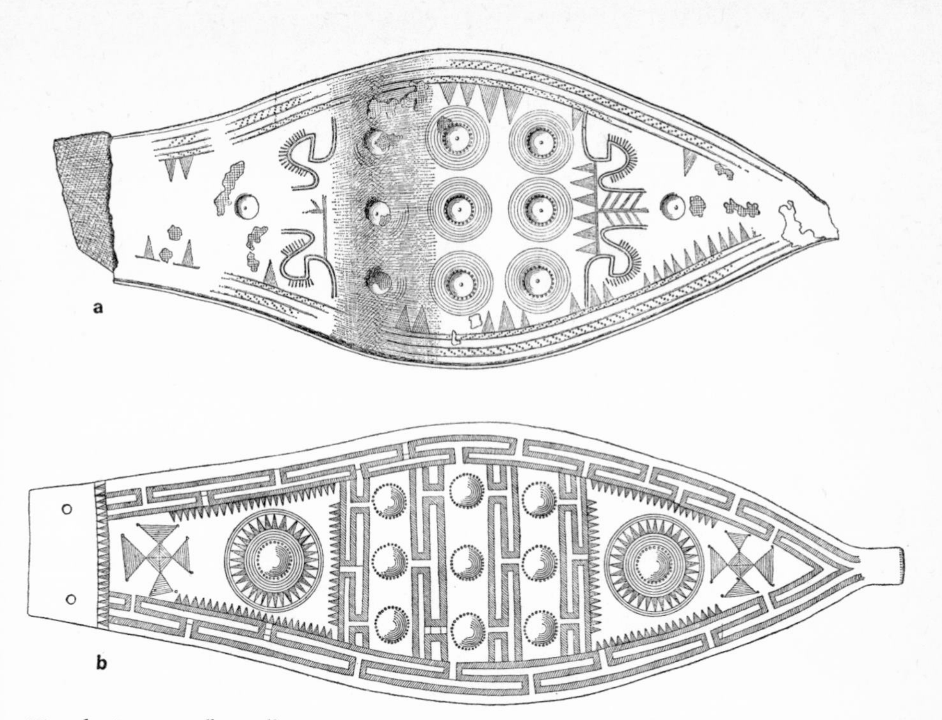

Fig. 26. Bronze girdles, Villanovan II: a has halves of double bird boats in highly stylized form, b has T-shaped meanders and Balkan crosses at ends. 1:3

It is possible that the wheel pendants are another form of the 'sun disc'. Plates 131, 132

I have already mentioned among the undated Villanovan objects a wheel-shaped pin-head, but in Villanovan II there appears a more elaborate type with pendants hanging from it and little birds sitting on it. This seems to be another expression of the idea of circles or 'sun discs' and birds that we have already seen on helmets, bronze vessels and girdles. *Fig. 27a*

Two silver filigree bracelets came from a very rich cremation grave on Monterozzi. The filigree may owe something to imported technique from the higher centres of civilization to the east, but it may also have local roots in the spirals with undulating ends common in Villanovan I. *Fig. 27c*

Silver was used for a few other small objects of Villanovan II. Since this metal was rare in Italy before this period, which corresponds to the time of the first Greek colonies in southern Italy and Sicily, its use may be another sign of foreign contacts.

A few 'scarabs' are also reported but the only one of which even an illustration survives comes from the Warrior's Tomb to be referred to later. Nevertheless scarabs or anything that looked like a scarab to early excavators would probably point to foreign trade either Greek or Phoenician that we have already seen at the end of Villanovan I.

Fig. 27b

Bell-shaped pendants are also important as harbingers of oriental influence in Period III.

Many of the older fibulae died out before Villanovan II began, and several others only survived into its opening years. But the leech-shaped fibula now became increasingly important, and this developed into the exaggerated leech type. There was also a tendency to lengthen the catch, and one variety of leech-shaped fibula has three birds' heads protruding from the bow. But others retained the old disc-shaped foot, though this had by now lost the spiral from which it had been originally derived. Another leech-shaped fibula is of electrum and has an early example of granulated ornament and wire filigree, both techniques of eastern origin. A quite different kind of fibula related to the older serpentine type has pairs of knobs on the bow and a very long catch.

Plates 134, 135, Plate 137

Plate 138

Fig. 31a

THE WARRIOR'S TOMB

The greatest of all Villanovan burials at Tarquinia was discovered in 1869 in an enormous sarcophagus on Monterozzi near the Primi Archi. As with many great tombs discovered in Italy in the last century, doubts have been cast on its integrity. I have discussed this more fully elsewhere and will merely say here that I believe in the essential authenticity of the tomb. The

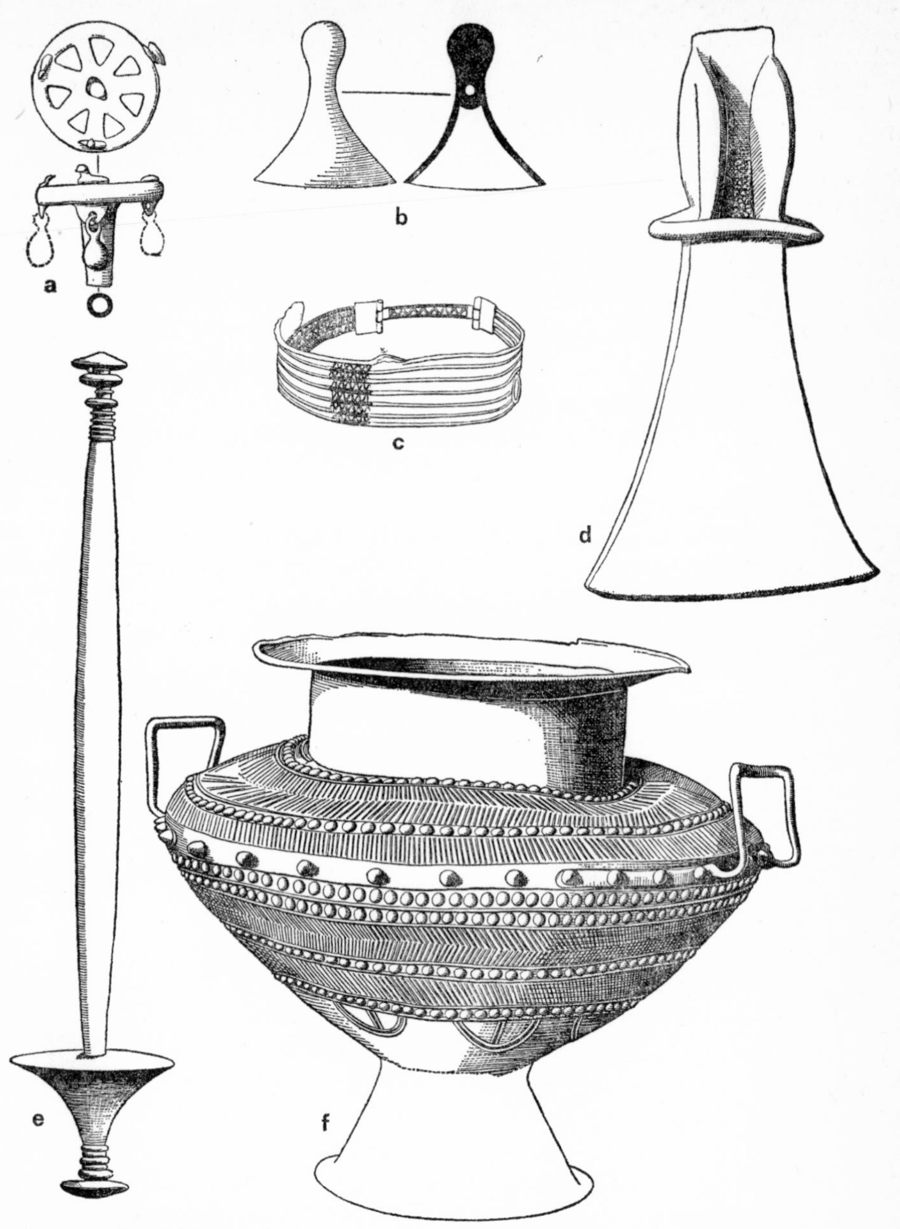

Fig. 27. Objects of Villanovan II: a, pin-head; b, bell-shaped pendant; c, silver filigree bracelet; d, axe (palstave); e, spindle; f, bronze amphora (c–f after Monumenti dall'Instituto). a–e, 1 : 2; f, 1 : 4

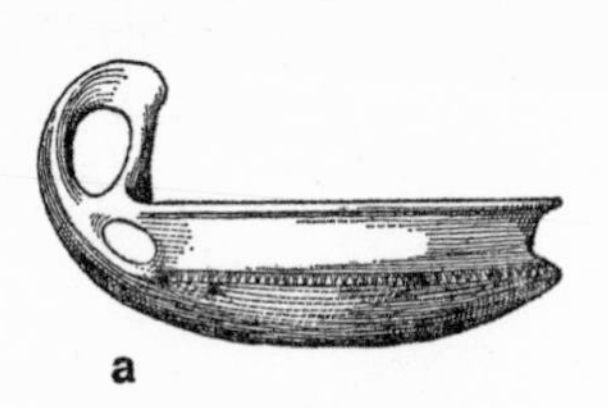

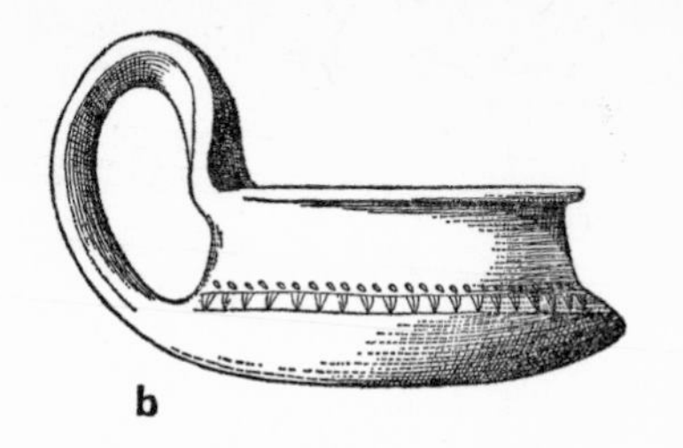

best authorities for what it contained are two careful contemporary accounts by the German archaeologist Helbig and the set of drawings published by him. The objects with one exception are reasonable for Villanovan II, and so are the combination of influences, Villanovan, central European, Greek and eastern. The single exception is a silver plate on which Helbig himself was not entirely clear.

Plates 139–141

There were no less than fourteen painted vases of Greek type, an oinochoe, a skyphos and an askos as well as bowls, plates and small jugs. They all probably belong to the second half of the eighth century, and many if not all are the products of Greek or Greek-trained potters in Italy rather than imports from Greek centres. Opinions vary about what part of the Greek world influenced their making and in this connection the Cyclades, Rhodes, Cyprus and Crete are most often mentioned. The drooping-tailed birds, whose descendants are common Period III, occur on several vases and are sometimes connected with Rhodes. The bird-shaped askos has affinities with Crete or Cyprus, although its head seems to be that of a horse, an element connected with the Villanovan taste for unlikely combinations of animal forms. The oinochoe with its rounded body and conical neck mimics a Cypriot metal shape also known in Italy.

Fig. 28

Other pottery included a bottle-shaped jug, a cup with a binocular handle and one with a single-looped handle, all standard Villanovan forms. There is too a two-handled cup

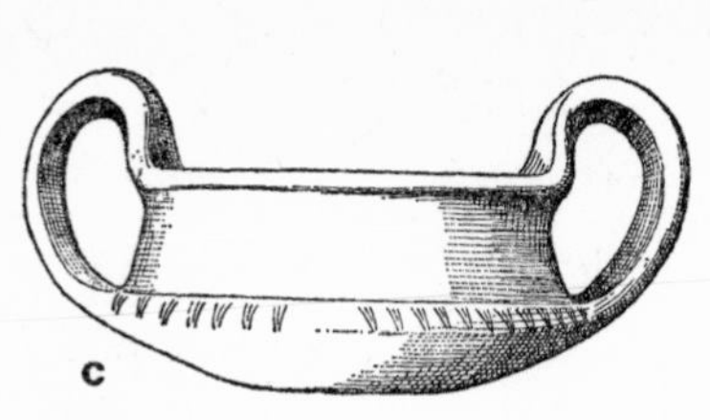

Fig. 28. Pottery from the Warrior's Tomb of Villanovan II on Monterozzi: a–c, cups; d, bottle-shaped jug; e, f, cup-shaped vessel with openings (after Helbig). a–d, 1 : 4; f, 1 : 2

e

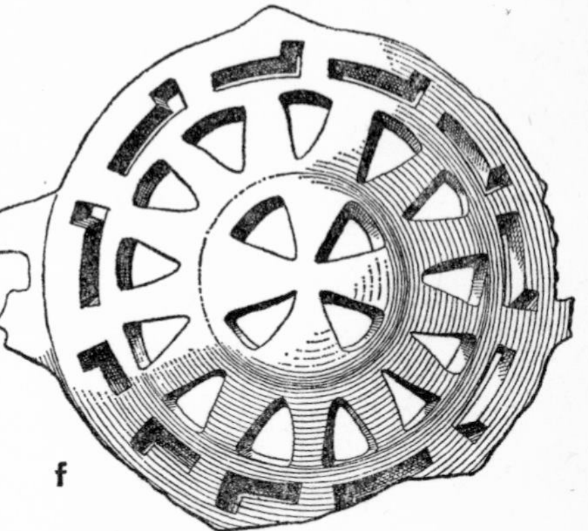

of a kind which first appears in Villanovan II, but which continues in Period III. There are also two vessels shaped like cups with a variety of different openings in them, and these openings may reflect Cyprus or Greece.

The finest of the bronzes is a magnificent shield decorated in the same style as some of the larger bronze vessels from other graves in Villanovan II. The most surprising is a shoulder piece, the first known from Europe since the Mycenaean ones from Dendra, but unfortunately Helbig's drawing is less clear than his others. The warrior's weapons were an enormous spear and two bronze axes. Parts of harness include bits for a pair of horses, eight pointed knobs with slots at the back for two straps crossing at right angles, a tube-cross for a similar purpose and some openwork bronze discs like the wheel pendants already described but more complex.

Fig. 30e

Fig. 29

Fig. 30a, b, d

Bronze vessels included an amphora and a bronze flask of types already mentioned in Villanovan II, as well as a hemispherical cup.

Fig. 30c

Of the gold objects, other than the fibulae described below, the chief example is a pectoral. I have already referred to a plainer contemporary bronze pectoral with the same basic scheme of ornament. But the one from the Warrior's Tomb has

Fig. 31f

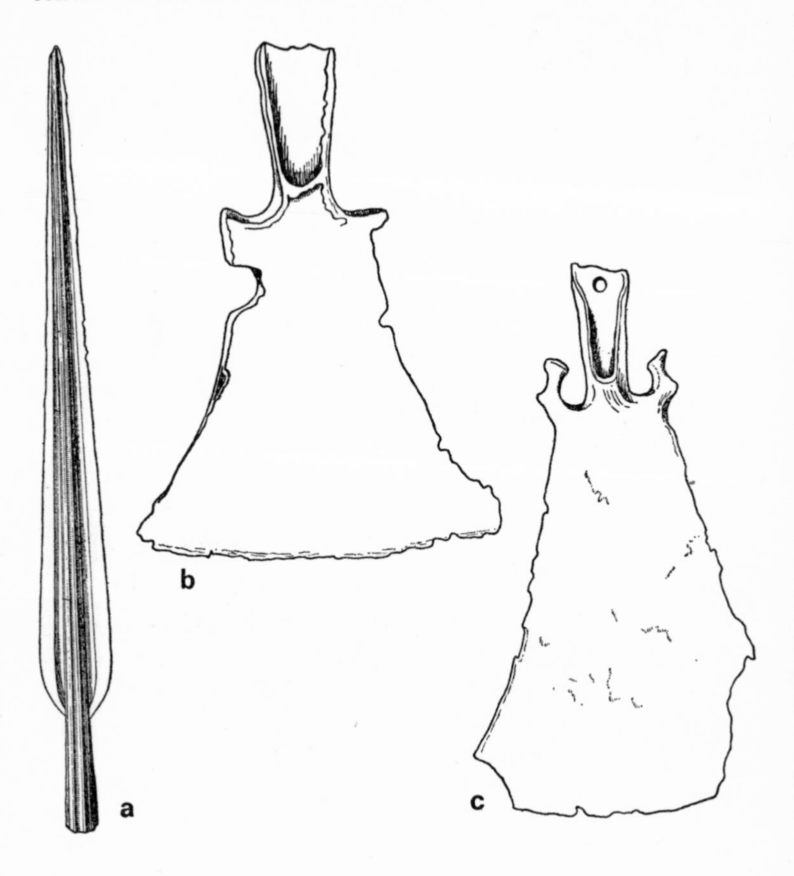

Fig. 29. Weapons from the Warriors' Tomb of Villanovan II on Monterozzi: a, spear (after Helbig); b, c, axes (palstaves). a, 1:5; b, 1:2; c, 1:6

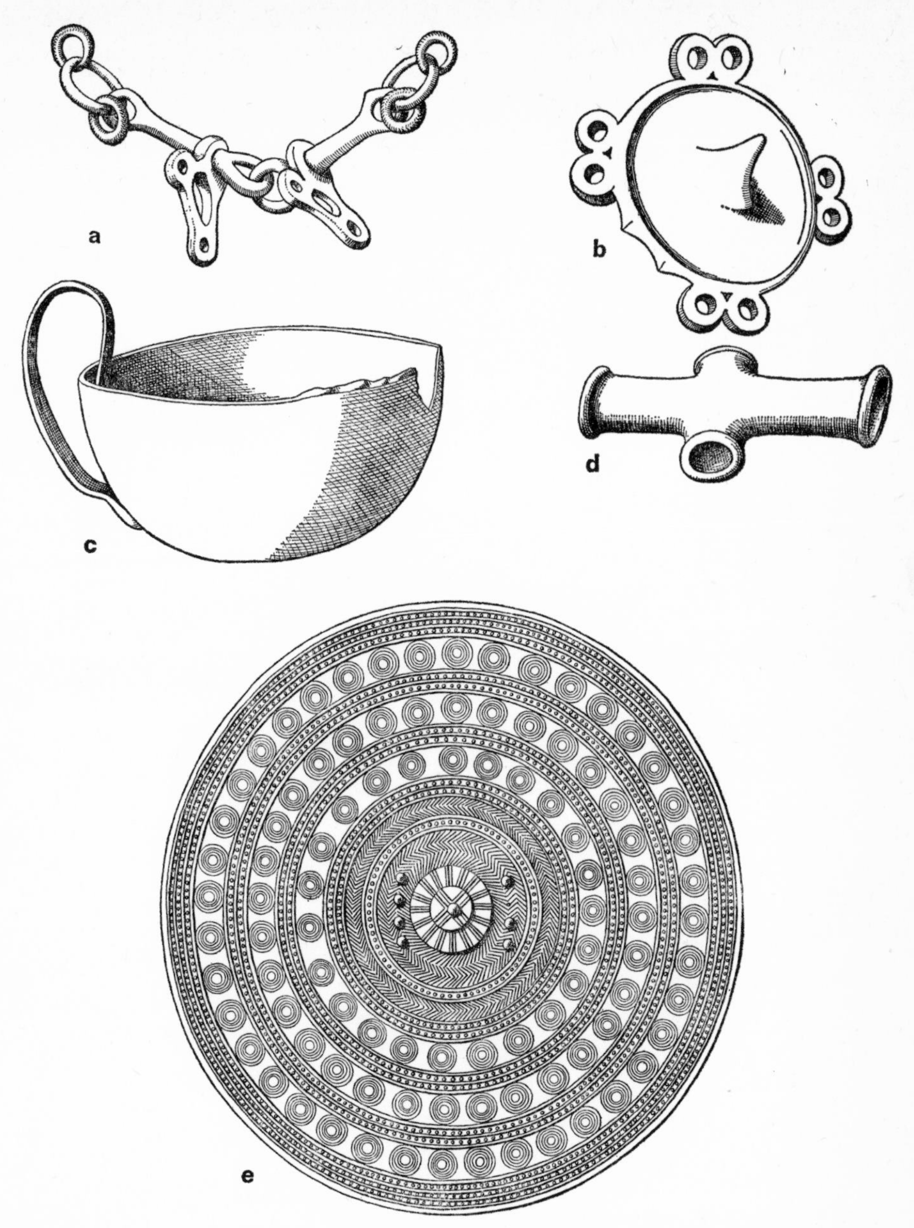

Fig. 30. Bronzes from the Warrior's Tomb of Villanovan II on Monterozzi: a, bridle bit; b, pointed knob; c, hemispherical cup; d, tube-cross; e, shield (after Helbig). a, 1:4; b–d, 1:2; e, 1:8

Fig. 31. The Warrior's Tomb of Villanovan II on Monterozzi: a, gold and silver serpentine fibula with pairs of knobs; b, animal fibula; c, signet ring with scarab; d, g, silver cups; e, Navicella fibula of bronze; f, gold pectoral (after Helbing). a, b, d–f, 1 : 2

birds not quite like those on the painted vases, concentric circles that resemble standard Villanovan decoration, a kind of arcading recalling that on one of the cap helmets of this same period and two sets of three Y-shaped ornaments that are to be explained by the stylized lotuses on the Avvolta shield of Period III.

Fig. 23

Plate 156

The most notable silver objects are a cup with a single looped handle and a fluted base like some pottery cups of Villanovan II, and a two-handled cup matching the pottery one also from the Warrior's Tomb. The silver and bronze signet ring with a scarab is a Phoenician type.

Fig. 31d, g

Fig. 31c

The fibulae all had the elongated catch, and some had leech-shaped bows made of bone and amber segments in the old Villanovan style or an enlarged but hollow bow of the new kind called a navicella or 'little boat' fibula. Another new shape in bronze was the animal fibula. Others were of gold and silver with pairs of knobs and in one case filigree. The long catches, the navicella form, the animal fibula and the pairs of knobs all foreshadow Period III.

Fig. 31a, b, e

CHAPTER IV

Villanovan Background I: Italy before the Villanovans

THE ITALIAN BRONZE AGE

FOR THIS WE MUST TAKE a long look back into the past of both Italy and middle Europe. From about 1400 BC we find in Italy the Apennine Bronze Age, contemporary with the latter part of the central European Middle Bronze Age. This consisted of older local elements with some intrusive ones from the western Balkans. It was strongest in the Adriatic coastal areas of central and southern Italy but spread gradually across the peninsula to the other side, and some think that it was at least partly responsible for the introduction from across the Adriatic of Indo-European tongues, the linguistic ancestors of Latin and related Italic languages. A later phase called Subapennine and contemporary with the early part of the central European Late Bronze Age begins about 1200.

The Apennine people were largely herdsmen who moved every year from the two shores of the peninsula into the central mountain chain and occupied scattered villages and caves. But in fertile Apulia in the south-eastern heel of Italy there were more permanent Apennine sites, and these included the famous trading post of Scoglio del Tonno near Taranto that had Mycenaean contacts. Apennine burials, which contain unburnt skeletons, are very poor and are found near or even within the settlements, but in the Subapennine phase agriculture and bronze made some progress among the Apennine inhabitants, due in part to the example of the agricultural settlements called terremare in the rich Po Valley north of the Apennines.

Also at the same time there were in the Po Valley in the Middle Bronze Age cemeteries in which the cremated remains of the dead were buried in urns covered by bowls. These were in fact what in middle Europe are called urnfields. Urnfields were known as early as this in Hungary and the Balkans, though what connection existed between those of northern Italy and those of eastern Europe is quite uncertain. In the Late Bronze Age the northern Italian urnfields took on a more central European look, suggesting new settlers from over the Alps, but at the same time substantial local elements in them point to a mixing of populations. The people of the terremare in the Po Valley were in some degree responsible for these northern urnfields, though relatively few terremare can be directly connected with them. On the other hand the north Italian urnfields have a much wider distribution than the terremare, indicating that there is much here still to be investigated.

APENNINE ELEMENTS IN VILLANOVAN

Since at Tarquinia the Villanovans lived in a substantial town that must have been supported by an area of farming country around it, its economy was clearly much more advanced than that of the Apennine Bronze Age inhabitants. At the same time there are Apennine elements in its pottery, and the fine dark polished ware sometimes used for smaller pots resembles the finer Apennine fabrics. Apennine cups also often had an angular profile, and something like this can be seen in certain Villanovan ones. Also handles of some Apennine cups are surmounted by animal-heads or a pair of horns, and such handles can also be seen in Villanovan. A curious cup of dark polished ware which has a tubular spout in the middle and little depressions ranged in a ring around it, seems to have something to do with the lids of Apennine milk-boilers. These were lids with raised sides and a large hole in the middle surrounded by little holes, whose purpose was to allow the boiling milk to rise through the holes and then to run back into the pot without

Fig. 32a

Plates 35–39, 99, 100, 106, 107

Plate 108

Fig. 32b

spilling. This Villanovan cup is not the lid of a milk boiler, but it seems to echo the same shape.

As for decoration on pottery, an element common to Apennine and Villanovan is the meander, but since this is also common to the Balkan urnfields and to Geometric Greece, the source of Villanovan meander is not clear. A few other scraps of Apennine ornament recur in Villanovan such as the angular pattern on a jug.

Plate 21

One would expect a majority of the Apennine elements at the beginning of Villanovan, but that is not what one finds. Instead they appear in very tentative fashion early in Villanovan, rise to a climax toward the end of Villanovan I and in early Villanovan II and then fade again along with Villanovan as a whole. This does not support the idea of a gradual evolution from Apennine to Villanovan, even if one takes the Previllanovan urnfields into account. One possible interpretation might be that the late Apennine people lived alongside the Villanovans at Tarquinia, and that the two groups gradually merged, so that the bulk of the Apennine elements appear not at the beginning of Villanovan but in its later stages. Yet this may not be the whole answer, for Villanovan graves became increasingly rich as time passed, and more and more different

Fig. 32. Apennine pottery: a, cup from Filottrano; b, lid of milk-boiler from the Caverna Pertosa (a after Trump, b after Radmilli). a, 1 : 4

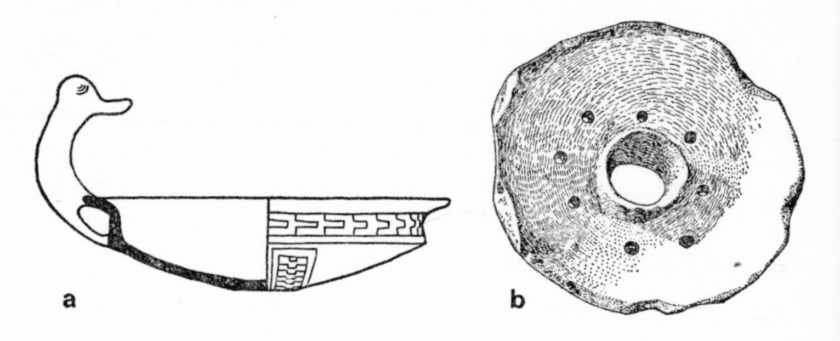

kinds of pots were included in them. Hence the chance of Apennine elements appearing in the pottery was greater in later graves. Thus some Apennine features may have been part of Villanovan from the beginning.

At Tarquinia we have only graves, but two other Villanovan settlements have been recently excavated. The British School at Rome has been working at Veii in southernmost Etruria, where the Etruscan city on its plateau was preceded by a number of Villanovan villages, each with its adjacent cemetery on a knoll below the plateau's rim. The excavation of one of these villages produced only a small proportion of Villanovan ware but a much larger amount of Subapennine pottery. Yet the two belonged to the same people at the same time. Evidently the inhabitants of Veii were more Villanovan in their cemeteries and more Apennine in their kitchens. Pottery-making at this level of civilization is generally a home industry of the women, and it may be that the Villanovan newcomers did not have women enough to go around, causing some to settle down with local wives. This recalls the legend of the early Romans who solved the same problem by seizing the Sabine women.

The excavations of the Swedish Institute in Rome at San Giovenale in southern Etruria also contribute more suggestions. There a small Etruscan city was situated on the usual plateau, but the plateau had also accommodated a Villanovan village and near it an Apennine one. The Apennine village was largely Subapennine in date and had been destroyed in a violent conflagration, but despite the fact that the Villanovan village lay so near it, not a single Villanovan sherd was found at the Apennine one. Evidently no Villanovan ever even threw rubbish there. Perhaps the Villanovans had destroyed it and hence regarded it as *infelix*. But again the Villanovan village and the Subapennine one contained similar bowls of dark polished ware and lids of milk-boilers, and one may suspect that, if the Villanovans destroyed the village, they kept its women. I should add that this interpretation is strictly my own, and it should not be attributed to my Swedish hosts.

THE EARLIER PREVILLANOVAN URNFIELDS

Fig. 33

I have already referred to the urnfields of northern Italy in the Po Valley between the Apennines and the Alps. A few, as I have said, go back to the Middle Bronze Age, while more belong to the Late Bronze Age, and indeed by that time scattered urnfields appear elsewhere in the peninsula. Still, they do not replace the basic Apennine culture but become a new element contemporary with it. Indeed in the Marche in eastern Italy the debris of dwelling sites shows a fusion of the new urnfielders and the older Apennine people into a unified culture. Elsewhere the urnfields, often isolated deep in Apennine territory, have contained pots that embody Bronze Age elements, again suggesting a mixing of populations. Otherwise these urnfields differ greatly among themselves, suggesting that they belonged to new settlers of various kinds. Some elements may have connections with northern Italy, eastern central Europe or the Balkans, but the poverty of the graves makes it hard to trace their antecedents with any assurance. They might represent groups of displaced persons from any of these parts of the urnfield world who settled sporadically in Apennine Italy.

Among the oldest datable urnfields in Aegean terms are Pianello in the Marche, and Timmari in Apulia, both near the coast, for these contained violin bow fibulae such as occur in Greece late in the Mycenaean Age. At Pianello there is also the figure-of-eight fibula that occurs in Mycenaean III C (1200–1050). But both also have the arc fibula that in Greece appears in the eleventh century BC. Besides, Timmari has produced a razor of the roundish rectangular kind such as belong to the very beginning of Villanovan I, and on it may be an engraving of a double axe, another possible Aegean link.

Fig. 34c

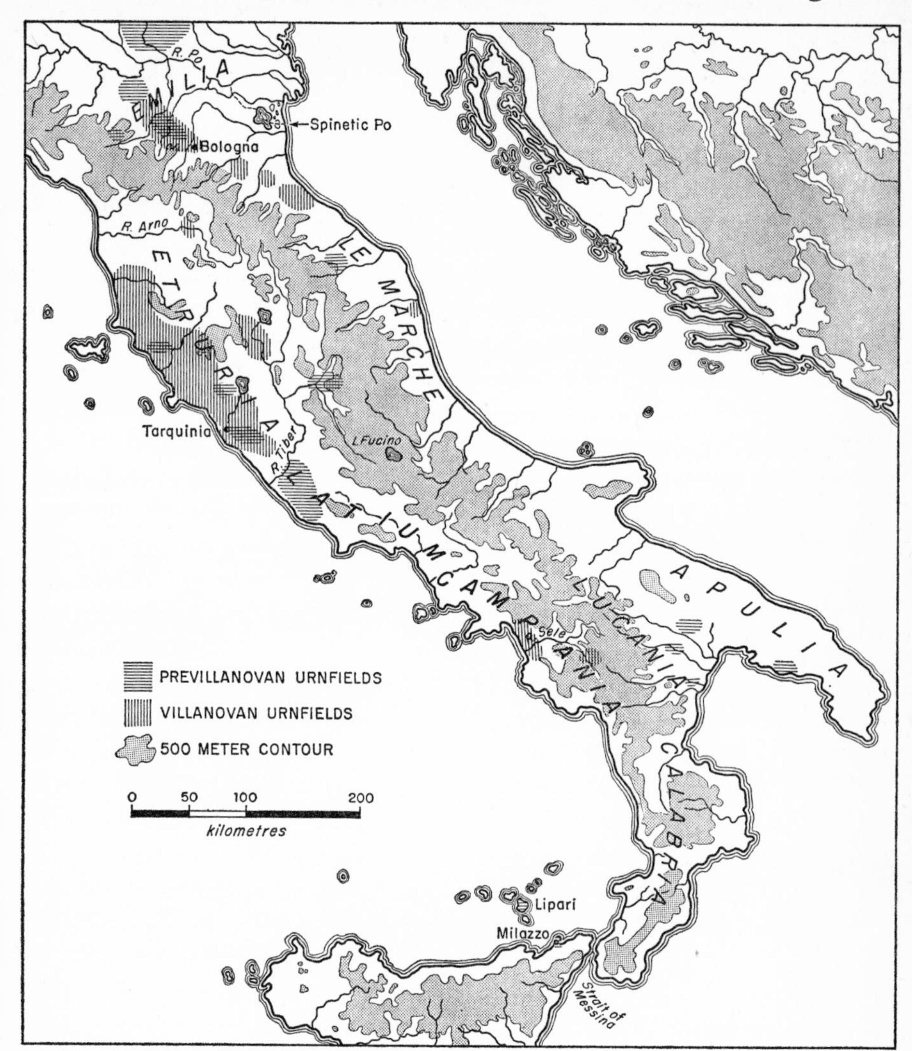

Fig. 33. Map of the Italian urnfields

A third urnfield in Apulia has been found at Torre Castelluccia close to the coast, and a few central European bronzes in it suggest that it had begun by 1200. It was beside an Apennine settlement which also yielded late Mycenaean and Submycenaean pottery belonging to the twelfth and eleventh centuries. Here the juxtaposition of the urnfield and the Apennine site suggests a connection between them, and the Mycenaean wares show that the area was also in contact with the Aegean Bronze Age in its final years. In addition there are traces of urnfields in Lucania and slighter ones in Calabria.

As for the relationships of these urnfields within Italy, the pots from Pianello in eastern Italy have both similarities to and differences from those of the northern Italian urnfields. But by the time one reaches Timmari in the far south-east, the northern resemblances are fewer and the differences greater. At the same time the links between Apulia and the Mycenaean world are quite clear. It may also be remembered that these cemeteries belong both to the period of continental urnfield expansion and to the contemporary cycle of sea-borne disturbances that shook the Aegean and the eastern Mediterranean at this same time. From a geographical viewpoint urnfields near the coasts like Timmari and Torre Castelluccia and far from other urnfields raise the question of whether some of these urnfielders may have arrived by sea.

The Lipari Islands and Milazzo on the adjacent coast of Sicily have been the scene of brilliant excavations by Bernabò Brea and Cavalier. At each there is an acropolis providing an ideal stronghold for sea people interested in traffic passing through the Strait of Messina. The people of Lipari took full advantage of their position from the Neolithic to the end of the Bronze Age, and so did the inhabitants of Milazzo, though apparently not so early.

In Lipari the Middle Bronze Age is entirely different from that of Apennine Italy. It was an extension of the Aegean and

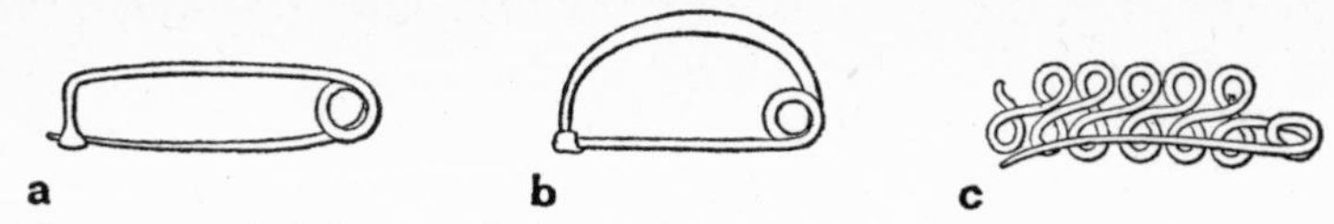

Fig. 34. Greek fibulae: a, violin bow fibula; b, arc fibula; c, figure-of-eight fibula (after Furumark)

the eastern Mediterranean, and it includes pottery of Mycenaean III A (1425–1300 BC) and a little of III B (after 1300), though Apennine pottery was also imported from the mainland. This period ended in violence, and on the acropolis of Lipari over the ruins of the Middle Bronze settlement there appeared a quite new and different culture, frankly Subapennine. There were also bucket-shaped pots, some of which may have contained cremations of children, and such pots occur in central and southern Italy. They were domestic utensils at Torre Castelluccia but were used for cremated burials in the Previllanovan cemeteries in Latium. Clearly the newcomers were from Italy and may be identified with the Ausonians who in Greek tradition did indeed come to Lipari from Italy. This period is called Ausonian I after them. None the less trade with the Mycenaean world did not cease, for fragments of Mycenaean pottery have been found, though authorities differ as to whether they belong to Mycenaean III B (1300–1200) or to III C (1200–1050). This phase was evidently short, since it is represented by a very thin layer over the Middle Bronze Age ruins.

The succeeding Ausonian II continued the same culture but mixed with new intrusive elements. The houses recall Previllanovan Iron Age ones on the Palatine overlooking the Roman Forum. Some pottery resembles that of the Previllanovans, while other pots recall the eastern Meditterranean and Anatolia, and a few fragments look like Greek Geometric. In the cemetery of this period the older graves contained unburnt bodies stuffed into huge pots, an old Anatolian custom known also in

Greece and Sicily, but the later graves were cremations in bucket-shaped pots like those of Ausonian I. In short, Lipari was at this time occupied by inhabitants who included both Subapennine and urnfield elements but who also had eastern connections.

Opposite Lipari on the Sicilian coast is the acropolis of Milazzo. There the Middle Bronze Age cemetery contained inhumed skeletons in huge jars, and the culture was of an Aegean-eastern Mediterranean type. But this was supplanted by people who buried in a Previllanovan urnfield, and some of the urns resemble those of Timmari, though a few were of the bucket-shaped kind found in Lipari. These cremations in urns contrast sharply with the older Sicilian custom of uncremated burials in rock-cut tombs, natural caves or big jars. The acropolis of Milazzo has also produced some pottery that corresponds to Ausonian II on Lipari, and some of the same ware has been found deep in the interior of Sicily at Morgantina.

Clearly the new settlers at Lipari and Milazzo came from Italy and represented a mixture of Apennine and urnfield people repeating a situation already seen on the Italian mainland. Indeed urns at Lipari and Milazzo, as at Timmari, could be covered by bowls like those in northern Italy which were the predecessors of the true Villanovan cover-bowls. Also these settlers at Lipari and Milazzo were in touch with the Aegean and eastern Mediterranean, and they both appeared at about the same time, perhaps somewhat after the period of disruption in the Aegean and the Near East. Besides they obviously came by sea to Lipari and Sicily, and I have already suggested that the urnfield settlements in Apulia represent in part sea-borne newcomers. Could some of the new arrivals represent an overflow into the central Mediterranean of the disturbers of the peace further east, who also contained urnfield elements? Did they mix with the Subapennine inhabitants of southern Italy and did different mixtures of these peoples move on to Lipari and

Milazzo? There is no answer to the questions, but they may be worth bearing in mind.

SOUTH-EASTERN SICILY

Here no urnfields or Apennine pottery have as yet been found, but the events at Lipari and Milazzo had parallels in the south-east around the great harbour of Syracuse. In the Middle Bronze Age there were numerous unfortified settlements of the Thapsos Culture along the shore. The roots of this lay in the Aegean and Anatolia, and trade with the Greek world is shown by pottery of Mycenaean III A (before 1300) and a little of III B (1300–1200). This in fact repeats the contemporary situation at Lipari.

Then suddenly, at about the same time as the Ausonian seizure of Lipari, the old culture vanished from the shore, and the inhabitants fled inland to established new cliff-girt settlements in the mountains. The most important of these is Pantalica which gives its name to the new culture. Its first period, Pantalica I, contained no true Mycenaean pottery, but there are evidences of connection with the Aegean, Rhodes, Cyprus and the Levant which suggest a date in the twelfth and eleventh centuries BC. In any case the abandonment of the prosperous coastal settlements shows that the danger was a maritime one. Were the raiders from Italy, or was this an extension of the disturbances that were disrupting the Near East and the Aegean at this time? Again we can only pose the question without having a ready answer. Nevertheless the Pantalica Culture continued to maintain tenuous connections with the Aegean and eastern Mediterranean lands. Using these as best one can for chronological links, I would suggest that Pantalica I lasted down to the eleventh century, that Pantalica II belonged to about the eleventh-tenth centuries and that Pantalica III began about the tenth century. Pantalica III in any case died out in

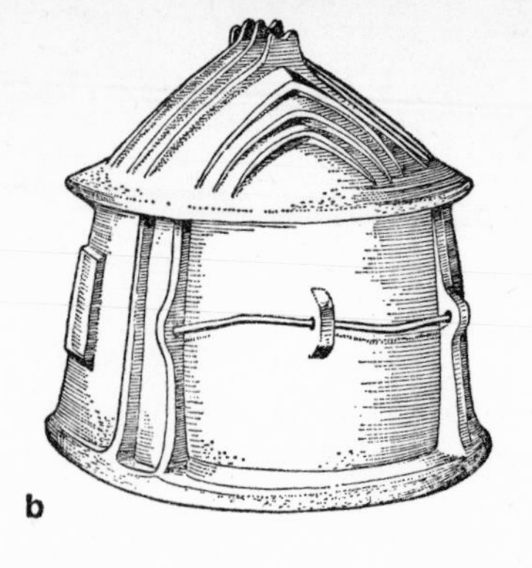

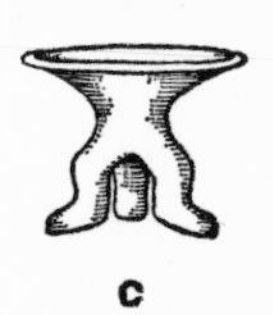

the second half of the eighth century when the Greek colonization of eastern Sicily began. I mention these later phases of the Pantalica Culture because they are useful for the dating of Villanovan I.

LATER PREVILLANOVAN URNFIELDS

In Rome and in the adjacent Alban Hills there were more urnfields. Unburnt burials are also found, but they are later. Indeed some of the cremations are in pozzo graves like the Villanovan ones but most cannot be called Villanovan, since the characteristic two-storied Villanovan urns are very rare. Their connections with the urnfield world of Europe remain to be investigated, but their pottery clearly owes a good deal to the late Apennine Bronze Age, and some of the elements are traceable to the Aegean.

Fig. 35b
Plate 143

One possible post-Minoan Cretan element is found in the house urns, the predecessors of the Villanovan ones, and one example of this Latian type came from the vicinity of Tarquinia. These differ from the Villanovan ones in having pairs of horns on the roofs, and these recall pairs of horns on Late Minoan and post-Minoan pottery coffins. At the same time the Cretan analogues of the house urns are much smaller; they were not for cremated human remains and are found not in tombs but in

Fig. 35. Pottery from Latium and Euboea: a, pot with small cup attached, Roman Forum; b, house urn from Grottaferrata, Latium; c, pottery tripod, Roman Forum; d, pottery tipod, Xeropolis, Euboea (a–c after Müller-Karpe, d after Popham and Sackett)

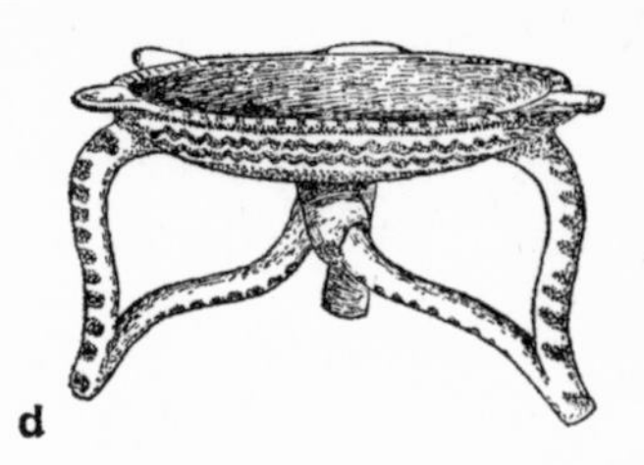

houses. But some doors of the Cretan models are strikingly like the Latian ones. Both have a projection on either side of the door for a rod to hold it in place and another in the middle of the door for the rod to pass through. Such a model could of course only reproduce a building in which no one lived, since the door could only be fastened from the outside. This suggests a shrine rather than a dwelling, and the idea of shrines gains support from somewhat similar human figurines contained by some Cretan and Latian examples. Possibly in Italy the house urns became shrines for the cremated bones of some people of special importance. In the Latian cemeteries, as at Tarquinia, house urns were comparatively rare. House urns very like Italian ones are of course a feature of the Bronze Age of the southern Baltic lands, but the northern examples are not clearly older than their Italian counterparts.

There is also a kind of pottery tripod in the Latian urnfields that consists of a dish supported on three curved legs that meet underneath it. The best parallel elsewhere for this kind of tripod is an Early Protogeometric one of about the eleventh century recently found in Euboea by the British School at Athens. This Euboean tripod has three 'flying buttresses' derived from the legs of a kind of Cypriot tripod that begins somewhat earlier. In the Euboean example these buttresses connect the rim with the legs, but they were not needed in the sturdier Latian ones. Other

Fig. 35c

Fig. 35d

resemblances to the Aegean are the asymmetrical pots called askoi and also the trick of attaching little cups to larger pots. Such little cups and some other resemblances also occur in Villanovan.

Fig. 35a

Similarities between Latium and the Aegean are to be seen too in some bronzes, including fibulae and miniature weapons. Among the miniature weapons is the sword with a curved T-shaped hilt, a feature common both to the Aegean and the Near East. These new Aegean elements arrived in west central Italy with the Previllanovan urnfields and have no connection with the Apennine Bronze Age. Yet these newcomers were not really in the Aegean tradition, though they had come under some degree of influence from the post-Mycenaean world. Basically they seem to be an offshoot of the European urnfields, though in Latium they mixed with the older Apennine inhabitants. As is the case of the southern urnfielders in Italy, their sites are within reach of the sea. The oldest stage of these urnfields belongs probably in the eleventh to tenth century BC.

In southern Etruria there are some Previllanovan urnfields, mostly small, and also some scattered objects such as a house urn from Tarquinia, an urn from Vulci, and another with no history in the museum at Tarquinia. The contents of these urnfields are allied to those of Latium. The two most important are Allumiere and Sasso Furbara, and these and other places where Previllanovan graves have been found are for the most part within reach of the sea.

Plate 143
Fig. 36c, e

The urnfield at Allumiere was relatively large and contained pozzo graves, some with stone receptacles as in true Villanovan. No graves seem as early as the earliest at Pianello, Timmari or Torre Castelluccia, and certain urns, like the two mentioned above, approach the true Villanovan shape. Some resemblances in ornament occur, including a few seated figures of Villanovan type. But the fibulae are more archaic and have the spiral wire feet from which the Villanovan spiral disc was derived.

Fig. 36a, b

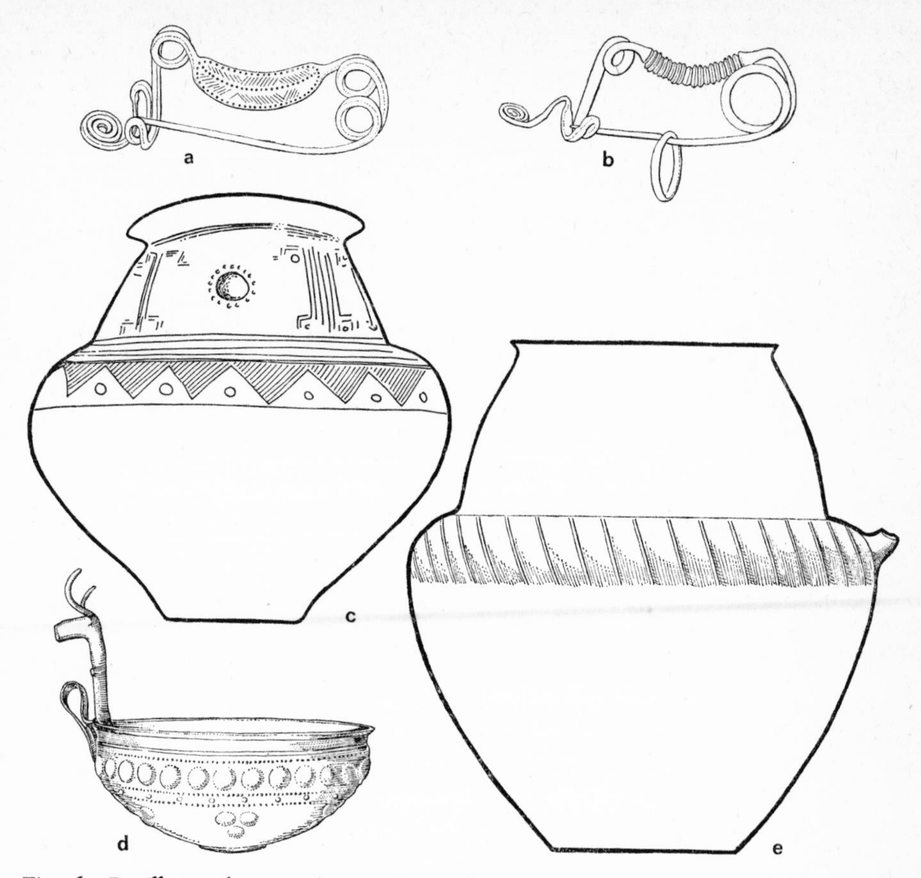

Fig. 36. Previllanovan bronzes and pottery from southern Etruria: a, b, fibulae from Allumiere; c, urn in the Museo Nazionale, Tarquinia; d, bronze cup from Coste del Marano; e, urn from Vulci (a, b after Colini, c after Säflund, d after Müller-Karpe). a, b, 1:2; c–e, 1:4

The relationship of the Previllanovans to true Villanovans in Etruria is hard to define. The Previllanovan cemeteries are generally not in the same places as Villanovan ones, and hence there is no such continuity as exists between Villanovan and Etruscan, for many of the Villanovan cemeteries were grouped around the plateau settlements that became the Etruscan cities of later times. Allumiere and Sasso Furbara are to some extent exceptions to this. There was no great Etruscan centre at either place, but there are Etruscan settlements, cemeteries and scattered tombs around Allumiere, while at Sasso Furbara there exists a whole sequence of tombs from Previllanovan through true Villanovan to Orientalizing Etruscan.

Allumiere and Sasso Furbara could be the seed from which Villanovan sprang, but the wider the view that one takes, the greater are the difficulties in accepting this too readily. The original Villanovan centres in Etruria were indeed in the south within reach of the coast, and those further north and the further inland were later and more provincial. But across the Apennines in the Po Valley there is the great Villanovan centre of Bologna which is at least as old as any Villanovan in southern Etruria. This militates against the theory of the origin of the whole Villanovan culture in southern Etruria, for then Bologna should be later. Neither does it support an origin at Bologna, for in that case the cemeteries in northern Etruria should be earlier and those further south more provincial and later. But this is the very opposite of what seems to be the case. The two parallel Villanovan settlements, one in coastal Etruria and the other north of the Appenines and not far from the Adriatic, could perhaps be explained as roughly simultaneous settlements of the same people who came by sea to Italy, one to the western side and the other to the eastern. The Previllanovans of Allumiere and Sasso Furbara might then have been less ancestors than related forerunners who also arrived by sea. I shall allude to the traditions relevant to this idea in Chapter 9.

As for chronology, the Previllanovan tombs of southern Etruria seem later than the oldest Italian urnfields that are contemporary with the last days of Mycenaean Greece, and still they seem earlier than true Villanovan at Tarquinia, which probably started about the tenth century BC. Hence the eleventh and tenth centuries might be as good a date as any for these Previllanovans of southern Etruria.

SOME PREVILLANOVAN BRONZES

Bronzes follow a different course from pottery among the peoples I have mentioned here, for they are much less clearly localized than the pottery of the different groups of Previllanovan urnfielders. One of these bronze forms, the roundish rectangular razor known in early Villanovan I, was used by both the Previllanovans and the inhuming people of the Trench Grave Culture of southern Italy. Another type of Previllanovan razor is almost identical with the elongated lunate kind used early in Villanovan I. This shape is common in north-western Jugoslavia and the adjacent part of Hungary at a time contemporary with Previllanovan and early Villanovan.

Also Previllanovan fibulae seem to be the basis for some Villanovan types. Central European urnfielders used many pins to fasten their clothes and relatively few fibulae, but in Hungary fibulae were commoner. Also the fibula with a spiral wire foot was commonest there too, and its occurrence at Mycenae shows that it is as old as the end of the Mycenaean Age. It was this spiral wire foot that was later hammered flat to make the disc of the Villanovan disc fibula. This does not mean that all inspiration for Previllanovan fibulae came from Hungary, for I have already referred to some types that resemble Aegean forms, and I will refer to others in dealing with Villanovan, but these shapes in Italy follow their own lines of development.

Fig. 27d

Fig. 29a, b

Figs. 25a, 26

Bronze axes of the kind called palstaves also appear in graves of Villanovan II. Simpler varieties of these are found in Italy with Subapennine and Previllanovan but are really forms of the older European palstave. They must always have been known to the Villanovans and are an example of an early form that did not appear in graves until Villanovan II. The same is true of the wide bronze girdle which does not appear at Tarquinia until Villanovan II. Yet these girdles seem much older in Italy, and they probably have a central European origin. Certainly their ornament comes from there.

Fig. 36d Finally something must be said about the famous bronze cups from the Previllanovan hoard of Coste del Marano near Allumiere. These are of central European background though made in Italy, but their bull-headed handles are not like central European bull-headed ones, and more probably were imitated from those found in Crete. If so they are an additional Aegean element in Previllanovan. Perhaps they found favour in Italy because horned and animal-headed handles in pottery had such a vogue among the Apennine people.

I have discussed these metal types separately from the pottery because their implications are different. Pottery at this level of society, as I have said, is usually locally made by the women. So a continuity in the shapes of pots implies a continuity in the female population and presumably some continuity in family life. On the other hand entirely new shapes of pots, and especially such a new idea as the making of urns to hold the cremated ashes of the dead, would seem to imply a break in this continuity indicating new people. As I have already emphasized, such breaks are seldom complete, and old forms continue beside the new ones indicating a continuation of elements of the older population mixed with newcomers.

Burial customs also have an ethnic significance since they are connected with the conservative forces of religion. Hence pots and burial customs are guides to who was who at this time, and they suggest that the cremating peoples of Italy including the Villanovans were a mixture of the older Apennine inhabitants with others.

But in societies of this level the working of metal is usually practised by a special caste of persons generally separate from the rest of the community. Hence such metal-workers might produce similar bronzes for a variety of cultural groups. When one also considers how easily small bronzes could be traded, it is clear that they have much less ethnic significance than pots which are more bulky and fragile.

CHAPTER V

Villanovan Background II: Balkan Elements

I HAVE ALREADY indicated that the Villanovans placed the cremated ashes of their dead in urns and buried them in cemeteries without tumuli, in other words in urnfields as in middle Europe. This mode of burial begins in the Hungarian Early Bronze Age, but the custom was soon taken up in the Middle Bronze Age after about 1600 BC in two areas of especial interest for this subject. They are Oltenia in south-western Romania and the adjacent Banat, now divided between Romania, Jugoslavia and Hungary. These two areas are the home of two-storied urns. Villanovan urns are also two-storied, and are the most prominent feature of Villanovan graves, for they are so large that in museum exhibits they dwarf all the other material. They do not repeat eastern European urns with any exactness, and most of their ornament is quite different except for the meander, but the similarity of the two-storied form is notable. The resemblance between Villanovan and Oltenian urns is especially striking if one compares the undecorated urns from both areas. The size, form and colour are quite alike.

Fig. 37

Fig. 38b, c

Double pots also are found in the Oltenian urnfields and are often connected by holes like Villanovan examples; in fact multiple pots with connecting holes have a long history in the Balkans. Grooved handles are likewise found in Oltenia as in Villanovan, though on different shapes of pots.

Fig. 38d

Fig. 38a

Still another form from these Oltenian urnfields of the Middle Bronze Age is the horned bird, and indeed the Oltenian representations of this mythical creature are the oldest known, but I shall discuss them later.

Fig. 39

Plate 145

Fig. 37. Map of Eastern Europe

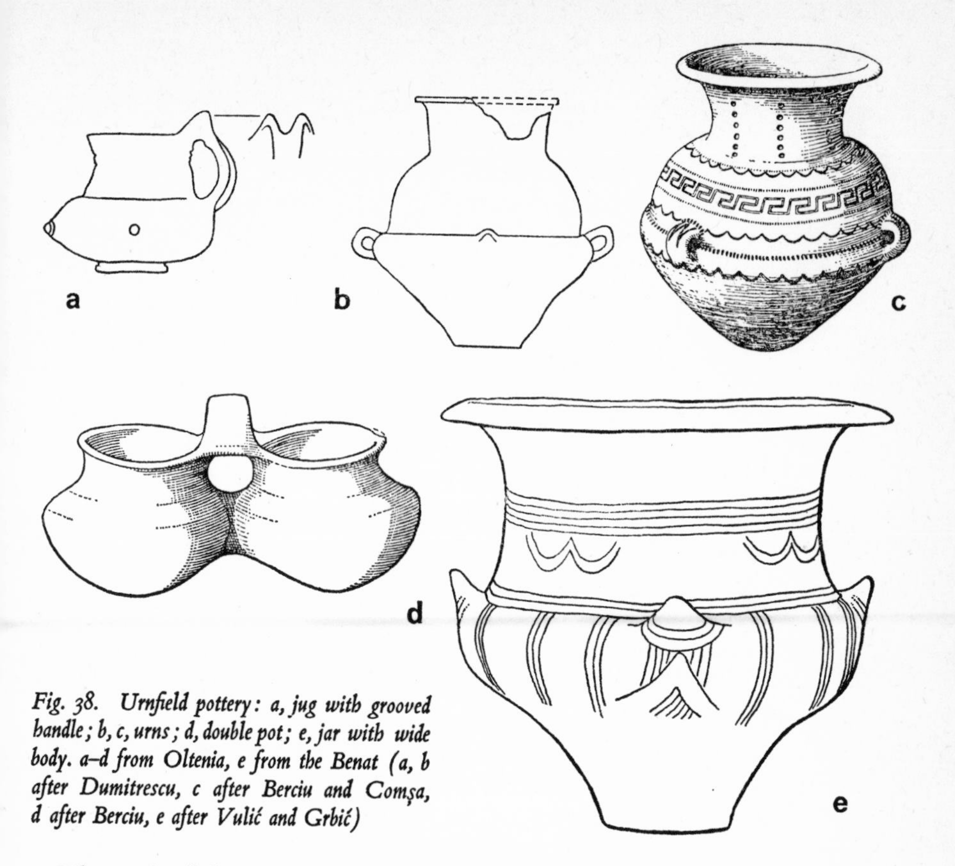

Fig. 38. Urnfield pottery: a, jug with grooved handle; b, c, urns; d, double pot; e, jar with wide body. a–d from Oltenia, e from the Benat (a, b after Dumitrescu, c after Berciu and Comşa, d after Berciu, e after Vulić and Grbić)

The end of this phase in Oltenia came perhaps about the twelfth century BC, and the Middle Bronze Age urnfields there are covered with a layer of sand suggesting a period of dry climate and the formation of dunes. Also at about this time urnfields with different urns appear indicating a movement of people from further west. This may be connected with disturbed conditions in central Europe suggested by the burial there of great hoards of bronze.

A later phase in Oltenia is represented by the cemeteries at Plopşor and Vîrtop. These are not urnfields but consist of tumuli containing cremations in two-storied urns which also

Plate 142

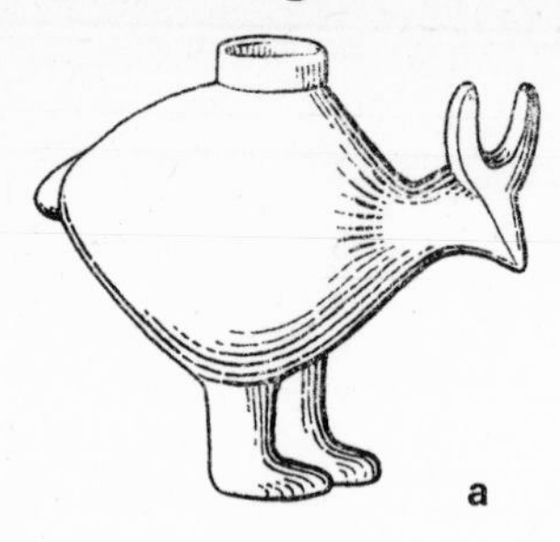

Fig. 39. Horned animal-birds: a, Vienna-Vösendorf; b, Oderberg-Bralitz, Brandenburg; c, Čičarovce, Slovakia (a after Müller-Karpe, b, c after Kossack). b, 1:4; c, 1:3

resemble Villanovan ones, while the diagonal fluting on the shoulders, reproduced in the drawing, also makes them look like some Previllanovan urns. Other resemblances to Villanovan are the double cups, sometimes with connecting holes, and a fruitstand recalling one from Tarquinia probably of Villanovan I. Some Romanian prehistorians place the beginning of Plopşor and Vîrtop before 1000 and others after 900 BC, but whatever the date, it is clear that forms with a resemblance to Villanovan had deep roots in Oltenia.

Fig. 36e
Fig. 9
Fig. 38d

In the Banat, with which Voyvodina may be included, the Middle Bronze Age urnfields have the same kind of two-storied urns as in Oltenia, but other kinds were used as well. Again we find double cups, but they are fewer and less apt to have connecting holes. Also there is a jar with a flaring rim, a wide body and a narrow foot with four big upward-pointing knobs on the shoulder, that recalls a pot from Villanovan I. But with the twelfth century BC this phase comes to an end as it did in Oltenia. Still in the twelfth and eleventh centuries two-storied urns recalling Villanovan ones were used in southern Transylvania.

Fig. 38d
Plate 19
Fig. 38e

In other Balkan areas, Bosnia and Macedonia, binocular handles are also found, though so far as I know, not specifically in urnfield contexts and not with very clear dates.

Of course these Balkan parallels to Previllanovan and Villanovan of Etruria are not precise, and there are many kinds of pots in these areas that have no parallels in Italy. But the

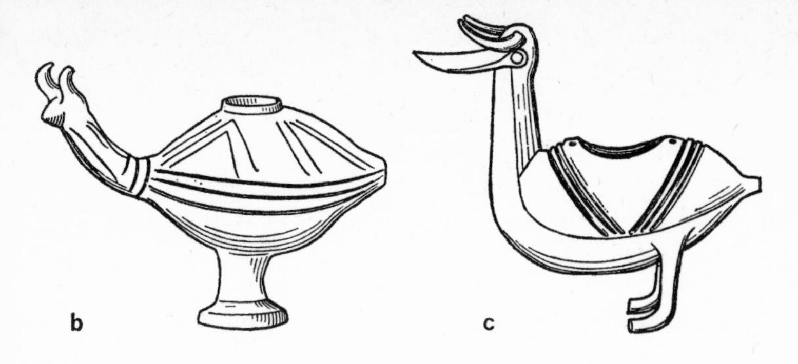

resemblances suggest that these settlers in Italy may have had a Balkan background.

One would imagine that the obvious way for Balkan people to migrate to Italy would be to follow the river valleys that lead northwestward toward the head of the Adriatic, and from there to descend into the Po Valley where the great Villanovan centre at Bologna would be the base for a further expansion southward into Etruria. But this plausible scheme is full of difficulties. If one follows the route westward from Oltenia and the Banat to the head of the Adriatic, one finds urnfields along it, but the further one goes toward Italy, the less the pottery looks like Villanovan. Also if Bologna had been the primary Villanovan base in Italy, one would expect the Villanovan cemeteries to be progressively later further south with the latest in southern Etruria, but this is the opposite of what occurs. Rather, it seems that Bologna in the Po Valley on the one hand and Tarquinia and similar centres in southern Etruria on the other are all of about equal age, and as one goes further north in Etruria toward Bologna the Villanovan cemeteries become later and more provincial. Hence it would appear that the Villanovan settlement in Etruria spread northward from the south rather than southward from Bologna, and that Bologna and its satellite settlements were a separate group.

All of this makes it hard to believe in a Villanovan settlement of Italy from the Balkans that went around the head of the

Adriatic. But if the Villanovans did not come by land, can they be explained by two nearly simultaneous settlements from the sea, one through the Adriatic going to Bologna on the eastern side of Italy and the other to southern Etruria on the western side? I shall refer in Chapter 9 to traditions that could be connected with two such settlements.

This chapter is short by comparison with the others dealing with the Villanovan background, but its material may be of greater importance than its length might indicate. Pottery-making among peoples of this level of civilization is, as already stressed, usually a household task of women. Hence, if types of pottery can be shown to have moved from one area to another, the implication is that the women who made them also moved. This in turn suggests that a migration took place that included at least some families. Consequently, if I am right in suggesting that the characteristic Villanovan urn and some other kinds of pots are of Balkan origin, their presence in Italy may have ethnic significance. At the same time the considerable differences between the Villanovan pots and their Balkan analogues would not point to a direct and rapid migration from the Balkans to Italy, but might be consistent with an indirect and slow one.

CHAPTER VI

Villanovan Background III: Central European Elements

THE CENTRAL EUROPEAN URNFIELDS

IN THE LATE BRONZE AGE in central Europe there were other urnfield peoples in addition to the earlier Balkan ones mentioned in the last chapter, but their art, like that of the Balkans, included representations of circular 'sun symbols', birds and horned animal-birds. Indeed the basic forms of this art, probably magical or religious in content, were also shared by the Villanovans.

These Late Bronze Age urnfielders had an economy based on agriculture and stock raising, and some lived in substantial fortified settlements. They not only commanded the routes to the magic amber of the Baltic, but they also possessed bountiful sources of copper, tin and gold, and some were skilled in shaft mining. The metal-working crafts were especially highly developed in eastern central Europe, Hungary, Slovakia and Transylvania. The basic elements of urnfield culture had of course been learned from the Aegean and the Near East though by comparison with the civilizations of these areas, that of the urnfielders was illiterate and barbaric, if in other ways rich and vigorous. Access to supplies of metal and skill in working it made possible the development of a massive armament industry attested by numerous weapons in graves and also in the vast numbers of hoards of bronze, often very large. Even if one excludes votive hoards, the need to hide this great weight of metal in the ground bespeaks turbulent times, especially when one reflects that every hoard that comes to light today is one whose owners never came back for it.

From about 1200 BC and later these peoples began to expand. In Poland they pushed eastward while to the north their influence penetrated to Denmark and southern Sweden. To the south-west they spread into France and Spain, to the south over the Alps into northern Italy, and to the south-east into Greece. Signs of their penetration of Greece are the appearance of their weapons there at the time of the destruction and abandonment of Mycenaean palaces and settlements. But this need not imply that all urnfield penetrations were necessarily warlike, and their movements in many areas may well have included peaceful settlement and mixing with the older inhabitants.

As for chronology, there are two main periods, an Early Urnfield one which began in the thirteenth century BC and which lasted through the eleventh century, and a Later Urnfield Period from the tenth to the eighth century. The Early Urnfield Period can be connected with the chronology of late Mycenaean and Protogeometric Greece through urnfield bronzes found there. The end of the Later Urnfields and the beginning of the succeeding Hallstatt Iron Age can be linked with Italy in the eighth century when Greek trade and colonization there once more make it possible to relate Italian events to a Greek chronology now based on historical tradition. Early Villanovan at Tarquinia is about contemporary with the Later Urnfield Period of central Europe though not with its very beginning. The transition from Early to Late Villanovan in the eighth century at Tarquinia seems to have taken place at much the same time as the transition from the Late Urnfield Period to the Hallstatt Iron Age in central Europe.

CENTRAL EUROPEAN ELEMENTS IN VILLANOVAN

In the previous chapter I discussed the Balkan two-storied urns and multiple cups with connecting holes that resemble Villanovan ones. Occasionally these are also found in central Europe but these two-storied urns are unlike Villanovan ones in shape, and there is no such concentration of forms resembling Villanovan as in the central Balkans.

There are also some kinds of ornament on pottery common both to the central European urnfields and to Villanovan. The decorating of pots with bronze studs stuck in before firing goes back in Germany to the Early Urnfields, and it also appears in western Jugoslavia in the Later Urnfield Period. Similarly, making patterns on pots with very thin strips of metal is an Early Urnfield device in the Alps. But these are decorative elements distinct from the basic shapes of the pots themselves.

Central European elements are more numerous in Villanovan metal-work at Tarquinia than in pottery and include crested, bell and cap helmets of bronze, types that are all found in central Europe in the Early Urnfield Period and later, and hence are older there. The sockets of the bell helmet and one cap helmet are attached by casting on, the customary method in central Europe. At Tarquinia the first crested bronze helmets belong to mid and late Villanovan I, but a pottery replica occurs in early Villanovan I, showing that the form was then already known. The solitary bronze bell helmet and cap helmets with sockets are dated only to Villanovan as a whole, but the pottery replicas of these are here lumped together since they are hard to distinguish, and the oldest belongs to early Villanovan I. Cap helmets without sockets were never imitated in pottery and though the type is known from Bronze Age Italy, they do not occur in Tarquinia until Villanovan II.

Plates 54, 90–93
121, 122
Figs. 18, 23

Though these Villanovan helmets are ultimately of central European derivation, most of them differ in detail from foreign examples, and their ornament is more elaborate. In central Europe this ornament is found largely on other kinds of bronzes but was used sparingly on helmets. Thus it is clear that these helmets, though based on northern traditions, were not imports but were made in Italy.

Fig. 11

As for weapons, there is at Tarquinia a single antennae sword, and this belongs to mid-Villanovan I. Such swords are distributed largely in southern Baltic lands and central Europe, and there the earliest ones were clearly older than Villanovan. There are also numerous Italian examples of which several have been found in Etruria. Like the helmets, they are not imports, and must have been made in Italy since they differ in detail from the more northerly examples, but they are less numerous in Etruria than the short Villanovan swords already mentioned.

Plate 57

Fig. 36d

Bronze cups of urnfield derivation also occur in Villanovan I in forms traceable to central Europe where prototypes are as old as, or older than their relatives at Tarquinia. But since the famous Previllanovan ones from Coste del Marano in southern Etruria also belong to the same series, it is clear that such cups had reached southern Etruria even in the days of the Previllanovan urnfields. But as with other bronzes, most of these Villanovan cups do not repeat exactly the forms of central Europe, and so are probably Italian products under central European inspiration. By Villanovan II bronze cups had developed feet, sometimes very high, and other peculiarities quite unlike the trans-Alpine ones, and by the same period the Villanovan artisans had developed other shapes of bronze cups not traceable at all outside Italy.

Fig. 22a, b

Plate 127

Fig. 24a, c

In Villanovan II, especially toward its end, large bronze vases were placed in the richer graves, and among these are situlae or buckets with swing handles. The bronze situla had long been known in Hungary, but it had handles on the sides. Swing handles had a long history in central Europe from the Early Urnfield Period down to the Hallstatt Iron Age, but they belonged originally to hemispherical cauldrons quite different in shape from the situlae. It was only in the Hallstatt Iron Age beginning in the eighth century that swing handles were attached to situlae, and these are found chiefly in central Europe and in Italy north of the Po.

The situlae from Tarquinia differ somewhat from the true Hallstatt ones in form and ornament, and, like the bronze cups of Villanovan II, they are provided with high feet. Here we have another example of how craftsmen in Italy could transform a foreign type to suit the tastes of their customers.

Other large bronze vases of late Villanovan II have a handle on each side and may be called amphorae. One kind of amphora at Tarquinia belongs to a group whose origin may have been in western Hungary, but which has a wide distribution in central Europe and even in the southern Baltic countries. This group belongs to a late stage in the Later Urnfields and to the Hallstatt Iron Age, in other words slightly before and contemporary with Villanovan II at Tarquinia. Another kind of amphora, an Italian derivative of those already mentioned, has a concave neck and resembles the pottery urns of the Arnoaldi Period at Villanovan Bologna, which begins in the seventh century. Still a third kind of amphora is in the shape of a two-handled Villanovan urn. At the same time, one should not separate all these amphorae too sharply; probably those less like central European ones were Italian responses to a new form derived from the north.

Plates 123, 124

Figs. 27f, 41

Plate 123

Plate 124

Bronze girdles also appear in the graves of Villanovan II. In early Villanovan II there is one consisting of a bronze band of uniform width. In late Villanovan II there are several of the wide kind with tapering ends that covered only the front of the body, while the rest must have been of perishable material. The girdle of uniform width has much older parallels north of the Alps, but the very simplicity of its shape deprives such comparisons of much meaning. I will return later to its ornament.

Plate 130

Figs. 25, 26

The broad girdles are rather like other objects in central Europe and even in the Balkans. Some of these may have also been girdles, and they range in date from the Middle Bronze Age to the Later Urnfield Period, but there are also early parallels in Italy. An object of stag's horn from a Bronze Age terramara in the Po Valley seems related in shape, and an apparent fragment of a bronze one belongs to a Late Bronze Age hoard near Livorno. At Bologna an early Villanovan grave contained a replica of the bronze form made of horn. Hence the origin of the broad girdles worn by some late Villanovan ladies at Tarquinia is not clear; it could have been in central Europe, in Italy or in both. But wherever it first originated, the Bologna example seems to have been much older than Villanovan II beginning at Tarquinia about 750 BC. This is an excellent example of a kind of object that was apparently long in use before it was placed in graves.

Plate 73
Plate 133

There are also various kinds of bronze ornaments with an urnfield background. Spirals with undulating ends emanate from north-western Jugoslavia, where related forms go back to the latter part of Early Urnfield times. Disc pendants began in Villanovan I and, despite resemblances to eastern Mediterranean ones, they have closer parallels in the Early Urnfield Period in Germany, and the openwork circular pendants, often wheel-shaped and sometimes called 'sun-discs', are deeply rooted in the very early Urnfield cultures of south-eastern Hungary and western Romania, which are definitely older than Villanovan.

Plates 131, 132
Fig. 20a

In general one can say that various kinds of bronzes of central European origin were used by the Villanovans of Tarquinia. But while they reflect central Europe, they were not imports but were made by immigrant craftsmen or their Villanovan apprentices to suit the tastes of Italian customers. Tarquinia and the other major centres of Etruria were perhaps by now sufficiently strong economically to attract such craftsmen from far and wide.

Fig. 10a, b

This brings us to the various kinds of decoration on Villanovan bronzes at Tarquinia, the first of which is the *engraved geometric style*. This includes parallel lines with cross-hatching between them, zigzags, herringbones and hatched triangles. A relatively simple example of this sort of decoration arranged

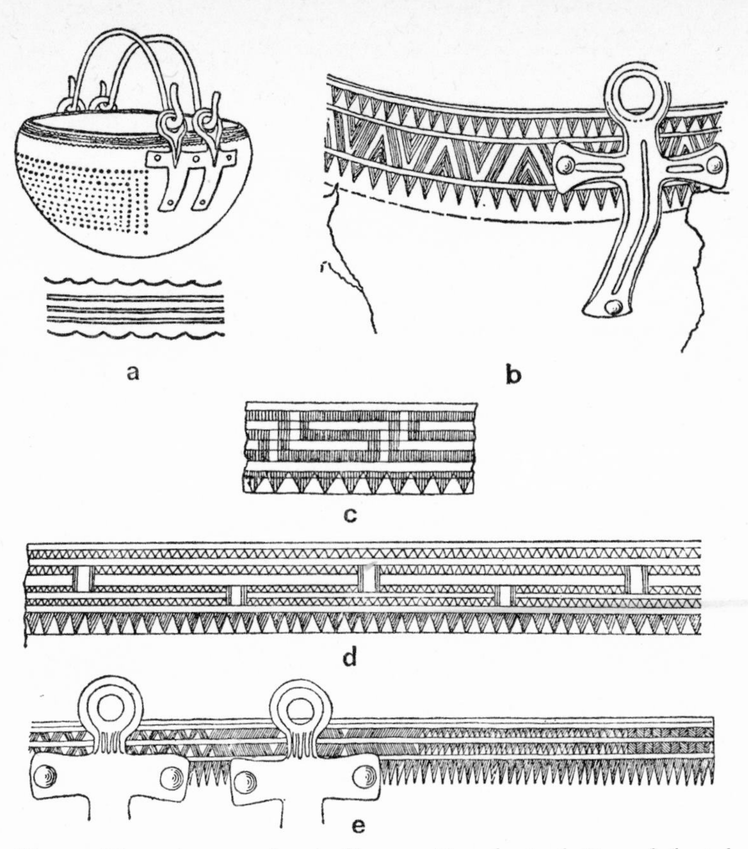

Fig. 40. The music paper style on cauldrons: a, Transylvania; b, Denmark (central European import); c, Istria; d, Austria, with T-shaped meanders; e, Germany. a, e, Later Urnfield Period; others Hallstatt Iron Age (after Merhart)

along parallel lines with cross-hatching and zigzags is seen on a sword scabbard of the beginning of Villanovan I and on another undated one that may also be early. This resembles what the great German prehistorian Merhart called the 'music paper style' native to eastern central Europe, and based on parallel lines arranged below the edges of cauldrons. On the cauldrons the resemblance to music paper is pronounced, but Italian craftsmen bent the lines to fit the scabbards of swords which

Fig. 10a, b

makes them less like music paper. Such ornament as that on the scabbards already mentioned has parallels in Merhart's Later Urnfields, contemporary with and somewhat older than Villanovan, for there one sees cross-hatching and zigzags between parallel lines. *Fig. 40e*

A more developed example of this style including meanders and hatched triangles is seen on a scabbard of late Villanovan I. The stags here have Balkan analogies, but the geometric ornament of zigzags, hatched triangles and T-shaped meanders may be compared with the late version of Merhart's music paper style on the rims of cauldrons that really belongs to the Hallstatt Iron Age. Both include the relatively rare T-shaped meander. These later cauldrons were made chiefly in the eastern Alps, and the reason for the transference of the workshops probably was that towards the end of the Later Urnfield Period central Europe was invaded by pre-Scythian horse nomads from the Russian steppes. This invasion may have driven the craftsmen of eastern central Europe to seek safer homes further west. *Fig. 10c* *Fig. 40c, d*

In Villanovan II the engraved geometric style on bronze really comes into its own. There is another scabbard very like the one of late Villanovan I, and it must be a product of the same workshop. Also there are girdles with similar hatched meanders including T-shaped ones and hatched triangles that are closely paralleled on the rims of cauldrons of the Hallstatt Iron Age. Another bronze girdle has a frame of little semicircles, a survival of a pattern from the rims of cauldrons of the Later Urnfield Period. *Fig. 22c, d* *Fig. 25b, 26* *Figs. 25a, 40a*

Another form of the engraved geometric style on bronze is a band of big zigzags, and this is also found on the rims of cauldrons of the Hallstatt Iron Age. In Tarquinia in Villanovan II it sometimes occurs on the handles of big bronze cups. *Fig. 40b* *Fig. 22b*

Two other elements of the engraved geometric style on bronze have closer analogies with the Balkans than with central Europe. I have already mentioned one of these, the deer engraved on *Fig. 10c, 22c, d* scabbards. The other is the Balkan cross with triangular arms seen at the ends of one of the girdles, evidently older in the Balkans than at Tarquinia. *Fig. 26b*

Another form of decoration on bronze at Tarquinia is *embossed ornament*. There are three varieties of this:

1. Bosses of equal size.
2. Rows of large and small bosses.
3. Raised ridges often with rows of bosses of equal size.

All of these begin in the Early Urnfield Period considerably before Villanovan, and adjuncts to them, especially in the Later Urnfield Period, are large bosses often stamped and surrounded by concentric circles.

Bosses of nearly equal size occur in Villanovan I on a few small things, and also on an undated cap helmet with a face, if we exclude the two large bosses representing the eyes. Plate 91

Rows of large and small bosses are much more numerous in Villanovan I and occur for example on a crested helmet, a cylindrical container, two cups and two gold plated bronze ornaments. They also occur on three helmets, Villanovan but otherwise undated. Plates 54, 57, 71, 72, 90, 92, 93 *Fig. 18*

Raised ridges and bosses often of the same size occur only once in Villanovan I on a hollow bronze object belonging to the middle of the period. Though this ornament of ridges and bosses occurs early in the Urnfield world, most examples belong in the latter part of the Later Urnfield Period and to the Hallstatt Iron Age. At Tarquinia it becomes much more prominent in Villanovan II. Plate 68

In Villanovan II bosses of equal size are found on a girdle and also on a bronze pectoral, where there are in addition large bosses surrounded by concentric circles. Large and small bosses in Villanovan II continue on various conspicuous bronzes: two cap helmets, an amphora, a censer, and a cup. Plates 129, 130 Plates 121, 122, 124, 126 *Fig. 22a, 23*

I have already mentioned that raised ridges and bosses of equal size began in the Early Urnfield Period in central Europe, but this kind of decoration flowered especially in eastern Germany and Poland towards the end of the Later Urnfield Period and in the Hallstatt Iron Age. Examples from Tarquinia of Villanovan II include a situla, a flask, an amphora and the shield from the Warrior's Tomb. The amphora has a likeness to the example from Prenzlawitz in Poland, but the flask is an outspokenly eastern Mediterranean form which has acquired typically European ornament. Here again one may see northern craftsmen and their Italian followers adapting a foreign style to kinds of bronzes for which it was never intended.

Figs. 24b, c, 27f, 30e

Fig. 41

Another similar kind of decoration from central Europe and the southern Baltic is pendulum ornament which occurs only once at Tarquinia on a bronze cup probably of Villanovan II, but the cup itself is of local shape.

Plate 127

Fig. 41. Amphora from Prenzlavitz, Poland (after Merhart). 1–4

I have already mentioned the conspicuous place of *birds* in the magical or religious art of the urnfields. Indeed birds far outnumber animal and human figures, and representations of them go back to the Middle Bronze Age in the urnfields of Oltenia, the Banat and southern Hungary. With them are sometimes associated wheel-like ornaments often called 'sun discs'. These birds come into central Europe with the beginning of the urnfields there in the Late Bronze Age. First of all there are single birds in the round, which appear during the Early Urnfield Period, but in Italy they are later, and appear for example in the hoard of bronzes found at Monte Primo contemporary with the Previllanovan urnfields. Among the material at Tarquinia that cannot be dated more closely than to the Villanovan Period as a whole are some that are not entire single birds in the round but birds' heads which serve as the figureheads of pottery models of boats.

Plates 76, 77
Fig. 17

Whole birds in the round are found on a few wheel-shaped heads of pins in Villanovan II. The wheel-shaped pin-head is a Bronze Age heritage, but the combination of birds with a circular ornament recalls again the motifs of the urnfields. Also in Villanovan II birds' heads rise from some of the fibulae.

Fig. 27a
Plates 134, 135

Another form widely distributed in the urnfield world is the double bird with one body and a head at either end. Such double birds occur at Tarquinia in early Villanovan I on the roofs of house urns and on a cylindrical bronze container of late Villanovan I. In Villanovan II there is a fine example in relief on a bronze girdle. A Villanovan pottery model of a boat with a bird's head at either end also resembles a double bird and corresponds to a boat-shaped pendant with two birds' heads from northern Romania.

Plate 8
Fig. 5
Plates 58, 130
Fig. 17
Fig. 42b

The boat with a bird's head at either end is depicted also on helmets and a bronze amphora, but the boat is freighted with an ornamental 'sun disc'. Here again we have the combination of birds and a circle. This bird boat with the 'sun disc' is

Plates 93, 124
Figs. 19, 23b

generally made with rows of larger and smaller bosses, and it appears in Hungary in the latter part of the Early Urnfield Period, though the bronze vessels on which it is displayed were very widely traded in Europe. The earlier examples of this pattern were much the best, but later they degenerated. The birds' heads lost their crispness of line, and the disc is often reduced to a boss with concentric circles around it. The central European vessels with this later form of the motif were evidently of eastern Alpine manufacture, perhaps because the artisans had been driven westward by the pre-Scythian nomads from the steppe, but their products were still widely traded. Some workshops may have been set up in Italy itself, since the Later Urnfield forms occurring there are distinguishable from those of central Europe. At Tarquinia the best example of the bird boat and 'sun disc' is on a crested helmet which is not precisely dated but which might belong to Villanovan I. Here we see the later urnfield form of the design in which the disc is a boss surrounded by concentric circles that are stamped instead of being made with little bosses. Other examples belonging to Villanovan II are a cap helmet and a bronze amphora, but in these the pattern seems to have degenerated even further into mere pairs of birds' heads facing each other. A quite different use of the pattern is seen in a pair of cast bronze cheek-pieces of a bridle belonging to Villanovan I, where the 'sun disc' is represented by the badly corroded central ring through which passed the ends of the bit.

Fig. 42f
Fig. 42a
Plate 93
Fig. 19
Plate 124
Fig. 23b
Plate 56

Another urnfield design consisted of birds' heads all facing the same way, though in central Europe this was generally engraved on weapons. In Villanovan II at Tarquinia this appears in the technique of large and small bosses on a cap helmet. But could this not be a further degeneration of the bird boat in the hands of Italian craftsmen who had quite forgotten the boat.

Plate 121

Still another form is the double bird boat in which one boat is upside down as though mirrored in water. This double bird

Fig. 42d

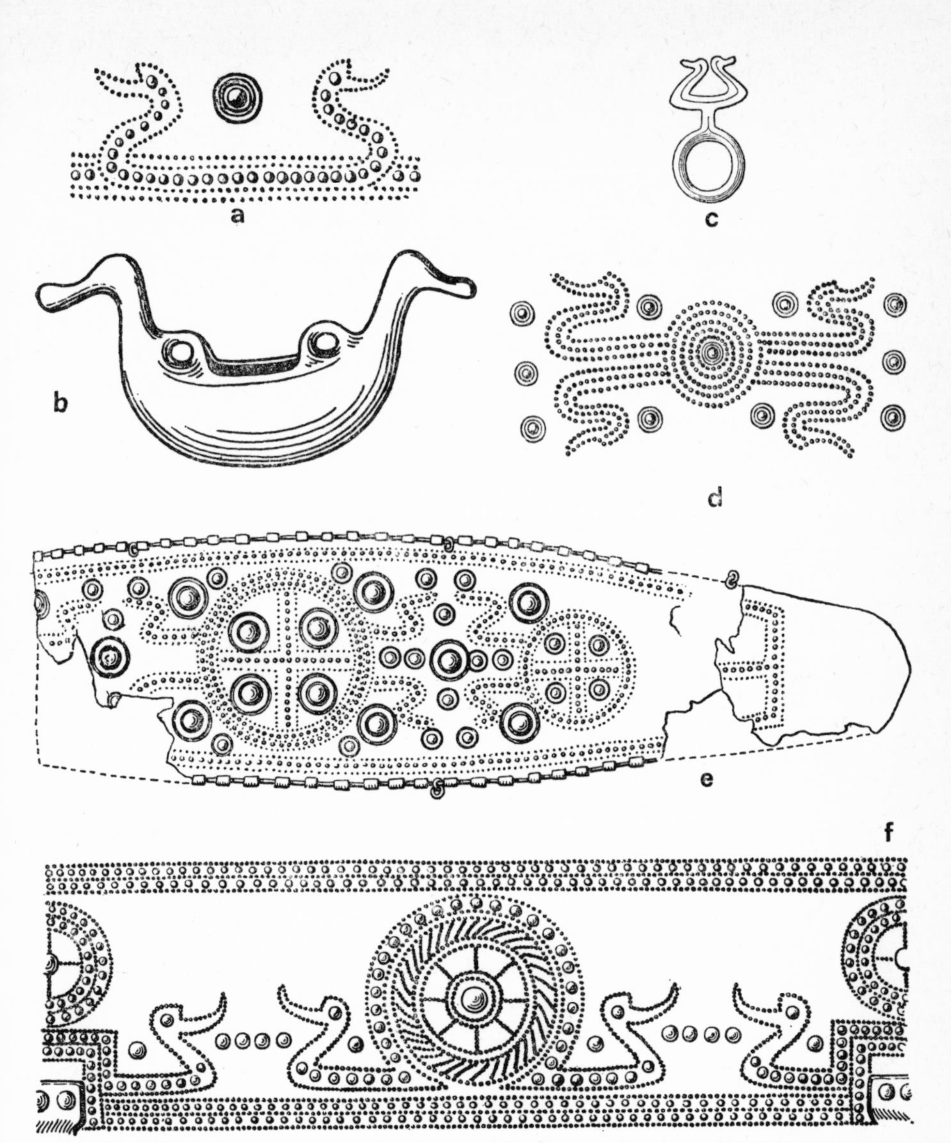

Fig. 42. Bird ornament of urnfield origin: a, later urnfield bird boat, Pomerania; b, boat-shaped pendant, Romania; c, double bird and circle, Bavaria; d, double bird boat, Este, Italy; e, double bird boat and half a double bird boat, Bologna; f, earlier urnfield bird boat, Denmark, imported from Central Europe (e after Orsi, others after Kossack). c, 1 : 2

boat is at home in north-eastern Italy and Austria in the Hallstatt Iron Age. The design does not occur at Tarquinia, but I have mentioned it to explain a degeneration of it that I call half a double bird boat; this consists of the 'sun disc' with one pair of birds' heads projecting from it. This is found at Villanovan Bologna, and an example with one head much corroded is seen on a bronze girdle of Villanovan II. More degenerate ones appear on other girdles.

Fig. 42e
Plate 130
Figs. 25a, 26a
Fig. 13b

A much stylized expression of the same thing is probably to be seen on the pairs of birds' heads on the circular handles of razors that begin late in Villanovan I and continue into Villanovan II.

Single birds either engraved or stamped are also an element in the art of the Later Urnfield Period and the succeeding Hallstatt Iron Age. The Later Urnfield examples were engraved and had triangular tails, and at Tarquinia this form is seen on a girdle of Villanovan II. In the Hallstatt Iron Age birds were often made with a stamp, as on a situla of Villanovan II at Tarquinia. Another kind of Hallstatt Iron Age bird has a mane-like crest, and this appears at Tarquinia at the end of Villanovan I in the double bird surmounting a cylindrical container. In Villanovan II it is also seen in the engraved birds on girdles.

Fig. 25a
Fig. 24a
Plate 58
Figs. 25a, 26a

Another very peculiar form is the horned animal-bird. This mythical creature must have been of great importance to the urnfield peoples including the Villanovans, and, since a number of examples have been found in graves, they may have been prized personal possessions. It could be simply a bird with a pair of horns on its head, or it could have the body of a bird with an ox-like head. In Italy it could have four legs, often stumpy and vestigial, and there are pottery examples of this kind from Tarquinia belonging to mid Villanovan I and Villanovan II. These look at first like figures of oxen, but their plump rounded bodies are more like those of birds, though one

Plate 48
Plate 115
Plates 49, 109

would not think of them as birds without the rest of the series. The most famous one from Tarquinia is the bronze example which has the form of a quadruped bird with the head of an ox and a lid of the same shape with another ox-head. The wheels on which this is mounted recall the frequent combination of the bird and the 'sun disc' in the art of the urnfields. It is not dated more closely than to the Villanovan Period as a whole.

Plate 86

I shall mention here only a few of the Balkan and central European examples of the horned animal-bird in order to illustrate the various forms at different times. The oldest birds with horns, come from urnfields of Oltenia and belong to the Middle Bronze Age, while others from near Vienna belong to the Earlier Urnfield Period. Another attributed to the same period is from Brandenburg and has a bird-like body and long neck but with ox horns on its head. A Slavonian example from Beravci dates from the beginning of the Later Urnfield Period. All these are of course older than Villanovan in Italy. A fifth from Slovakia is simply a bird with horns and is variously attributed to the Later Urnfield Period or the Hallstatt Iron Age. Italy provides the Villanovan example from Bologna that also has the plump rounded body and long neck of a bird as well as the four stumpy legs like some at Tarquinia. Finally the horned bird from the Isis Tomb at Vulci of the first half of the sixth century BC shows a decided Villanovan reminiscence in the true Etruscan period.

Plate 145

Fig. 39a, b

Plate 146

Fig. 39c

Plate 144

Two other objects from Tarquinia do not really belong to the urnfields but to the pre-Scythian nomads from the Russian steppe who invaded urnfield territory toward the end of the Later Urnfield Period, and these must have reached Italy from central Europe. One of these objects is an openwork pendant of bronze from an undated Villanovan grave, and the other is the tube-cross from the Warrior's Tomb of the very end of Villanovan II.

Fig. 20e

Fig. 29d

In concluding this chapter, it seems fair to say that there is a difference between the Balkan elements in Villanovan as contrasted with those of central Europe. The apparently Balkan types of pottery have been described in Chapter 5, and I have already emphasized their possible significance with regard to ethnic movements. By contrast many kinds of bronzes and their ornament are basically central European, and they do not suggest more than migrating craftsmen, but these craftsmen and their local followers transformed their wares into new modes to suit the taste of an Italian clientele. Elements common to both the Balkans and central Europe such as birds, 'sun-symbols' and the horned animal-bird may be connected with religious beliefs held by the Urnfield peoples in general, including the Villanovans.

CHAPTER VII

Villanovan Background IV: Aegean and Eastern Mediterranean Elements

I HAVE ALREADY ALLUDED to the Aegean connections of the Previllanovan urnfields in Italy. Some of these were slight, but the urnfields of Latium at Rome and in the Alban Hills had more substantial Aegean links, as did the adjacent ones in southern Etruria. These connections with the Aegean and the eastern Mediterranean became still more important in Villanovan I, increased further in Villanovan II, and became dominant in the Orientalizing Period III after 700 BC. These connections are to be found in a wide variety of objects.

The asymmetrical vessels known as askoi are of eastern inspiration. At Tarquinia some in the shape of birds occur in both Villanovan I and II, but they are headless, either because they never had heads or because the heads are broken off. Bird askoi have a long history in the Bronze and Iron Ages further east, and are found especially in the Iron Age along the great commercial route that ran between Cyprus, Rhodes, Crete and Italy, but those at Tarquinia are locally made and are not imports.

Plates 47, 78, 111

Another kind of askos is that representing the horned animal-bird. This mythical creature, at home in eastern Europe, sometimes assumed among the Villanovans the form of the Cypriot and Aegean animal askos with a basket handle, a curious combination of disparate ideas peculiar to Italy. One example at Tarquinia belongs to mid-Villanovan I and another to Villanovan II.

Plates 49, 109

There is also a ring-shaped askos with a basket handle that had a ram's head on it when found, a simple example of more

Plate 48

elaborate vases of this kind in Mycenaean Greece and in Cyprus in the Iron Age. It is attributed to Villanovan I.

Plate 80

Another variety is a beaked jug common in Sardinia and recalling pots from Asia Minor and Cyprus in the Bronze Age, but it cannot be dated within the Villanovan Period.

Plate 143

Plate 8

In discussing the Previllanovan house urns from Rome and the Alban Hills, I took up their possible relationship with Crete. A house urn of this type was indeed found somewhere near Tarquinia, but the Villanovan ones from there represent a later version of this form. They are apt to have urnfield double birds on their roofs instead of horns, and their doors are less like the Cretan ones. Any connection with Crete is perhaps not direct but through the older Latian type.

Plate 79

Fig. 43a

The pottery 'candelabra' can only be dated to Villanovan as a whole. They are not really candelabra, since they have no sockets for candles, but a Cretan analogy comes from a Geometric tomb at Fortetsa near Knossos including material of the ninth and eighth centuries BC contemporary with Villanovan. This tomb contained two objects like Villanovan candelabra, but much smaller and belonging to the tradition of the Minoan tree with birds. Figures of birds were found with them and presumably belonged to them, but were not actually found attached. The Villanovan ones had no birds, but these Iron Age pottery trees from Crete are the closest analogies to the Villanovan candelabra.

Fig. 35a

Plates 45, 103

Little cups attached to larger pots occur in Previllanovan Latium and also in Villanovan I, and continue in Villanovan II. They feature in Late Mycenaean Greece and in Late Minoan and Postminoan Crete, as at the site of Karphi dating from about 1100 to 900 BC. Further east they are found in the Iron Age of Cyprus.

Plate 87

Pairs of small pottery wheels and pairs of little pottery horses probably represent model chariots and their teams, especially since they have been found in warriors' graves with pottery helmets. The chariots themselves were evidently of perishable material and were the predecessors of pottery models of chariots with their horses and also of actual chariots in Etruscan tombs of seventh century and later. Unfortunately the Villanovan ones at Tarquinia are only dated to the Villanovan period as a whole.

In speaking of chariots, I mean only the horse-drawn two-wheeled chariots, and I am excluding four-wheeled and other kinds of vehicles. There is of course no need to emphasize the Near East as the home of chariots, or their importance in Greece

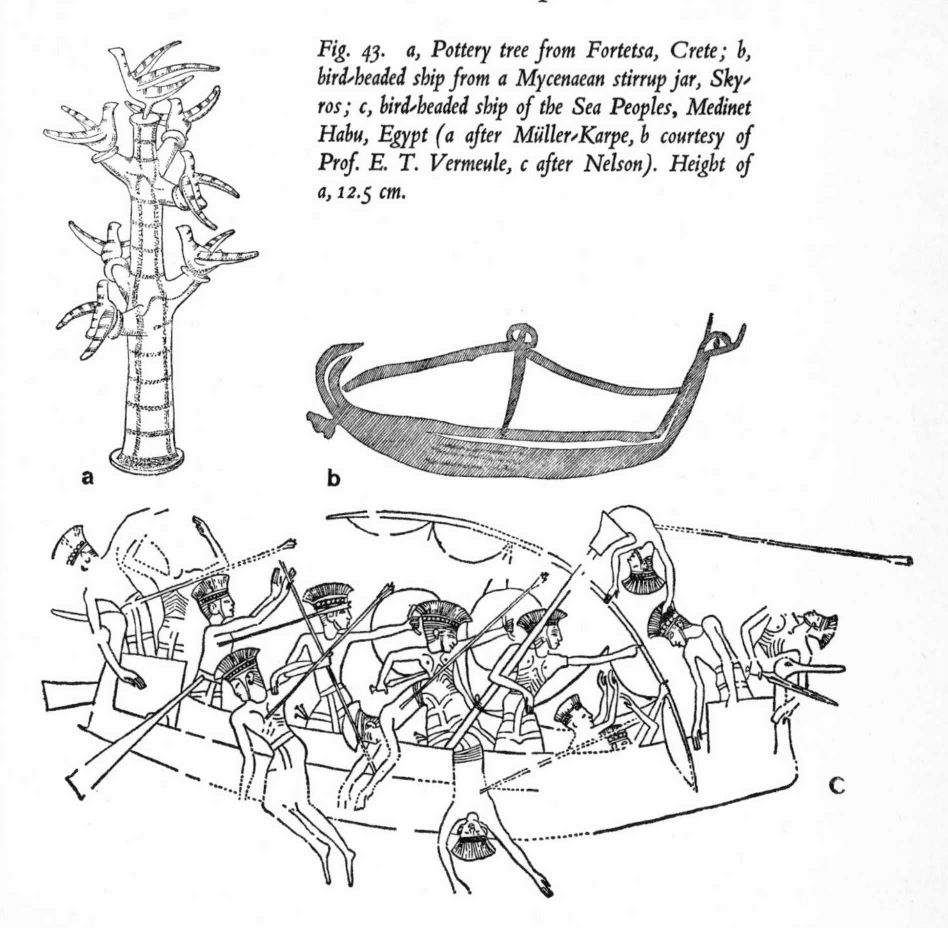

Fig. 43. a, Pottery tree from Fortetsa, Crete; b, bird-headed ship from a Mycenaean stirrup jar, Skyros; c, bird-headed ship of the Sea Peoples, Medinet Habu, Egypt (a after Müller-Karpe, b courtesy of Prof. E. T. Vermeule, c after Nelson). Height of a, 12.5 cm.

from Mycenaean times. There has been much discussion of chariots in central Europe in the Urnfield Period, but thus far there seems to be no reliable evidence there for the two-wheeled horse-drawn chariot. The argument that pottery models of spoked wheels in central Europe indicate chariots in the Urnfield Period is invalidated by the fact that in the urnfield cultures there is a group of small ceremonial wagons mounted on three or four spoked wheels. Hence I would attribute the chariots from Tarquinia to influence from the Aegean-eastern Mediterranean world.

Fig. 43b
Plate 76
Fig. 17
Fig. 42a, f

I have already suggested an urnfield connection for the birds. There is also a stirrup jar from the Aegean island of Skyros which has upon it a bird-headed boat, and the bird has an upswept beak like some figureheads of Villanovan boat models and the birds on urnfield bird-boats represented on bronze vases. This jar from Skyros dates from the earlier twelfth century, a time when the Sea Peoples were active in the eastern Mediterranean. Was this one of their ships?

Fig. 17
Fig. 43c
Fig. 42d

I have already referred to the Villanovan boat model with birds' heads fore and aft, and paralleled in the ships of the Sea Peoples portrayed by Rameses III on his temple at Medinet Habu commemorating his naval victory over these marauders in 1190 BC. These boats also recall the birdboats with a bird's head at either end on some urnfield bronze vessels.

Plate 50
Fig. 14d
Fig. 10b
Plates 88, 89

As elsewhere in the earlier part of the Iron Age, iron was rare, but it appears even in early Villanovan I, where there are iron rivets in a sword hilt and also an iron fibula. By late Villanovan I iron fibulae were frequent; there is also an iron sword that might be Villanovan I as well as other undated Villanovan swords and spears of iron. In early Villanovan II iron disappears completely, a circumstance that must be fortuitous, but it comes back in some quantity in late Villanovan II.

As for its point of origin, ironworking began in the Near East and spread westward to Greece well before the Villanovan

Period. Though it also reached Oltenia by about the twelfth century BC, it could have come to Etruria with the Balkan pottery already mentioned, but its basic source for Italy is probably the Near East and the Aegean.

The remarkable bronze mirror illustrated must belong to the very beginning of Villanovan at Tarquinia, since it seems to be the most archaic type from any of the cemeteries there. Its likely derivation is from mirrors of Mycenaean form found in Sicilian tombs of Pantalica I of about the twelfth and eleventh centuries BC, but the attachment of the handle is so like those of some rectangular razors from early Villanovan I at Tarquinia that it may be a local product. In any case this mirror is only a reminiscence of the Mycenaean world.

Plate 59

Plate 61

The Villanovans of Tarquinia had short swords of bronze or iron with eastern relationships, and bronze ones that go back to early Villanovan I. Bronze swords of this kind are also found in southern Italy in the Trench Grave Culture roughly parallel in time to Villanovan, and in the Modica hoard in Sicily of about the eleventh or tenth centuries BC. They have a resemblance to late Mycenaean swords, since both are short and have T-shaped pommels which are sometimes flanged. But the Mycenaean weapons generally lack the widening in the middle of the hilt often seen in Villanovan swords. The shoulders of Mycenaean swords are less rounded and are apt to be of quite different shapes from the Villanovan ones. Sometimes Mycenaean blades can be quite wide and flat, which is a contrast to the Italian swords, but others have ribs or grooves down the centre as in Italy. Recent studies have shown that characteristics of these Villanovan swords, the T-shaped pommel sometimes flanged, projections on the hilt and ribs or grooves on the blade, are essentially Levantine features of the second millennium BC. Probably one version of these Levantine swords was taken up in late Mycenaean times in Greece, while another version was in vogue a little later in the Italian Iron Age. So present evidence

Plates 50, 53, 88

Fig. 10b

is against these Villanovan swords being of Mycenaean origin, but neither does it point to any single home in the Near East. Perhaps it is best for the present to suggest merely that both late Mycenaean and Italian swords sprang from the same Near Eastern root.

Plate 74

Bronze tripods go back to early Villanovan I in about the tenth century and are related to the pottery tripods found in the early cremation graves in the Roman Forum dating from the eleventh to tenth centuries. I have also referred to the apparent prototype of these tripods recently discovered in Euboea and belonging to the eleventh century BC. The Greek example, which is of Cypriot derivation, resembles the Italian tripods in being a shallow dish with three curved legs that meet underneath it, a form quite different from most of the tripods in the Greek world. The newly discovered one from Euboea has 'flying buttresses' that connect the legs with the rim of the dish, a feature not found in Italy, but these are necessary in the Greek example because of its slender construction. The Roman ones do not need such supports because they are much sturdier, and some from Tarquinia do not need them either because they are of bronze.

Fig. 35c, d

Plate 65

Arc fibulae with leech-shaped bows and short catches begin in early Villanovan I and continue through Villanovan II. They may be of solid bronze or may have bows made of segments of bone or amber, but from my chronological study of these varieties, it seems that what counts is the shape of the bow and not the substance of which it is made. This tendency to thicken the bow of the arc fibula is noticeable in Protogeometric fibulae and early Geometric ones in Greece and in post-Minoan ones in Crete. Hence the development in the leech-shaped bow at Tarquinia was in step with the Aegean fashions.

Plate 62
Fig. 16

Another variety is the arc fibula with a twisted bow, of which all the dated examples at Tarquinia belong to the beginning of Villanovan I. Such arc fibulae with twisted bows are found in

Aegean lands following the Mycenaean Age, but those from Tarquinia are thicker than the Aegean examples and this suggests some lapse of time between them. This would correspond to the view that the Mycenaean Age faded away in the eleventh century BC and that Villanovan started in about the tenth century.

Another possible indication of Aegean connections is an old illustration of a bronze bird with raised wings from an undated Villanovan grave at Tarquinia. Birds with raised wings belong to the Minoan-Mycenaean tradition, and they continued in Crete in post-Minoan times at Karphi in about the eleventh and tenth centuries and at Fortetsa in the ninth and eighth centuries, but they are not found in the urnfield world.

Fig. 20f

Fig. 43a

A scarab and a pair of little figurines are perhaps attributable to late Villanovan I. They are not necessarily Egyptian imports, for many such things were probably of Phoenician manufacture and are also common in Greece. Greek traders and colonists were appearing in Italy in the first half of the eighth century, and Phoenician colonies were well established by then in the central Mediterranean. Since the Villanovans seem also to have been seafaring folk, the appearance of these Egyptianizing trinkets at Tarquinia is natural enough.

Fig. 15

Several more 'scarabs' are reported from Villanovan II when Greek connections were still stronger, and to the end of Villanovan II belongs the Warrior's Tomb with an outspokenly Phoenician broken-backed signet ring with a scarab set in it.

Fig. 31c

Vases of Greek type all belong to Villanovan II, are made of potter's clay, turned on the potter's wheel, and are painted in the Greek manner. Among them are a hydria and two cups, and they provide a sharp contrast to the coarse hand-made Villanovan wares. This is not to say that they were all imported, for most of them differ from genuine Greek vases in much the same way that urnfield bronzes at Tarquinia differ from central European urnfield bronzes. The reason may be the same, for

Plates 118–120

they were perhaps not imports but the work of immigrant potters and their apprentices working for Italian clients.

The decoration on these vases is often of Late Geometric type, and in this way they differ from the Protocorinthian vases that make up the bulk of the Greek colonial wares in southern Italy and Sicily. Some Tarquinian vases have been thought to reflect Euboea or the Cyclades among other areas of the Greek world. The connection between these Aegean islands and Etruria may have been through the Greek colonies at Pitchecusa and Cumae both close to Naples, which were founded by Euboeans in the mid eighth century BC. It is also interesting that these were the earliest Greek colonies in Italy and that they were closest to Etruria. The most probable explanation is trade in metals, in which Etruria was rich.

Plates 139–141

The vases from the Warrior's Tomb at the very end of Villanovan II are rather different, though they may also be locally made under foreign influence. As for the oinochoe, its shape, round body, conical neck, trefoil mouth and double handle all recall archaic Cyprus. The askos from the same tomb also resembles bird-shaped askoi of Cyprus and Crete, but, though the body is bird-shaped, the head is that of a horse with the high stiff mane rising between the ears, an example of the Villanovan propensity for combining unlikely animal forms. The skyphos also from the Warrior's Tomb has been compared to Rhodian examples, and so have its birds as well as those on the oinochoe and the askos. Other vases from the Warrior's Tomb have been thought to show the influence of the Cyclades, Rhodes and Cyprus.

Plate 117

Local pottery under Greek influence is certainly the work of Tarquinian potters in Villanovan II when external influences were at work, and the most important is a group of crater-like jars. These are essentially the old spheroid jars of red ware on a foot that go back to late Villanovan I. The ornament can also be in white paint in the Villanovan tradition, but the more sophisticated shape in Villanovan II may reflect the form of the Greek Geometric krater.

There are, besides, a number of miscellaneous pots, all quite different, whose manufacture involved the potter's wheel, purified clay and sometimes paint. The wide variety of such pots suggests experimentation in various directions by Villanovan potters. One of these is a wheel-made bowl of potter's clay with horizontal red bands that served as the cover for the hydria already mentioned as having been used as a cinerary urn.

Plate 116

Where fibulae with long catches are concerned the relationship to Greek types is not really clear. Fibulae with enlarged bows began early in Villanovan I, but at Tarquinia in Villanovan II they had at first somewhat lengthened, and then really long, catches. They resemble the fibulae with enlarged bows and long catches used even earlier by the Greek colonists in the south, though the root of the idea was probably in the long catches of the Italian serpentine fibulae. The serpentine fibulae with long catches now have pairs of knobs on the sides of the bow and also belong to late Villanovan II. Similar fibulae occur at the Greek colonies of Pithecusa and Cumae in graves of the second half of the eighth century BC. At the same time the British excavation at Veii may indicate that such fibulae with long catches were more of a Veian idea than a Greek one, and hence the relationship to the colonial Greeks remains to be decided.

Plates 65, 134, 135, 137

Fig. 31e

Fig. 31a

Silver first appears at Tarquinia in Villanovan II and was very rare in Italy before that time. Silver objects include a pair of filigree bracelets and a pair of cups from the Warrior's Tomb. The bracelets look like an elaboration of the older bronze spirals with undulating ends, and the cup with one handle and a fluted base is allied to current forms in pottery and bronze. As for the two-handled cup, this is the stage when cups with two handles begin at Tarquinia, and they become commoner in Period III. Most silver objects from Tarquinia belong to the

Fig. 27c

Fig. 31d, g

latter part of Villanovan II, and one is reminded that the earliest tombs of the Greek colonists in Italy at Pithecusa, Cumae and Syracuse contained silver, though the silver and bronze signet ring from the Warrior's Tomb is Phoenician. Perhaps the use of silver was inspired by these foreign contacts.

Fig. 31c

Fig. 24b

Flasks are of sheet bronze and belong to late Villanovan II. They are derived from the pottery 'pilgrim flasks', long used in Syria, Palestine, Cyprus and Crete. But the Tarquinian bronze examples are decorated in the central European tradition with rows of large and small bosses or in the ridge-and-boss style, and must have been made by the same craftsmen who produced the other bronze vessels of Villanovan II with similar decoration. Thus they constitute an interesting example of the mixing of two cultural traditions, one from the eastern Mediterranean and the other from the heart of Europe.

Plate 125

The simple undecorated bowls of late Villanovan II are not very reliable indicators of cultural relationships, but quite similar ones are found in Syria and Palestine in the latter part of the Late Bronze Age and in the Iron Age and also in Cyprus in the Iron Age.

Plate 138

Granulation was popular in Period III and later in Etruria, but the earliest example at Tarquinia is a small and coarse one on an electrum fibula of late Villanovan II. The technique was very old in the Near East and often employed by Phoenician jewellers and sometimes by Greek ones as well. The same was true of the small amount of filigree on this fibula.

Plate 128

A pair of bits with horse-shaped cheek-pieces came from a grave of Villanovan II, but numerous others have been found in Etruria and at Villanovan Bologna. The closest analogies come from Luristan, the part of Iran immediately east of Mesopotamia, but the bits to which they belong are different in Luristan and Italy and so is the style of the cheek-pieces. At the same time those from Luristan are believed to belong to the eighth and seventh centuries BC, which is their date in Italy.

Also it is hard to find analogies elsewhere except for a few isolated examples in the Alps and central Europe which probably represent Villanovan exports or their provincial imitations. Hence, despite differences, Luristan may be the source of the Italian ones. There has indeed been much recent discusson of the trade that connected various parts of the Near East and specifically Luristan with Italy; thus the horse-shaped cheek-pieces do not stand alone. There is, for example, the divided pommel of the short sword from the great seventh-century Etruscan burial from Palestrina called the Bernardini Tomb. This kind of divided pommel is also a contemporary form from Luristan.

None the less these cheek-pieces have undergone a transformation on their way to Italy, for the horses are not Iranian but of a breed related to Greek Geometric ones. Furthermore they are in many cases combined with birds, as horses often were in Greek Geometric art. Hence it looks as though this type, though basically from Luristan, had been filtered through the Aegean on the way to Italy. But the Villanovan spirit is apparent in the horses' bird-like beaks, another example of odd combinations of animal forms that is characteristically Villanovan.

Belonging late in Villanovan II are bell-shaped pendants, and close parallels come from an Urartian cemetery of the early first millennium BC at Igdyr in eastern Turkey. There are also more or less contemporary parallels further north in Georgia which have bird-like handles recalling an example from the cemetery of Le Rose near modern Tarquinia. Again the ancient kingdom of Urartu in modern Armenia may seem strangely remote from Etruria, but there were other Urartian influences there in Period III, and these little pendants may be their harbingers.

Fig. 27b

Fig. 20b

Openwork decoration of triangular holes belongs late in Villanovan II and occurs on two pottery vessels from the Warrior's

Fig. 28e, f

Tomb. Such ornament is found in pottery in Cyprus and Greece in the Iron Age.

Stylized lotus buds were long-lived favourites in the Near East, and they are to be seen in an abbreviated form without their centres on the pectoral from the Warrior's Tomb of the end of Villanovan II, where they appear as two sets of three Y-shaped ornaments. They may be seen in a more authentically Near Eastern form in the Bocchoris and Avvolta Tombs of Period III.

Fig. 31f

Plates 156, 160

GENERAL CONCLUSIONS

Influences from the Aegean, already seen in southern Etruria and Latium in the Previllanovan Iron Age, became more prominent in Villanovan at Tarquinia and were joined by others with a more eastern flavour. Among these is the short sword of Levantine origin favoured by the Villanovans of Etruria over the long sword from central Europe. This suggests that they were accustomed to the Near Eastern way of fighting. At the same time the Villanovans were not an Aegean or Near Eastern people but European urnfield folk. If they imitated Aegean or Near Eastern forms, they did so strictly in their own terms. All this raises the question, to which I will return in the next chapter, as to whether they reached Italy by way of the Aegean and the Near East. In Villanovan II these foreign elements increased greatly in importance, and this heralds the Orientalizing Period III which was also semi-Greek.

Chapter VIII

Period III

WITH PERIOD III we reach the orientalizing phase of civilization at Tarquinia that starts about 700 BC. In it are found the first inscriptions in the Etruscan language, and hence we need not hesitate to call the people of Period III the Etruscans of history. As for the town of Tarquinia, its inhabitants continued to bury in the old Villanovan cemetery on Monterozzi which now expanded, though the eastern cemeteries of the Villanovan Period were abandoned. Tarquinia was indeed like the other older Etruscan cities in having Villanovan cemeteries associated with it.

Plate 173

At the same time, the scene changes markedly in Period III, though little precise information is available, for grave-robbing, old-fashioned excavations and the failure to keep together the contents of many tombs deprives us of much information. One can none the less fall back on some generalities. The influences from eastern and central Europe, so important in Villanovan days, no longer reached Tarquinia, though there was a strong Villanovan survival. At the same time Greek and Near Eastern influences became much greater than before, and this was due to various factors. First there was increasing contact with the Greek colonies in southern Italy. Also the Phoenicians were already well established in Carthage, Malta, western Sicily and Sardinia. Hence the Etruscan cities, now developing further economically due to their mineral resources, had ample opportunities for Greek and Near Eastern contacts through trade.

But there were at the same time marked changes in burial custom. Cremation, which was declining in Villanovan II, became very rare, and the use of sarcophagi for inhumations apparently disappeared also. Inhumation in trench graves continued from Villanovan II, but as at other Etruscan sites, a

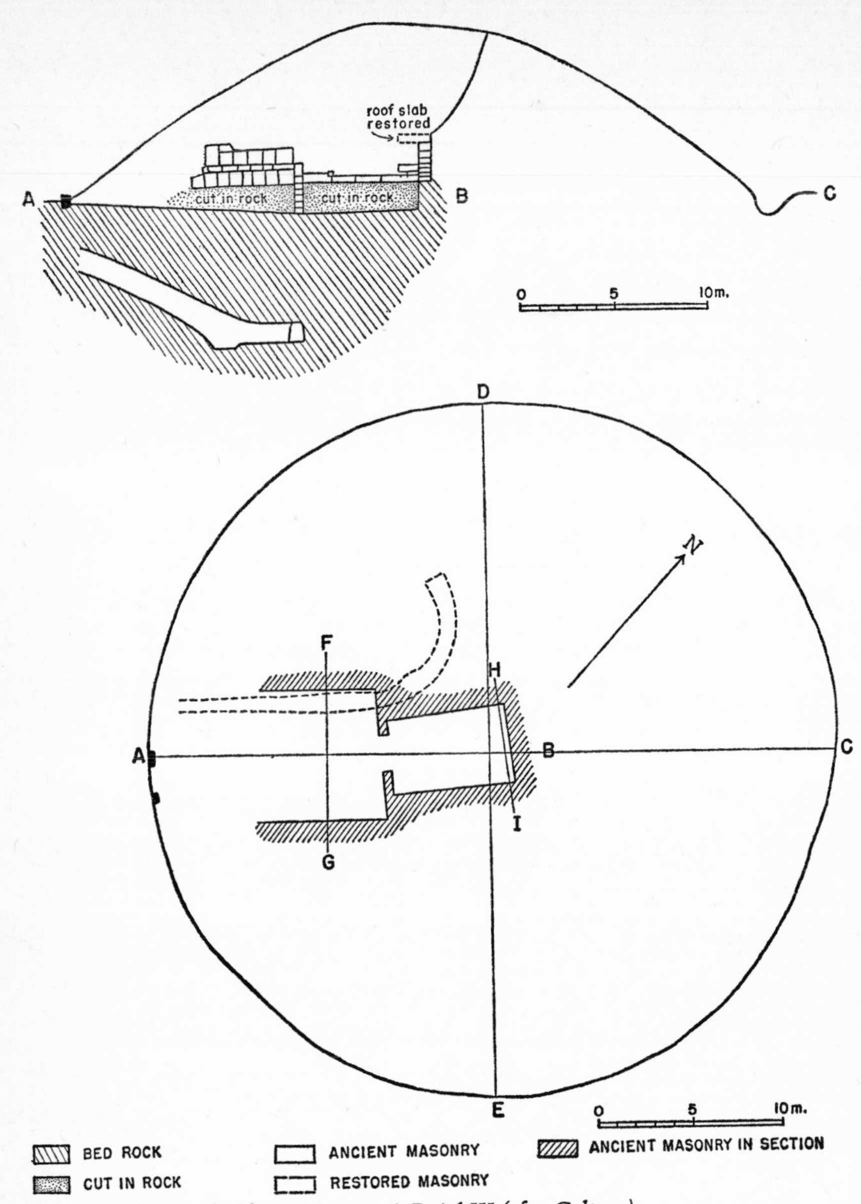

Fig. 44. The Tumulo del Re, Monterozzi, Period III (after Cultrera)

large number of inhumations were in chamber tombs, in some cases at least covered by a tumulus. Inside they might be provid- ed with benches, either built or rock-cut, for the repose of the dead. The Avvolta Tomb under a tumulus was probably later than some of the others, and consisted of a rectangular chamber roofed with stone slabs supported by lintels carried on a pair of columns. Chamber tombs with wall paintings and sometimes more elaborate plans are later still and are beyond the scope of this book.

Figs. 44–47

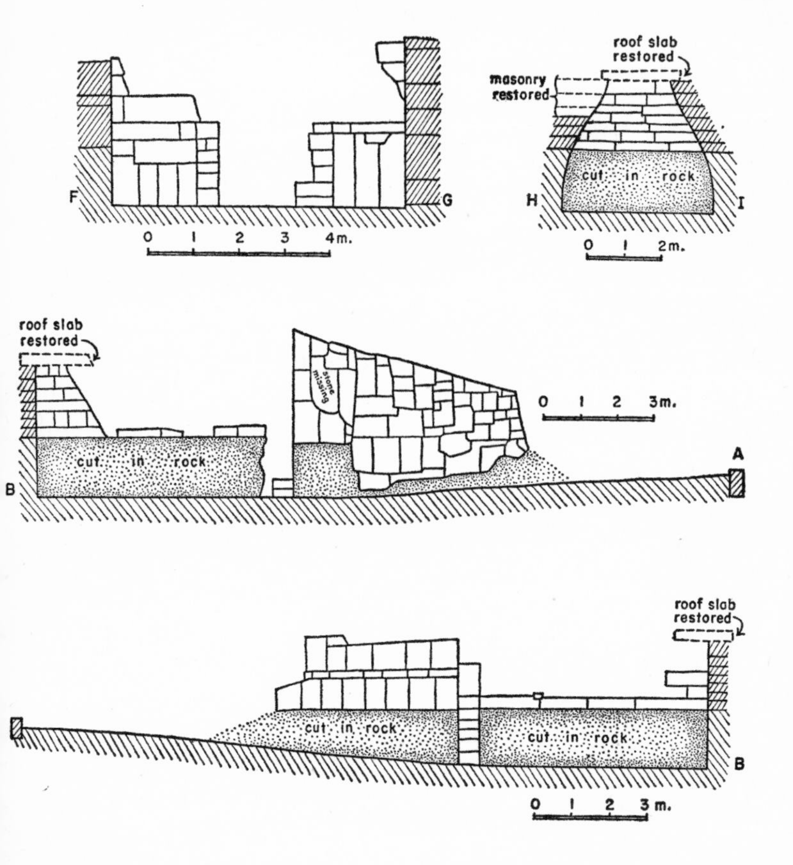

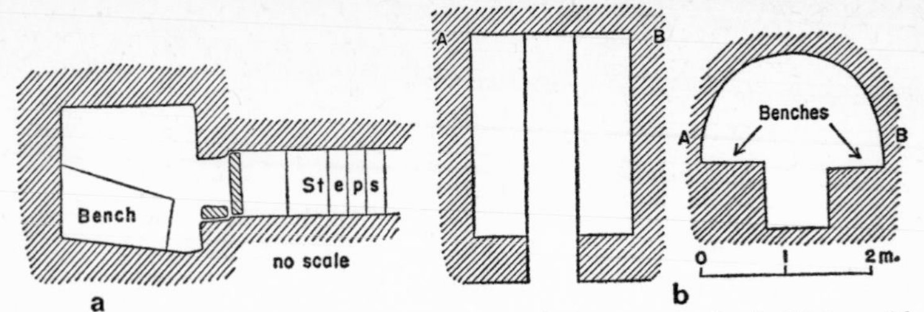

Fig. 45. Chamber Tombs on Monterozzi, Period III: a, at the Casale Madonna del Pianto (under tumulus); b, Romanelli's 92

What were the reasons for these changes? Greek and oriental elements might be due in part to commerce, and the adoption of inhumation seems to have been the result of an internal evolution that began before Period III. Chamber tombs might also be due partly to internal causes, for they bespeak a rising prosperity accompanying increasing trade. It is sometimes argued that such tombs covered with stone slabs are really enlarged trench graves, for trench graves were also covered with slabs. If they were made larger and provided with entrances, they would become simple chamber tombs which might evolve further into the more elaborate varieties. There may be some truth in this view, and indeed chamber tombs, either cut in the rock where it is soft, or built of masonry where the stone is suitable, occur at various times and places in the ancient Mediterranean world.

All the same, chamber tombs and tumuli are new elements that now appear in Etruria with stronger influences from the east, and however much chamber tombs may be due to local evolution, their course may have been guided by external factors. In this connection Greece is not very helpful; for, though little tholos tombs of Bronze Age tradition continued in use in Thessaly and Crete, these tombs represented a fading tradition outside the main stream of Greek developments in the seventh century. On the other hand burial chambers of various kinds were common in western Asia and Cyprus, and have varying degrees of similarity to tombs in Etruria including some in the

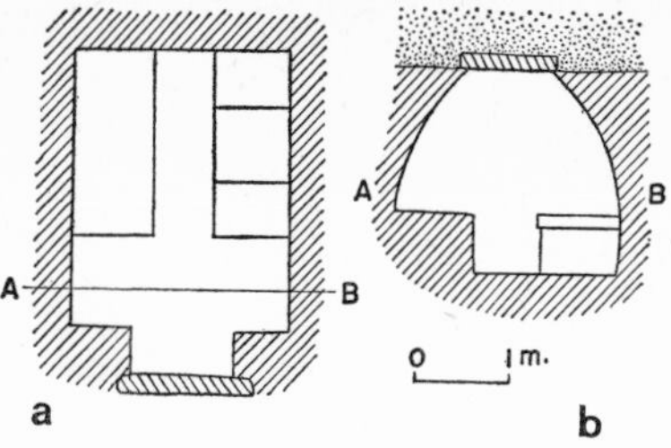

Fig. 46. Chamber Tomb with Fish Oinochoai, Monterozzi, Period III: a, plan; b, section; c, interior view (after Marchese)

Urartian kingdom in eastern Turkey with benches comparable to Etruscan ones. But tumuli with chambers were much more a feature of Asia Minor than elsewhere; one need only mention the famous cemetery called Bin Tepe or the Thousand Mounds at Sardis believed to belong in part at least to the Mermnad dynasty that ruled in Lydia in the seventh and sixth centuries BC. These chamber tombs under tumuli in Asia Minor may be considered with other western Asiatic influences at this time in Etruria. Though the chamber tombs at Tarquinia may in part contain an element of the old trench graves, this does not apply to the tumuli. Unlike many other parts of early Europe, Etruria and indeed most of Italy is not a land where tumuli are common, and reputed Apennine ones near Caere are more likely to be Etruscan. Some chamber tombs at Populonia contained Villanovan material, but Populonia was a conservative place where even Villanovan I seems to have overlapped with Period III. Hence the tombs there may not be as early as they seem.

If chamber tombs and tumuli really represent some new elements, they pose an interesting question. Burial customs in most societies are treated with conservatism, and, though they change gradually with the passage of time, sudden and radical innovations are rare. Often such innovations follow the arrival of new and different people in the area. Was that what happened at Tarquinia and elsewhere in Etruria?

There are indeed two currents of Near Eastern influence discernible in Etruria at this time, a Syro-Cypriot one with a strong Egyptian flavour, and an Asiatic-Continental one connected with Asia Minor, northern Syria, and other areas further east. A possible answer to why influences from these areas now came to Etruria may be found in the history of these lands. In the second half of the eighth century the Assyrian kings embarked upon a policy of expansion in Syria, and by the earlier seventh century most of the area was under firm Assyrian control with revolts crushed, though some coastal cities, mostly Philistine and Phoenician, still enjoyed a nominal independence. These Assyrian conquests were accompanied by the customary atrocities, and one can imagine that with each new advance the coastal towns would be crowded with refugees seeking to escape overseas. These people might include persons of wealth with their households and treasure as well as artists

Fig. 47. The Avvolta Tomb, Monterozzi (under a tumulus), Period III (after Carlo Avvolta)

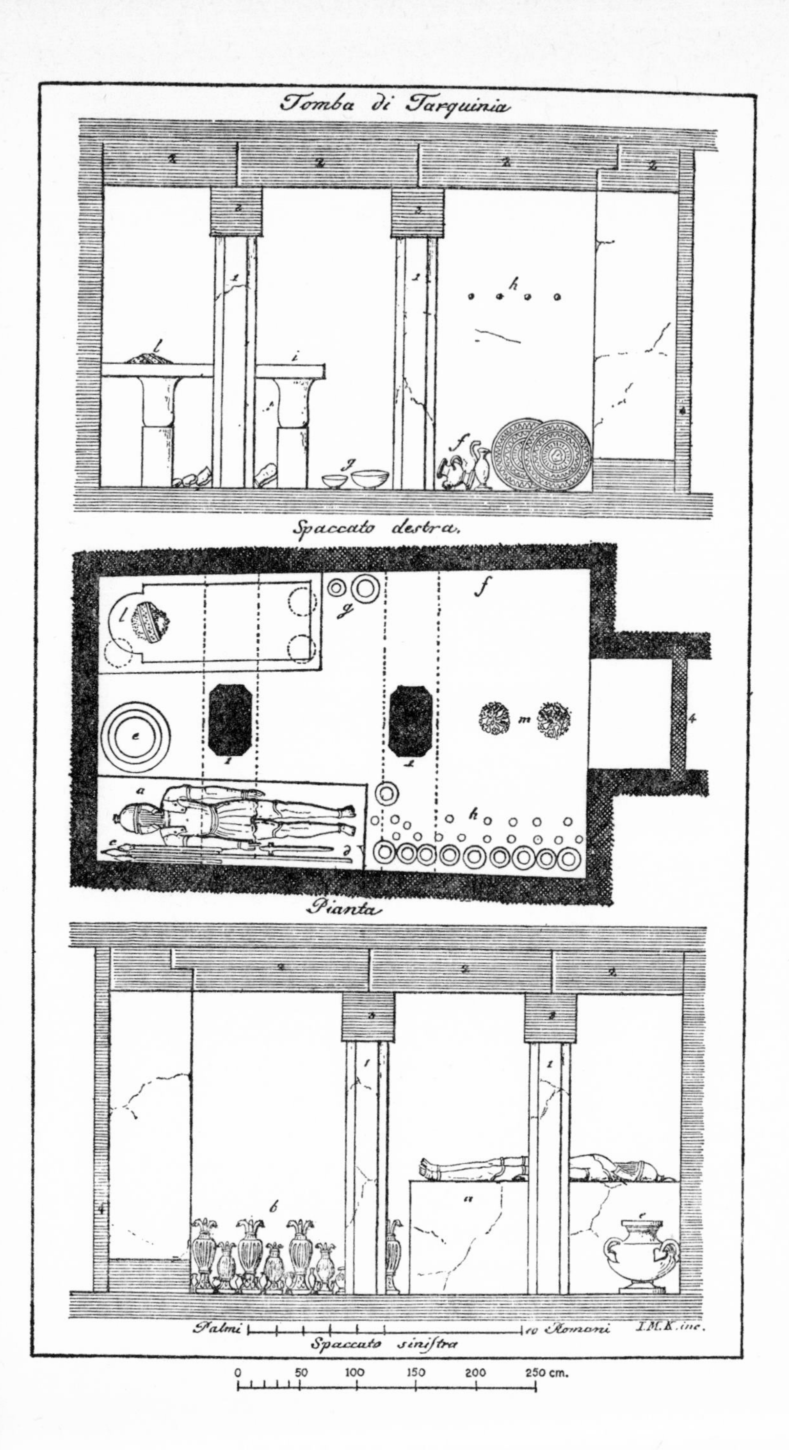
Tomba di Tarquinia
Spaccato destra.
Pianta
Palmi
10 Romani
I.M.K. inc.
Spaccato sinistra
0
50
100
150
200
250 cm.

and craftsmen. Hence trade with Phoenician colonies in the central Mediterranean need not be the only source of influences in Etruria from this direction.

Similarly if one turns to Asia Minor and adjacent areas, one finds a parallel situation, for in 714 BC the Cimmerians from north of the Black Sea attacked the Urartian kingdom in eastern Turkey. Later they moved westwards destroying Gordion, the Phygian capital; then between 667 and 664 and again in 652 they attacked Lydia. The ravages of such barbarous invaders in these civilized kingdoms may have been as terrifying as the Assyrian assaults on Syria, and one can imagine that the ports of Asia Minor might also be thronged with refugees all seeking ships bound for more tranquil lands. Such refugees might have included the wealthy intent on saving themselves and their possessions as well as artists and craftsmen.

Since all this was happening just when Near Eastern influences were becoming more marked in Etruria, it seems possible that these Assyrian and Cimmerian attacks might account in part for the currents coming from the Near East, and this might well include the introduction of chamber tombs and tumuli from Asia Minor. But this does not necessarily mean that 'the Etruscans' came from Lydia at this time, though the famous story of their Lydian origin given by Herodotus has been cited in this connection.

As for Greek influences in Etruria in the seventh century, the tradition of Demaratus may provide a parallel for the historical events in the Near East. The story in question comes from very late sources and hence must be treated accordingly, but in essence it is this. Demaratus, a member of the Bacchiads, the ruling family of Corinth, amassed a great fortune in trading with Etruria, but when the Bacchiads were driven from power in the mid seventh century BC, Demaratus fled to Tarquinia, where he had many friends. He took with him as much of his wealth as he could and also a number of followers including artisans. According to some versions of the story, he played a large part in introducing Greek culture into Etruria, married a Tarquinian lady of noble birth and became the forebear of the Tarquin kings of Rome.

This tradition coincides in a way with the appearance of pottery of Corinthian type and other Greek influences in Etruria at the time, but this pottery was in vogue in the Greek colonies in southern Italy even earlier, and they must also be given a share of credit for influencing Etruria. Demaratus is even said to have introduced the alphabet into Etruria, but the Etruscan form of it resembles the alphabet of Cumae, the Greek colony near Naples, more closely than it resembles that of Corinth. Perhaps Demaratus' association with the Tarquins caused many stories of Greek contacts to cluster around his name, but there may still be some kernel of truth in the tradition that a Greek from Corinth, like the Near Eastern displaced persons that I have already postulated, sought refuge in Etruria with his followers.

I shall now take up some of the more important Villanovan survivals as well as Greek and Near Eastern elements. As for the Villanovan ones, Tarquinia continued to occupy the plateau where the Villanovan settlement had been, and, as already mentioned, the very important Villanovan cemetery on Monterozzi grew larger.

Fig. 3

As for pottery, the ordinary wares of the seventh century were continuations of Villanovan ones, but only a very few Villanovan urns can be as late as the beginning of Period III. One is from Romanelli's Tomb 66, a pozzo on Monterozzi, that was found a long distance from other Villanovan pozzi and in an area of tombs of the seventh century and later. This grave contained in addition to the urn a crested pottery helmet of Villanovan type with more elaborate decoration than earlier ones, but its late date is indicated by a locally made oinochoe or wine jug based on a Protocorinthian type with ornament

Plate 149

Plate 148

Plate 150

Plate 166 close to that on the skyphos from the Bocchoris Tomb of early Period III.

Plate 154 Another Villanovan survivor is the bottle-shaped jug with a handle suggesting a horned animal found in the Chamber Tomb of the Madonna del Pianto, while the horned animal-bird also appears, though in a much damaged state, on a plastic animal vase from another chamber tomb. The spheroid jars of red ware also have descendants both with and without *Fig. 48* feet. The Bocchoris Tomb, another chamber, contained such a jar without a foot, and, though its ornament embodies foreign forms, some of this is in the old white paint that goes back to Plates 152, 153 the Villanovan house urns. A pair of such red jars on feet but now with decorative ribs comes from the Trench Grave with a Geometric Oinochoe and must belong to the beginning of Period III, while a much more developed type with a lid and a foot comes from the somewhat later Avvolta Tomb. The Trench Plates 157, 151 Grave with a Ring-shaped Bull Vase contained the vase that gives it its name, and this was another example of the old red ware. The dark polished ware also continued in a more refined form and tended in the direction of the later black bucchero. At the same time it assumed more elaborate shapes such as the big Plate 155 cup that may have come from the Bocchoris Tomb. Another form of this ware is seen in the small amphora from the Plates 44, 115, 164 Bocchoris Tomb, a shape perhaps descended from the more primitive Villanovan amphorae of southern derivation.

Some metal forms also continue into Period III, though most of them go no further back than Villanovan II. These include Plate 163 the sharply curved razor, the animal fibula, a bronze flask and a Plate 156 bronze amphora. The shield probably from the Avvolta Tomb *Fig. 30e* continues the tradition of the shield from the Warrior's Tomb of late Villanovan II, but with new decorative elements. Fibulae with enlarged bodies and long catches or the serpentine kind with pairs of knobs on the sides also continue from Villanovan *Fig. 49b* II. The Fossa with a Bronze Tripod is so called from its tripod

Fig. 48. Spheroid jar, Bocchoris Tomb of Period III, Monterozzi. 1:6

which is a Villanovan survivor, and the mounted warriors on the legs wear crested Villanovan helmets.

In connection with these Villanovan survivals at Tarquinia, Villanovan elements from other Etruscan cemeteries of this time and later may be mentioned. I have suggested that the pairs of pottery horses and pairs of pottery wheels from Villanovan graves represent model chariots and their teams, and both model chariots and actual ones have been found in Etruscan tombs of the seventh century and later. The famous silver sword with a gold hilt from the Bernardini Tomb is basically a continuation of the short swords of Villanovan days, despite its oriental hilt. The gold filigree bracelets, such as came from the Tomb of Bes at Vetulonia, seem to be descendants of the silver filigree ones of Villanovan II at Tarquinia, and ultimately of the bronze spirals with undulating ends of Villanovan I, though

Plate 87

Fig. 27c

true filigree might also owe something to foreign influences. Furthermore, there are pottery model boats in tombs of the seventh century and later that represent an old Villanovan custom. There is too the splendid horned bird from the Isis Tomb at Vulci that shows that this mythical Villanovan creature was alive in the Etruscan mind even in the sixth century.

Plate 147

As for elements from the Greek and Near Eastern worlds, it is difficult to deal with them in a tidy fashion, for Greece also came under oriental influences at this same time, though without the chamber tombs and tumuli that in Etruria suggest Near Eastern settlers. Still, owing to these orientalizing influences in Greece, it is not really possible to make a complete separation between Greek and oriental elements in Etruria. Indeed it has been argued that oriental influences were transmitted to Etruria largely by the Greeks, and one cannot deny some justice in this view. None the less I shall try to divide the material from Tarquinia into elements that seem more Greek and those that seem more Near Eastern.

The most important of all the Greek elements was the appearance of the Etruscan alphabet apparently derived from that of the Greek colony of Cumae near Naples. Vases of Greek type are now far more numerous at Tarquinia than in Villanovan II, and as before most of them were probaby made in Etruria. Though the old geometric kind of decoration had a long survival, the more important relationships are now with the Greek colonies in Italy, where the Protocorinthian and Corinthian styles were popular, rather than with the Aegean islands, Rhodes and Cyprus as in Villanovan II. Indeed the story of Demaratus may perhaps imply connections with Corinth itself. As before, these Greek types of vases contrast sharply with the local wares of Villanovan descent because they are made of light-coloured potter's clay and painted in styles of Greek origin, though often in a provincial manner. I shall refer here only to a few examples.

Plate 173

The oinochoe from the Trench Grave with a Geometric Oinochoe has the round body and conical neck recalling the one of Cypriot shape seen also in the Warrior's Tomb of Villanovan II, but this one has Late Geometric ornament. It might indeed be placed in Villanovan II, but it was found with a painted cup in a somewhat later style, and also with two red jars with ribs that are characteristic of Period III. Besides, it was found in a zone of tombs of Period III and a considerable distance from any of Villanovan II.

Plates 139, 153

Plate 152

Examples of the Protocorinthian type are the skyphos from the Bocchoris Tomb and the oinochoe from Romanelli's Tomb 66. These are local products, probably from the same workshop, and belong to the earlier seventh century. There are also some vases with fish that recall Cumae. As examples of Corinthian type I illustrate two locally made olpai.

Plates 166, 150

Plates 167–170

Other elements from the Greek world are the horses related to the Greek Geometric breed that appear in the fibulae from the Bocchoris Tomb and on the feet of the bronze tripod. A bronze figurine from trench grave 9 on Poggio Gallinaro is also related to Greek Geometric ones. The warriors on the red jar from the Bocchoris Tomb have Greek prototypes, and so have the griffins' heads on the lid of the jar probably from the Avvolta Tomb, though in this case there are oriental prototypes as well.

Plate 163

Fig. 49b

Plate 171

Fig. 48

Plate 157

As for Asiatic elements, a few samples of the Syro-Cypriot current with an Egyptian flavour may be mentioned. These include numerous objects of faience and glazed composition, such as vases, scarabs, and figurines, some representing Egyptian deities. Many of these were probably of Phoenician manufacture, but the most important of all, the Bocchoris vase inscribed with the name of the Egyptian king Bocchoris who reigned briefly toward the close of the eighth century, is according to recent opinion a genuine Egyptian piece and not a Phoenician imitation as has been previously suggested. If so,

Plate 159

Plate 165

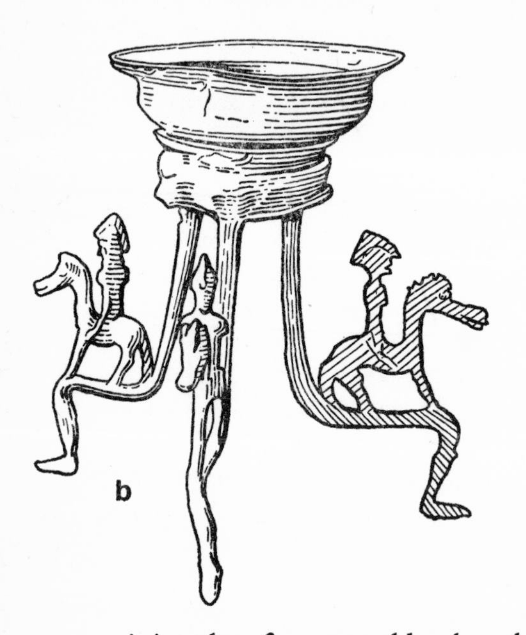

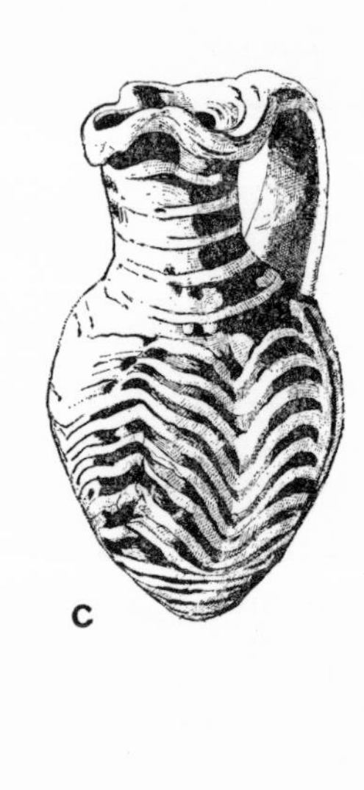

Fig. 49. Objects of Period III from Monterozzi: a, gold plaque from the Bocchoris Tomb showing the goddess between sphinxes; b, c, bronze tripod and glass jug from a trench grave (a after Montelius, b, c after Monumenti dall'Instituto). a, Approx. 2:1; b, c, 2:3

it is only a few years older than the vases of Greek type from the same chamber tomb. The acrobatic dancing girl on the lid of the red jar from the Bocchoris Tomb is also derived from an Egyptian form.

Fig. 49

I have already mentioned a kind of oinochoe with geometric decoration but whose shape recalls Cypriot ones, and another element perhaps from the same quarter is the series of crenellated towers on the same red jar from the Bocchoris Tomb. These resemble the towers represented on the so-called Phoenician bowls often thought to have been made in Cyprus.

Phoenician connections are also possible for the monkeys or apes that ride the bronze horse-shaped fibulae from the Bocchoris Tomb. The Phoenicians apparently imported these animals from India, and the distribution of representations of them corresponds with the areas of Syrian and Phoenician trade. Ostrich eggs from Tarquinian chamber tombs also probably reflect Phoenician trade, since the Phoenicians were breeders of ostriches and made bowls from their eggs.

Plate 163

The goddess between two sphinxes on a gold plaque from the Bocchoris Tomb represents an old Near Eastern concept, the Mistress of the Beasts, though this penetrates Greek art as well. Other goddesses also with long girdled dresses and locks of hair but with folded wings came from the chamber in the Tumulo del Re and had been the supports of a bucchero cup. In addition, ornament related to the Near Eastern sacred tree was found in the Tumulo del Re. Such ornament also accompanied by rosettes and a guilloche is found for example on the Nimrud ivories of the late ninth to late eighth centuries. The gold pectoral always attributed to the Bocchoris Tomb, but which came from another chamber tomb at Tarquinia, also has oriental ornament of guilloches, rosettes, Phoenician palmettes and 'lions'.

Fig. 49a

Fig. 50a, b

Fig. 50c

Plates 161, 162

Fig. 50. Objects of Period III from Monterozzi: a–c, Bucchero goddesses and sacred tree, originally supports for a cup from the Tumulo del Re; d, 'ivory panther' from the Chamber Tomb of the Bronze and Gold Pectoral (a–c after Cultrera, d after Montelius). d, 1 : 2

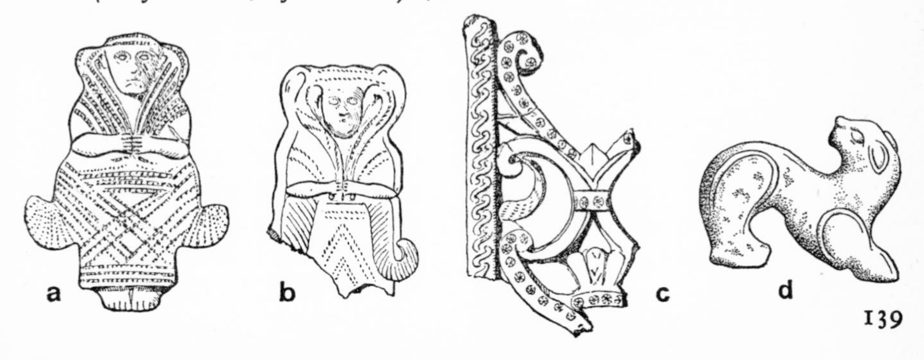

Another favourite Near Eastern motif is the lotus bud, already seen on the pectoral from the Warrior's Tomb; this is now found on the handles of a big amphora from the Bocchoris Tomb and on the shield from the Avvolta Tomb, which has other Near Eastern elements as well. In the trench grave that contained the bronze tripod was also found a glass jug derived from a considerably older Near Eastern type, but this is probably an imitation made in Italy.

Plates 156, 160

Fig. 49c

As for the Asiatic-Continental elements, there are first of all the pottery stands for pots. A fine example made of pottery derived from the old Villanovan red ware came from the Bocchoris Tomb; another was in the Chamber Tomb with Fish Oinochoai, and the Avvolta Tomb contained a pot and stand combined in one piece. The one from the Avvolta Tomb is also in part the successor of the old spheroid jars, sometimes ribbed, that stood on feet. But these stands and their pots are also the ceramic counterparts of the bronze stands and cauldrons from the great Etruscan tombs at Caere and Praeneste, whose parallels are found in Urartu in eastern Turkey and elsewhere in western Asia, though they were also known in Greece. One wonders how much of the oriental ritual for which they were intended penetrated to Etruria. 'Ivory panthers' from the Chamber Tomb of the Bronze and Gold Pectoral might have Phrygian connections. Elements with ultimate roots in Persia may be the two lions with a joint head on the handles of a bucchero cup, and so may the human feet of the bronze tripod. The horsemen on the tripod are almost legless, a feature found in Greece and Cyprus but likewise in Luristan, Syria and the land of the Hittites in Asia Minor. They are also armless like some Syro-Hittite terracottas.

Plate 158

Fig. 46c

Plate 157

Plates 26, 152

Fig. 50d

Plate 172

Fig. 49b

To sum up the evidence from Period III, inhumation had almost entirely superseded cremation, but that process had already begun in Villanovan II and might indicate influence from southern Italy. But the appearance of chamber tombs and especially chambered tumuli seems a marked departure from established burial custom, and even though chamber tombs might have a partially local explanation, these changes can be interpreted as indicating new settlers. Other Near Eastern elements might point to contacts or influences as the result of trade either directly with Near Eastern peoples or with the Greeks of the Orientalizing period. But these explanations do not altogether account for the change to chamber tombs and especially chambers in tumuli. If these are Near Eastern, then we may guess that not all the other Near Eastern elements were merely due to trading contacts.

But there are also strong arguments for substantial Villanovan survivals, more especially the continuity of the site as a whole and of the cemetery on Monterozzi. Also the objects of this period abound in foreign forms, although these are often embedded in a Villanovan matrix. The bronze tripod of Villanovan descent has oriental and Greek elements, but its horsemen wear Villanovan helmets. The big red jar from the Bocchoris Tomb is in itself of Villanovan origin, and so is its white painted decoration, the warriors on it however are ultimately Greek, the towers Cypro-Phoenician and the acrobatic dancer on the lid Egyptian. The examples could be multiplied, but the main point to be made here is that even though new settlers attracted by the mineral wealth of Etruria may have come in Period III from Syria, Asia Minor and adjacent lands where invasions had produced unsettled conditions, they mixed with the Villanovan population in somewhat the same way that the Villanovans had previously mixed with the Apennine Bronze Age people.

Fig. 49b

Fig. 48

Chapter IX

Invaders and Traditions

I HAVE ALREADY MENTIONED the resemblances between urnfields in the central Balkans and Villanovan ones in Italy, and I have also suggested the possibility that the Villanovan and perhaps some of the earlier urnfields near the Italian coasts might be explained as the cemeteries of sea-borne settlers who mixed with older inhabitants. These settlers first appeared during the period of the urnfield expansion and the upheaval in the Aegean and Near East when the Mycenaean world and the Hittite Empire disappeared. In Greek tradition it was the period following the Trojan War, now dated to 1250 or a little later, when the Tyrsenians and their Pelasgian kinsmen were reported to have been in the Aegean. The Greeks also applied the name Tyrsenians to the historical Etruscans, and the departure of the Tyrsenians from the Aegean according to Herodotus refers to this period. Furthermore there are discernible urnfield elements among the disturbers of the peace in the civilized lands of the eastern Mediterranean at this time, but unfortunately they are scanty, and they contain nothing that can be called Villanovan. Still, since there is little evidence that forebears of the Villanovans came overland from the Balkans to Italy, there is always the possibility that they and perhaps some other urnfielders near the Italian coasts arrived by sea and were connected with movements from the heartland of Europe into the Aegean and the eastern Mediterranean. All this is of course mere speculation, but, if borne out by future discovery, it offers a possible means of reconciling archaeological evidence with tradition.

As for barbarian penetrations into Greece, we find that life in Macedonian settlements using Mycenaean pottery was interrupted by strangers who made coarser wares resembling those of central and eastern Europe, and probably this was another reflection of movements of urnfield peoples in the Balkans that I have already mentioned. Also graves of the late thirteenth century in Epirus contained Danubian bronzes as well as a Mycenaean dagger.

Further south there are more signs of trouble not far from 1200 BC. The fortifications of Athens, Mycenae and Tiryns were strengthened, and a defensive wall was built at the Isthmus of Corinth with towers on its northern side indicating the direction of the danger. None the less major Mycenaean centres were destroyed, while others fell into decline or were abandoned, though Athens and other places survived, and some even revived for a time. But the old Mycenaean way of life was never the same again, and it was gradually replaced by the Geometric Iron Age on a lower level of civilization.

At the time of these destructive attacks and later there appear in Greece bronze swords, spears, daggers, shields bosses, fibulae and long pins which are not derivable from Mycenaean forms. The weapons are characteristic of the central European urnfields while the fibulae and pins have Balkan parallels. Also the central European swords indicate a new mode of fighting that was non-Greek. Not all of these foreign bronzes were direct imports into Greece, for some differ in detail from the true urnfield ones and may have been made in Greece, but their roots are clearly in central and eastern Europe. Neither did they all come at once but indicate a succession if intruders and a long period of contact between Greece and people from the lands to the north. They also represent currents coming from that direction at a time when Greece was weak; this is the reverse of the earlier current, when Greece was strong, which bore various Mycenaean forms including armour northward into central Europe. Also this was the period when the urnfielders were beginning to expand in other directions around their periphery, and urnfield weapons in Greece could indicate intrusions paralleled elsewhere.

In Greek tradition of course the invaders were Dorians, but the Dorians are faceless archaeologically, while the bearers of the central European panoply are nameless. Yet they can hardly be the same, since it is difficult to see how the Dorians, rustic Greeks from northern Greece, could have come with central European armament. Thus they may represent a different facet of the disturbances of this period and may have filled a power vacuum to the south. Some northerners may also have taken service under Mycenaean rulers, for contemporary Pharaohs recorded barbarian attacks against them and the hiring of erstwhile attackers as mercenaries. Whatever happened, the Dorians may have lived in Greek tradition because they were Greeks, while the more northerly folk could have been absorbed by the Hellenic population and thus lost their identity.

Also at the end of the Mycenaean Age the dead were sometimes buried in cists made of slabs. This was not unknown previously in Greece, but such cists were also used in the southern Balkans in areas where cremation was not universal. In Greece these cists sometimes contain arc fibulae and long bronze pins of kinds known at this time in the southern Balkans. Pins are scarce in Mycenaean Greece after its opening phase with Schliemann's shaft graves at Mycenae, but pins are very plentiful in central Europe. Also the skeletons in some of these cists suggest physical types connected with the lands north of Greece.

The Protogeometric Period beginning in the eleventh century BC saw the beginnings of the cemetery of tumuli at Vergina in Macedonia where inhumed burials and rare cremations were accompanied by a central European flange-hilted sword and by Danubian, local Macedonian and Protogeometric pottery. Also from Protogeometric times and later there are numerous small bronze birds such as were part of the culture of the urnfields, and in Greece these include the urnfield double bird and even the horned bird. Another sign of change especially in

Attica at the very end of the Mycenaean Age is cremation, and this increases in Protogeometric times. A shift in burial rite from inhumation to cremation is not in itself significant, and indeed Attic amphorae were used for the ashes rather than urnfield urns. But the amphorae may be decorated with the meander, a design new to Greece though with a long history in the Balkans. Perhaps these vases made of light-coloured and refined clay and with painted ornament would have seemed more attractive to the newcomers than their own much coarser urns, especially if one of their own motifs were prominently displayed on them. Furthermore these amphorae were accompanied by arc fibulae, long pins and figurines all with Balkan analogies. Such graves may also contain shield bosses and swords of ultimate urnfield type, though the swords are now of iron. All of this suggests new settlers from the lands north of Greece, who would have come after the initial attacks on Mycenaean centres and who eventually merged with the older population.

In Crete too there are signs of change, but their meaning is unclear. Some sites were destroyed though not simultaneously, while others continued, but new towns appeared on defensible heights as though in response to danger. Also the population tended to move away from the coasts into safer inland areas. Along with this there was sporadic cremation, and long pins, fibulae and urnfield swords also appear. It is of course easy to exaggerate the foreign elements in Greece and Crete, and any barbarian settlers must have been absorbed by the indigenous folk, but with these foreign elements, there went a drastic change in the Bronze Age way of life.

As for Asia Minor, there is first of all Troy. A generation or so after its destruction by the Greeks coarse pottery appears there related to that of eastern Europe, indicating settlers from that quarter, but soon the site was abandoned perhaps as a result of a new calamity. The Hittite realm collapsed not far from this time, and its capital Bogazköy was destroyed. The destroyers were presumably the Phrygians who are believed to have come from Europe. At Gordion, the Phrygian capital, coarse, black, hand-made pottery appeared at about this time, but it did not last long; this suggests barbarian invaders, possibly Phrygians, who were soon absorbed.

Down the coast of Asia Minor Miletus was destroyed though it had been heavily fortified not long before. On some of the eastern Aegean islands towns were wrecked or abandoned, and cremations and rare urnfield swords have been found. In southern Asia Minor, Syria and Palestine cities were devastated, and in Cyprus Bronze Age places were wrecked, while the foreign trade of the island declined. The important city of Enkomi was destroyed three times between the later thirteenth and mid twelfth centuries and was finally abandoned in the eleventh. In Cyprus, too, there occur European swords, spears, fibulae and long pins. It would be going beyond the evidence to insist that these European bronzes were all brought by the destroyers, but as before they accompany disaster.

In this connection the Syrian site of Hama is of especial interest, for about 1200 BC a new phase of the city's life began on a much lower cultural level. The new inhabitants buried their dead in urnfields, and, though the urns were non-European painted pots, a parallel to the amphorae used at Athens, they were accompanied by bronze and iron swords of urnfield derivation and by European fibulae.

The next step is to see what literary evidence there is for the destroyers in western Asia, and it is clear that they were of many different sorts. The Homeric Greeks and the supposedly European Phrygians accounted respectively for Priam's Troy and the Hittite Empire, but the Sea Peoples known from Egyptian and Hittite sources are credited with much of the rest. Even as far back as the fourteenth century we hear of people called Shardana, Shakalash, Danauna and Lukki. The Shardana are suspected of being Sardinians either from Sardinia or a people who later settled there. If the Danauna were Greeks (Danaoi) and the Lukki were Lycians from southern Asia Minor as some have suggested, other peoples than urnfielders were involved. These various peoples posed no particular threat until the reign of Merneptah of Egypt (about 1232–1224), but he had to fight off a combined force of Sea Peoples including Akaiwasha, probably Achaean Greeks, and Tursha who may have been Tyrsenians, which, as we have seen, was a Greek name for the Etruscans. Somewhat later Rameses III (about 1198–1166) repelled three more attacks of Sea Peoples who included Tursha and also Peleset, often equated with the Philistines of the Bible and the Pelasgians ('sea people') of Greek tradition. In these attacks the Egyptian forces included mercenaries of some of the same tribes as the attackers. The most dangerous invasion was that of about 1190, for then the naval attack was supplemented by a migrant hoard of men, women and children moving in ox carts which overran the whole area from northern Syria to the borders of Egypt. To commemorate his victory over them Rameses III illustrated on the walls of his temple at Medinet Habu near Luxor the naval battle in which the Shardana and the Peleset were defeated; their long low ships with the head of a water bird fore and aft are reminiscent of the bird-boats depicted somewhat later in the art of the urnfields. If anyone wonders how inland urnfielders could have become sea people, one need only point to the Vandals of Carthage, previously a people of inland Europe, who became a piratical scourge in the fifth century AD in the Mediterranean, and who even sacked Rome.

Fig. 42a, b, f
Fig. 43c

As for the Peleset, or Philistines, their settlement in Palestine followed their defeat in Egypt, but their remains are unhelpful in the matter of their origin. Some have thought that they came from Asia Minor or from Europe, and indeed they sometimes practised cremation; but they had by this time adopted a mixture of Mycenaean, Egyptian, and Near Eastern culture that disguises their origin. In this regard they may have followed the practice of many other barbarian peoples who moved into more civilized regions, discarding their own material culture and taking over elements of more advanced ones with which they came in contact. As for the Tursha, if they are the Tyrsenians of Herodotus who left the Aegean apparently after the Trojan War, that is after 1250 or a little later, their appearance in Egypt about 1232–1224 might fit chronologically. In general it seems that these disturbers of the peace were of many kinds and apparently included Greeks and people from Asia Minor among others. This was not a war between barbarians on one side and civilized peoples on the other, but a period of turbulence beginning with the breakdown of two great powers, Mycenaean Greece and the Hittite Empire. Both barbarous and civilized peoples were found among the attackers, and great kings hired barbarians to fight other barbarians. Within the framework of the evidence there is also room for some European urnfielders.

Finally, one might draw a broad parallel between three barbarian movements in Europe, those of the urnfield peoples, the Celts of the Iron Age and the Germanic tribes who overran the Roman Empire. All of them had learned much from the great civilizations of the Mediterranean, and all penetrated the three southern peninsulas of Europe, Greece, Italy and Iberia. Often the higher the civilization of an invaded area, the fewer are the archaeological remains of the barbarians, this applies to Greece in all three invasions, Urnfield, Celtic and Germanic. In the case of the Germanic tribes in Italy, their threat caused Rome to be fortified by the Aurelian wall paralleling the strengthening of defences at Mycenaean centres, but this did not preserve the city from eventual capture. As in Greece, the invaders were on a lower level of civilization, and the traces that they have left are hardly enough to suggest that they ever seized the Eternal City. Indeed in Italy they absorbed many cultural elements from their surroundings, and at Ravenna the art and architecture of the Gothic kingdom centred there are those of contemporary Italy and have nothing to do with the Germanic antiquity.

I have said all this simply to indicate that while there is no specific evidence that the presumed Balkan forebears of the Villanovans ever passed through the Aegean-eastern Mediterranean world, what we know of this period provided an opportunity for them to have done so. Not only was it the time of the urnfield expansion in Europe, but in the view of Homer Thomas there were also contemporary movements on the steppe whose repercussions were felt in Oltenia in the central Balkans. Hence there may have been reasons for an exodus from that area. This could also explain how the Villanovans, who may have arrived in Italy by sea, happened to have both Balkan and Aegean-eastern Mediterranean elements in their culture. One would have to suppose also that those who went to Italy did not have sufficiently close contact with Aegean-Near Eastern civilizations to pick up more than a smattering of elements before they moved away. Since the cultures of Italy then were not highly developed, the Villanovans would not have been tempted to abandon their own ways as completely as did other barbarians settling in areas of high civilization. All of this does not, of course, tell us what really happened, but only suggests what might have happened. Nevertheless it will be worthwhile to compare it with the ancient traditions about the Tyrsenians.

But before taking these up, something should be said about the general framework of ancient legend in which they belong. The sources of these legends vary enormously in age, and if they have any significance, it is only in their broadest outlines. They deal mainly with central and southern Italy and Sicily and touch the north only occasionally. Beginning with settlers 'seventeen generations before the Trojan War', they bring a series of peoples and heroes to Italy chiefly from Greece and the Aegean area and to a lesser extent from across the Adriatic.

There is very little mention of anyone coming from the north or the west. Naturally, ancient authors were much more likely to bring the peoples of early Italy from the civilized lands with which they were familiar rather than from the barbarous and less known north and west, but still the general picture given by the legends has a correspondence, however generalized, to what we learn from the prehistory of the southern part of the Italian peninsula and Sicily from the Neolithic onward, when the flow of culture through the Mediterranean was indeed from east to west.

Greek tradition also had much to say about Tyrsenians in the Aegean in the period of the Trojan War and later, and also about the Pelasgians who were said by Thucydides to have been a branch of the Tyrsenians. Sir John Myres long ago recognized that the Greeks had two apparently contradictory ideas about the Pelasgians. One was that they were a sea people connected especially with the northern Aegean toward the end of the Mycenaean Age. The other was that they were an ancient pre-Greek people in Greece. Myres aptly compared these contradictions to the old ideas in England about the Druids. Everyone knew that the Druids were the priests of the Celts, but all sorts of ancient remains were called 'druidical', though the real Druids never had anything to do with them. Myres accordingly distinguished between the 'actual' and 'theoretical' Pelasgians in Greek tradition, and here I shall concentrate on what seem to be references to the former. The most important references to Tyrsenians and Pelasgians are in Herodotus and Thucydides, both of whom lived in the fifth century BC, and though later authors gave other versions of the traditions, they added little and indeed beclouded them by trying to rationalize them into connected accounts.

Since the Pelasgians were said to have been a branch of the Tyrsenians, I shall consider them in some detail and will even be so bold as to offer a rationalization of my own. This is of course not history but is rather a synthesis of what Greeks in the fifth century BC thought had happened many centuries before. In the *Iliad* the Pelasgians appear as allies of Troy and evidently lived not far away, but in the *Odyssey* they appear in Crete which is the first hint of them as sea people. Herodotus tells how they moved to Attica where the Athenians gave them land in return for which they built the Pelasgian Wall on the Acropolis. This wall belongs very late in the Mycenaean Age and is one of the fortifications apparantly occasioned by threats from the north already mentioned. Did Priam at Troy and, somewhat later, the Athenians ally themselves with the barbarians in time of trouble as the Pharaohs did in Egypt? In any case the alliance with the Athenians ended in a quarrel; the Pelasgians were expelled a generation or so after the Trojan War and went to the northern Aegean island of Lemnos and elsewhere, but they took vengeance by kidnapping some Athenian women attending the festival at Brauron, which gives them the aspect of sea raiders. Their presence in Lemnos recalls the famed Lemnos stele with its inscription in a language that resembles Etruscan. They were still in Lemnos when the Persians annexed the island about 505 BC, but on its capture by the Athenians, they went to the northern Aegean peninsula of Chalcidice. In the time of Herotodus the Pelasgians lived in a city called Creston, and among their neighbours were Tyrsenians, while Thucydides says that the eastern arm of Chalcidice, the Acte peninsula, was inhabited by Pelasgians who belonged to the Tyrsenians who once inhabited Lemnos and Athens. Another people in the vicinity according to Thucydides were the Crestonians, which suggests that Creston was not far away. There has been much discussion about where Creston really was, but if one considers what Herodotus and Thucydides both said in conjunction with local geography with which they were personally familiar, it was certainly on or near the peninsula of Chalcidice in the northern Aegean.

This brings us to Herodotus' famous story of the Tyrsenian migration from Lydia. The chronological implications in Herodotus make it quite possible that he thought that this migration took place not long after the Trojan War, or after about 1250. According to the story, half of the population of Lydia was forced to emigrate by a prolonged famine. These folk went to Smyrna where they built ships and sailed away under command of Tyrsenos, son of the Lydian king. After passing by many nations in turn, they arrived in Italy in the land of the Umbrians where they founded cities and where, says Herodotus, 'they have lived ever since'. Also they changed their name to Tyrsenians after their leader Tyrsenos. Herodotus uses the name Tyrsenians for these migrants and for the historical Etruscans of his own day. His statement that they founded cities in Italy and 'have lived there ever since' recalls the Villanovans, whose cemeteries are the earliest remains connected with the Etruscan coastal cities. One must at the same time face the fact that in the Herodotean story the Tyrsenians' departure from Smyrna would seem to have been in the second half of the thirteenth century BC, while Villanovan at Tarquinia does not begin on my chronology until the tenth, and even if one includes the related Previllanovans of southern Etruria, one can hardly reach a time before the eleventh century. Could Herodotus' statement that they passed by many nations in turn before reaching Italy explain the gap between the departure of the Tyrsenians from Smyrna and the arrival of the Previllanovan and Villanovan urnfield peoples in southern Etruria? In any case one might imagine that an Aegean sea people like the Tyrsenians would be likely to use an Aegean port such as Smyrna and to leave at a time of famine.

Also, if there is little connection between Villanovan culture and that of Lydia at this time, cultural links with Asia Minor can be attributed more to Period III after about 700 BC when the Cimmerian raids in Lydia may well have driven refugees away to Etruria. Can it be that Herodotus telescoped two traditions into the same story, the departure of the Tyrsenians from Smyrna because of a famine not long after the Trojan War and the departure of Lydians escaping from the Cimmerians in the seventh century BC?

As for the famine in Asia Minor not long after the Trojan War, it seems to have been real enough. Merneptah of Egypt (about 1232–1224) sent relief shipments of grain to the Hittites, and a letter from the Hittite emperor to the king of Ugarit in Lebanon about this time alludes to a scarcity of food and also asks help against a military threat. Presumably these events were all connected with the same danger. There is also the more or less contemporary account of Madduvattaš of Zippašlā, a Hittite vassal evidently in north-western Asia Minor, who fled with his starving followers to the protection of the Hittite emperor who gave him supplies including seed, which suggests famine and devastation. It is easy to imagine that a famine in Asia Minor due to warlike conditions would motivate the departure of the Tyrsenians. Also Madduvattaš's enemies were the people of Ahhijava or 'Achaea', that is Greeks. We have already seen that Merneptah at about this time fought off a force including Akaiwasha and Tursha (perhaps Achaeans and Tyrsenians). This could be another chapter of the same story.

Other Greek traditions about the Tyrsenians, or Tyrrhenians as the Greeks sometimes called them, indicate that they were thought to have lived in Italy from very early times. The oldest Greek reference of all is in the Hesiodic Theogony composed not far from 700 BC, which says that the Tyrsenians were ruled by the sons of Odysseus and Circe. This places the Tyrsenians in Italy shortly after the Trojan War. In the fourth century BC Ephorus reported that before the founding of the Greek colony of Naxos in Sicily (734 BC) the Greeks were too afraid of the Tyrrhenian pirates to venture into Sicilian waters. Since the Greeks were thoroughly familiar with the coasts of southern

Italy and Sicily by the eighth century, Ephorus must have meant that his Tyrrhenians were already in Italy by that time.

We next come to a quite different story, that of Dionysius of Halicarnassus, who wrote in Rome in the first century BC, for he declared that the Tyrrhenians or Etruscans were indigenous to Italy and had not migrated from elsewhere. Dionysius was one of those late Greek authors who constructed romantic histories of ancient peoples, and, apart from his view that the Etruscans were indigenous, his work would be of little interest except that it embodies remarks by Hellanicus of Lesbos who, like Herodotus and Thucydides, wrote in the fifth century BC. According to Hellanicus, the Pelasgians were in the remote past driven out of their country by the Greeks and after leaving their ships on the Spinetic branch of the Po, they took Croton, an inland city, and proceeded from there to colonize Etruria. In Italy they took the name of Tyrrhenians. Using this and other material, Dionysius built up a story largely on references to the Pelasgians that relate to Myres' 'theoretical' Pelasgians rather than to his 'actual' ones. Dionysius' Pelasgians founded Spina at the mouth of the Spinetic Po, crossed the Apennines into Umbria where they captured Croton and from there colonized Etruria. Later at about the time of the Trojan War calamities caused most of them to abandon Italy, and their lands were taken over by the Tyrrhenians, who Hellanicus thought were a different people, though Croton according to him long retained its identity as a Pelasgian town.

Fig. 33

The value of Dionysius' ideas seems limited. Not only did he use references to Myres' 'theoretical' Pelasgians, but he says that they founded Spina, where the earliest remains belong to the sixth century BC, and that they captured Croton, identified with the inland Etruscan city of Cortona, where there is nothing as early as Villanovan. Yet all this would have happened before the Trojan War. Some scholars have thought that the Creston of Herodotus was not in Chalcidice but was Cortona in central

Italy, but this is not supported by the facts. The spellings of the names Croton and the Crotonians in Dionysius are quite distinct from those of Creston and the Crestonians of Herodotus and Thucydides, and, since these latter authors were themselves familiar with Chalcidice, and since they referred to the state of affairs there in their own day, it is a fair assumption that they knew whereof they wrote when they mentioned Creston, Crestonians, Pelasgians and Tyrsenians in the vicinity of Chalcidice. Hence to transpose Creston to central Italy would make nonsense of the whole Aegean geographical setting of the 'actual' Pelasgians as we find it in Homer, Thucydides and Herodotus.

Looked at in this light, it seems that Dionysius inherited from Hellanicus a story of the Pelasgians at Umbrian Croton and of how in Italy they took the name of Tyrrhenians. This seems like a garbled version of what Herodotus and Thucydides said about the Pelasgians and Tyrsenians at Creston near Chalcidice and of the settlers who changed their name in Italy to Tyrsenians. If so, was Hellanicus responsible for shifting the scene from the northern Aegean to central Italy, and was all this brought about by confusing Creston and Cortona?

Even so, there are two points of real interest in Hellanicus and Dionysius. One is the idea that the Pelasgians disembarked at the Spinetic Po, for Bologna, the great centre of the northern Villanovans is not far from it. If the Tyrsenians of Herodotus were the Villanovans of Etruria, may not their relatives, the Pelasgians, be represented in Italy by the Villanovans beyond the Apennines? Also the idea that the Etruscans were indigenous might correspond to my interpretation of the archaeology to the effect that, despite new settlements, there was some continuity of population in Etruria through the Bronze Age and Villanovan Iron Age to the true Etruscan civilization of the seventh century and later.

Italy itself gives us other relevant material. Roman tradition, though perverted by much tampering, also agrees that the

Etrusci were in Italy shortly after the Trojan War, for in Livy Aenas fell in battle against the Etruscan king of Caere. Varro even afforded a possible glimpse of Etruscan tradition itself; he quoted 'Etruscan histories' as saying that the Etruscans divided their era into ten ages. One can take Varro literally and arrive at a date of about 969 BC for the beginning of the first age or one can emend it slightly to reach a date of about 1049 BC. This, for what it may be worth, would approximate either my dates for the Villanovan or Previllanovan urnfield settlement of Etruria.

CHAPTER X

Who were the Villanovans and Etruscans?

HERODOTUS SAID THAT the Etruscans came from Lydia, and Dionysius said that they originated in Italy. This has often been the starting point for approaching the 'mystery' of Etruscan origins, but this approach was more appropriate to a time when knowledge of the ancient world was limited to the Bible and the classics, as when Dr Johnson remarked that all that could be known about the ancient world was already known. The modern approach of archaeology including European prehistory now must be considered, and the findings of archaeology indicate that Europe was inhabited in the periods under consideration by peoples of more advanced culture than the classicists suppose. Also their achievements had been steadily progressing for thousands of years before the Etruscan period, and this makes it increasingly difficult to agree with the older view of the classicists that the Etruscans must be explained by the settlement of a civilized people from the eastern Mediterranean world in an Italy that was inhabited, if at all, by mere savages. Indeed Etruscan culture and language have not been found in the eastern world but only in Etruria. Also the favourite idea of some classicists that the Etruscans only settled in Italy at the beginning of the Orientalizing Period from about 700 BC is a contradiction of everything that classical authors say, and their statements include Italian as well as Greek tradition.

The question, as I see it, is not where did the Etruscans come from, but where did the various elements come from that fused into the historical Etruscan nation in Etruria. I have already mentioned the Apennine Bronze Age and also the various kinds of Previllanovan urnfields, which indicate various sorts of cremating settlers mixing with the earlier Bronze Age inhabitants. Some of the settlers near the coasts of the peninsula came early in the period of continental urnfield expansion ultimately from the heart of Europe, though some elements of them might have arrived by sea. I have also mentioned the Previllanovan urnfields of this kind in southern Etruria that have a likeness to true Villanovan ones, but I have also indicated difficulties in deriving all Villanovans from them, if only because the Villanovans of the southern Etrurian coast seem older than those of northern and inland Etruria, while across the Apennines and within reach of the Adriatic is another Villanovan area whose metropolis, Bologna, seems at least as old as anything in southern Etruria. It might be that the Previllanovans of southern Etruria were related forerunners of the Villanovans who arrived by sea, while the real Villanovans there and beyond the Apennines represent settlements of closely related peoples who also came by sea respectively to the west and east costs of the peninsula. The recently discovered Villanovans of southern Campania would represent an additional settlement from the sea on the west coast of Italy.

I have not attempted to work out continental analogies for all the different kinds of Previllanovan urnfields, some of which contained central European features; but it seems to me that true Villanovan contains some rather fundamental elements traceable to the central Balkans. Yet the evidence is against central Balkan urnfield people moving overland to Italy around the head of the Adriatic.

The question then arises as to how all these urnfield people from the Danube Valley reached Italy. Some Previllanovan ones in northern Italy may well have crossed the Alps, but others from near the shores of central and southern Italy could conceivably be related to urnfield elements in the contemporary turmoil in the Aegean and eastern Mediterranean. Next, one must recall that the Italian coasts, especially in southern and to some extent in central Italy, had from the Neolithic been subject to sea-borne contacts from the east, and during the Apennine Bronze Age these contacts were represented by Mycenaean trade. Seamen in Aegean ports must always have known Italian waters and harbours, and may have been glad to serve those interested in going there. Also when folk with urnfield connections appear in the Lipari Islands and northern Sicily, we can be sure that they arrived in ships, though in these two cases their immediate point of departure was southern Italy. Moreover the unidentified enemies, who caused the inhabitants of the prosperous settlements on the eastern coast of Sicily to take refuge in the mountains, certainly came from the sea. So when the earliest Previllanovan urnfields with a few objects with Aegean parallels appear along the Italian shores, it raises the question of some connection with the contemporary unrest in the Aegean and eastern Mediterranean.

As for the Previllanovan urnfields of Latium, they include numerous Apennine Bronze Age elements but more Aegean parallels than the older Italian urnfields. They suggest non-Hellenic settlers from the Aegean in the dark post-Mycenaean Age, who may have originally come from Europe. Was it these people who appear much later in classical disguise in the pages of Livy and Virgil as Aeneas and his followers fleeing from fallen Troy? In any case these newcomers mixed with the previous inhabitants and settled in the neighborhood of the Alban Hills and Rome just as the Trojans and their descendants did in Roman tradition. With these Latian urnfielders the Previllanovan ones of southern Etruria were closely connected.

The next step is the settlement of the Villanovans themselves in Etruria, which is to be compared with the famous account of Herodotus about the settlement of the Tyrsenians who sailed from Smyrna and who founded cities where they were still living in Herodotus' own day. Since the Villanovan cemeteries are the oldest remains associated with the principal Etruscan cities of the coast, it would seem possible that it was the Villanovans to which Herodotus referred. Also the early Villanovans of Etruria had a limited number of Aegean and eastern Mediterranean elements in their culture including their way of fighting. But the chronology of Herodotus and the Villanovans does not really fit, because Herodotus evidently thought that they left the Aegean soon after the Trojan War, that is not long after about 1250 BC, whereas it does not seem to me that they reached Tarquinia until the tenth century. Can the intervening time have been taken up by Herodotus' statement that they passed by many nations in turn? Possibly the related Previllanovan urnfielders in Etruria were also embodied in Herodotus' story of the Tyrsenians. But in any case the coming of the Previllanovan and especially of the Villanovan urnfielders to Etruria represents the sharpest cultural break between the Apennine Bronze Age and the time when Herodotus wrote.

As for the northern Villanovans centred on Bologna, there is the story of Hellanicus who said that the Pelasgians left their ships on the Spinetic Po quite near this area, and indeed Thucydides knew of Pelasgians in the Aegean in the days after the Trojan War who were a branch of the Tyrsenians. It would be going beyond the evidence to put forward any firm conclusion that the Tyrsenians and Pelasgians actually were the Villanovans of Etruria and Bologna, if only because there is no real archaeological evidence of them in the Aegean and eastern Mediterranean, though there are some indications of urnfielders among the invaders there. We would have to suppose that unlike the Philistines, who settled in Palestine, and who may have been a branch of the Pelasgians, they did not stay long enough among peoples of advanced civilization to acquire more than a smattering of eastern elements, but moved on to Italy, where they settled among the local population whose culture was more lowly than their own. The lack of parallels to Villanovan or other Italian urnfield pottery in the Aegean might be accounted for by their purely hypothetical failure to settle anywhere for long until they reached Italy. But since the evidence is against the Villanovans having come overland, the Aegean route may be considered as a possibility especially in view of the legends, but it cannot be more than a guess in default of definite archaeological evidence.

If this should be the explanation of some coastal urnfielders in Italy including the Villanovans, they would fit the prehistoric pattern of settlement in the Mediterranean beginning in the Neolithic and continuing through the Bronze Age. In all these settlements whether in Malta, Sardinia, Spain or elsewhere, one has a sense of cultural currents coming from the east. But the cultures do not repeat the eastern Mediterranean with any exactness, and their homelands remain correspondingly hard to define with complete precision. Perhaps, like Herodotus' Tyrsenians, they had passed by many nations in turn but never stayed anywhere long enough to leave obvious traces. Perhaps also their material culture altered the further they went from home and the more they made new contacts along the way. Such may have been the progress of the ancient sea peoples of the Mediterranean from the Neolithic onward. All this is a great contrast to colonization by the more advanced peoples, the Phoenicians, the Greeks, and above all the Romans, who brought to their new homes the complete civilizations and languages of the old so that there is no doubt about who they were or whence they came. Also Apennine Bronze Age elements in Villanovan pottery indicate that, unlike most Greek and Phoenician settlers, they mixed to some extent with the people among whom they settled.

When we come to Villanovan II in the eighth century at Tarquinia, marked changes begin to be felt. Increased contacts with the Greek world and the Near East make this brief period a mere transition to the orientalizing Period III, and probably increasing trade in Etrurian metals lies behind the change. In Villanovan I some of the bronzes appear to be the work of immigrant craftsmen from central Europe or their local apprentices, but in Villanovan II this element increased markedly, and rising prosperity in Etruria as well as the attacks of nomads in the eastern Danube Valley may have driven the eastern Danubian craftsmen further west. Similarly, vases in the Greek Geometric manner suggests that Etruria also had an attraction for Greek potters, and oriental elements perhaps point to mounting Greek and Phoenician trade. At the same time inhumation began to increase at the expense of cremation; but this does not necessarily mean new settlers from abroad, for inhumation was deeply rooted in southern Italy, and at the great Etruscan city of Caere south of Tarquinia it had been practised along with cremation from the inception of Villanovan.

As for Period III, there were marked changes in burial rite consisting of the use of chamber tombs, some of which were under tumuli. While some chamber tombs may be enlargements of the trench graves for inhumations in Villanovan II, one may look in the main to western Asia for the source of these changes and especially to Asia Minor. It seems to me that such radical departures, especially when accompanied by other oriental elements, are more easily attributed to new and powerful settlers than to mere influences or contacts, and may well be the result of peoples escaping from the violence and disorder at this time in the Near East. As for Etruscan divination by examining the livers of sacrificial animals, this is clearly oriental, but it is not attested until much later, and consequently it is not clear at what period it came into use.

Vases of Greek inspiration became far commoner in Period III, and with them may be considered the tradition of the displaced Greek nobleman Demaratus, though this is no more than a sign of the times. But if the son of Demaratus could establish the Tarquin dynasty at Rome, may not the greatest

Etruscan tombs at Vetulonia, Caere and Praeneste be those of Near Eastern families who seized power in their respective cities and became just as Etruscan as the Tarquins? And yet we detect a fundamental continuity at Tarquinia from Villanovan times to Orientalizing, and in its chief necropolis, Monterozzi, foreign elements are often combined in a Villanovan matrix.

Next, there arises the thorny question of the language of the Etruscans, so different from that of their Italic neighbours. As its first inscriptions date only from Period III, it is tempting to think that it came then, but actually it was only at this time that the Etruscans learned the alphabet from the Greeks. Hence we have no way of knowing whether or how long before that it had been spoken in Italy. The classicists sometimes speak of it as a sign of Etruscan nationality, and indeed it was such a sign to the Romans, but here I am not dealing with the fully formed Etruscan nation known to Roman historians but with Etruscan beginnings. Also people change their language more readily than one might suppose. The Germanic Franks adopted a local form of Latin in Gaul; the Norse settlers in Normandy adopted French, while as Normans in England they later used English mixed with French elements. Hence in the formative period of a nation, language need not be identified with nationality.

The classicists also speak of the Etruscan language as an indication that the Etruscans came to Italy from somewhere else. In this regard they are thinking only of the Etruscans of history, while I am prepared to include their possible prehistoric forebears in Italy. Certainly some people at some time brought the Etruscan language to Italy, but if one considers the Etruscans as the sum of all the prehistoric inhabitants of Etruria, the possible horizons for the introduction of the language are many and extend far back in time.

Various views about the Etruscan language have been expressed, but there is a common element in some recent claims that it has resemblances to ancient languages of the Aegean and western Asia Minor. In this area there were two chief linguistic strata, the very ancient pre-Indo-European languages and the later Indo-European ones – Greek in Greece and in Asia Minor Cuneiform Hittite, Hieroglyphic Hittite, Lydian, Luvian, Lycian and several others. Of these Greek does not enter the picture, but attention is focused on the Indo-European tongues of Asia Minor, some of which were being written from the early second millennium BC.

First let us consider the view that Etruscan is related to the non-Indo-European group. Southern and central Italy received influences and probably settlers from the direction of the Aegean and Asia Minor in the Neolithic and Eneolithic, and the Villanovans themselves had Aegean-Near Eastern elements in their culture. One might even include the Near Eastern settlers of Period III, for one cannot rule out the possibility that they came from a surviving linguistic pocket of the old speech. There is also the puzzle of the Lemnos stele in a language like Etruscan. This Aegean island was in historical times inhabited by Pelasgians who were said to be a branch of the legendary Tyrsenians of the Aegean. Does the language of the stele substantiate the legend, or was Lemnos merely another surviving linguistic pocket like Etruria itself? Also if such linguistic elements could have come once, why should they not have been brought at different times by various peoples? Indeed some Italian scholars believe that such a language was once much more widely spoken in Italy but was pushed westward into Etruria by the advance of Indo-European speech from across the Adriatic, and this is held to account for the Indo-European elements deeply imbedded in it.

Another view is that Etruscan is related to the Indo-European languages of Asia Minor. If so, how did it get to Italy? Did the settlers of Period III bring it around 700 BC? Or did the Villanovans bring it? If the Villanovans brought it, was it because both they and the Indo-European speakers of Asia Minor all had roots in eastern Europe?

The impossibility of answering these questions at the present time means that no matter how much the language served to identify the Etruscans as a nation to their Roman neighbours, it does little to explain who the Etruscans were originally or how they acquired their language. The most that can be extracted from all this with regard to Etruscan origins is that the language has connections of some kind with the general area of the Aegean and Asia Minor and so do some of the cultures of early Italy; greater precision is as yet out of reach.

Finally it seems to me that in thinking about Etruscan origins we are on sounder ground if we put aside the theory of a migration that brought the historical Etruscans complete with language and culture from somewhere else, for present evidence is against it. Rather, we should look for the origins of the different elements that went into the making of the historical Etruscan nation. One might compare the situation to modern peoples like the British, the French or the Americans. No one would suggest that they came from somewhere else complete with their present languages and civilizations, for everyone knows that they are all composites formed of various elements with different languages. One need only recall that the British combine prehistoric peoples, Celts, Romans, Anglo-Saxons, Danes and Normans, while the French are made up of prehistoric peoples, Celts, Romans, Franks, Burgundians and others. The Americans combine British, Dutch, French, Spanish, Germans, Irish, Italians, and many more. In the case of the British, French and Americans there are historical reasons why one language became dominant. So it may well have been with the Etruscans, though with them we cannot identify the languages spoken by the different elements or discover the reason why one of them prevailed over the others.

Select Bibliography

Abbreviations

Ann. Inst.	*Annali dell'Instituto di corrispondenze archeologica*
BonnJbb	*Bonner Jahrbücher*
BRGKomm	*Berichte der Römisch-Germanischen Kommission*
BPI	*Bullettino di Paletnologia Italiana*
BSA	*Annual of the British School at Athens*
CVA	*Corpus Vasorum Antiquorum*
JHS	*Journal of Hellenic Studies*
JNES	*Journal of Near Eastern Studies*
JRS	*Journal of Roman Studies*
Mon. Ant.	*Monumenti Antichi*
NSc	*Notizie degli Scavi*
ProcPS	*Proceedings of the Prehistoric Society*
StEtr	*Studie Etruschi*

Tarquinia

AVVOLTA, C. Le Tombe di Tarquinia. *Ann. Inst.*, 1829, pp. 91–101.

BRADFORD, J. *Ancient Landscapes*. London, 1957. Chapter on Tarquinia.

HENCKEN, H. Tarquinia, Villanovans and Etruscans. *Bulletin of the American School of Prehistoric Research*, Vol. 23, 1968. This monograph contains many references to older publications.

MARCHESE, L. Tarquinia. *NSc*, 1944–45, pp. 7–22.

MORETTI, M. Tarquinia – La necropoli villanoviana 'alle Rose'. *NSc*, 1959, pp. 112–139.

PALLOTTINO, M. Tarquinia. *Mon. Ant.*, Vol. 36, part I, 1937. This monograph contains a large number of references to older publications.

PERNIER, L. Corneto-Tarquinia, I-IV. *NSc*, 1907, pp. 45–82, 227–261, 321–347.

Romanelli, P. Tarquinia-Saggi di scavo nell'area dell'antica città. *NSc*, 1934, pp. 438–443.
— Tarquinia-Scavi nella città. *StEtr*, Vol. 12, 1938, pp. 331–334.
— Tarquinia-Rinvenimenti fortuiti nella Necropoli e nel Territorio (1930–1938). *NSc*, 1943, pp. 213–261.
— Tarquinia-Scavi e ricerche nell'area della città. *NSc*, 1948, pp. 193–270.
— Scavi e ricerche nella città di Tarquinia. *Bollettino d'Arte*, Vol, 33, 1948, p. 54.
— *Tarquinia: la necropoli e il museo*. Rome 1954.

Italy

Åkerström, Å. *Der geometrische Stil in Italien*. Uppsala, 1943.
Alciati, G., Amorelli Falconi, M., Close-Brooks, J., De Agostino, A., Moretti, M., Passarello, P., Ridgway, D., Staccioli, R., Vianello, A., Ward Perkins, J. B. Veio. *NSc*, 1963, pp. 77–279.
Banti, L. *Il mondo degli Etruschi*. Rome, 1960.
Bérard, J. La question des origines étrusques. *Revue des études anciennes*, Vol. 51, 1949, pp. 201–245.
— *La colonisation grecque de l'Italie méridionale et de la Sicile dans l'Antiquité.* Second Ed., Paris, 1957.
Bernabò Brea, L. *Sicily before the Greeks*. London, 1957.
Bernabò Brea, L. and Cavalier, M. Civiltà preistoriche delle isole eolie e del territorio di Milazzo. *BPI*, Vol, 65, 1956, pp. 7–99.
— *Mylai. Società di Storia Patria per la Sicilia orientale*. Catania, 1959.
— *Meligunìs-Lipari I: La stazione preistorica della contrada Diana e la necropoli protostorica di Lipari.* Palermo, 1960.
Bianchi Bandinelli, R. Clusium. *Mon.Ant.*, Vol. 30, 1925, cols. 209–552.
Bloch, R. *The Etruscans*. London and New York, 1958.
— *The Origins of Rome*. London and New York, 1960.
Böethius, A., et al. *Etruscan Culture, Land and People*. Malmö, 1962; New York, 1963.
Buchner, G. Scavi nella necropoli di Pithecusa. *Atti e Memorie della Società 'Magna Grecia,'* 1954, pp. 1–11.

CAVALOTTI BATCHVORAVA, A., CLOSE-BROOKS, J., PASSARELLO, P., STACCIOLI, R., WARD PERKINS, J.B. Veio. *NSc*, 1965, pp. 49–236.

CIVILTÀ DEL FERRO *Documenti e Studi* (Deputazione di Storia Patria per le Provincie di Romagna), Vol. 6, 1960.

CLOSE-BROOKS, J. Considerazioni sulla cronologia della facies arcaiche dell'Etruria. *Studi Etruschi*, Vol. 35, p 323, 1968.

COLINI, G.A. Tolfa e Allumieri. *BPI*, Vol. 35, 1910, pp. 104–149, 177–204, and Vol. 36, 1911, p. 125.

DENNIS, G. *Cities and Cemeteries of Etruria*. London, 1878.

DUCATI, P. *Storia di Bologna*. Bologna, 1928.

DUNBABIN, I.T. *The Western Greeks*. Oxford, 1948.

EVANS, J.D. *Malta*, London, 1959.

FÒTI, G. The Principal Cities of Southern Etruria and Their Special Characteristics. In G. E. W. Wolstenholme and C. M. O'Connor, (eds), *CIBA Symposium on Medical Biology and Etruscan Origins*. London, 1959.

GÀBRICI, E. Cuma. *Mon.Ant.*, Vol. 22, 1913.

GIEROW, P.G. The Iron Age Cultures of Latium, Vol. 2, part 1. *Skrifter utgivna av Svenska Institutet i Rom*, Vol. 24, pt. 2, 1964.

GJERSTAD, E. Early Rome, II. The Tombs. *Skrifter utgivna av Svenska Institutet i Rom*, Vol. 17, pt. 2, 1956.

KASCHNITZ-WEINBERG, G. Italien, mit Sardinien, Sizilien und Malta. *Handbuch der Archäeologie*, Vol. 2. Munich, 1950, pp. 311–400.

KLITSCHE DE LA GRANCE, A. Allumiere, Tombe antichissime scoperte in contrada della Pozza. *NSc*, 1884, pp. 101–106.

MANSUELLI, G. and SCARANI, R. *L'Emilia prima dei Romani*, Milan, 1961.

MAXWELL-HYSLOP, K.R. Urartian Bronzes in Etruscan Tombs. *Iraq*, Vol. 18, pp. 150–67.

— Notes on Some Distrinctive Types of Bronzes from Populonia. *ProcPS*, Vol. 22, 1956, pp. 126–42.

MINTO, A. *Populonia*. Florence, 1922.

MONTELIUS, O. *La civilisation primitive en Italie*. Parts I, II, Plates. Stockholm, 1895–1910.

— *Die vorklassische Chronologie Italiens*. Stockholm, 1912.

MÜLLER-KARPE, H. Beiträge zur Chronologie der Urnenfelderzeit nördlich und südlich der Alpen. *Römisch-Germanische Forschungen*, Vol. 22, 1959.

— *Vom Anfang Roms*. Heidelberg, 1959.

— *Zur Stadtwerdung Roms*. Heidelberg, 1962.

MURRAY THREIPLAND, L. Excavations beside the North-West Gate of Veii, 1957–1958. Part II: The Pottery. *Papers of the British School at Rome*, Vol. 31, 1963, pp. 33–73.

PALLOTTINO, M. Sulle facies culturali arcaiche dell'Etruria. *StEtr*, Vol. 13, 1939, pp. 85–128.

— *L'origine degli Etruschi*, Rome, 1947.

— *The Etruscans*. Harmondsworth, 1955.

— *Etruscologia*. 4th ed. Milan, 1957.

— Nuovi studi sul problema delle origini etrusche. *StEtr*, 1961, Vol. 29, pp. 3–30.

PERONI, R. Per una nuova cronologia del sepolcreto arcaico del foro *Civiltà del ferro. Documenti e Studi*, Vol. 6, 1960, pp. 463–499.

— Allumiere-Scavo di tombe in località 'La Pozza.' *NSc*, 1960, pp. 341–362.

— L'età del bronzo medio e recente tra l'Adige e il Mincio. *Memorie del Museo Civico di Storia Naturale*, Verona, Vol. 11, 1963, pp. 49–104.

PIAGANIOL, A. Les étrusques peuple d'orient. *Cahiers d'histoire mondiale*, Vol. 1, no. 2, 1953, pp. 328–352.

RADMILLI, A. (ed.) *Piccola guida della preistoria italiana*. Florence, 1962.

RANDALL-MACIVER, D. *The Villanovans and Early Etruscans*. Oxford, 1924.

— *The Iron Age in Italy*. Oxford, 1927.

RICHARDSON, E.H. *The Etruscans: Their Art and Civilization*. Chicago, 1964.

RIDGWAY, D. 'Coppe cicladiche' da Veio. *Studi Etruschi*, Vol. 35, pp. 311–21, 1968.

RITTATORE, F. La necropoli di Canegrate. *Sibrium*, Vol. 1, 1953–54, pp. 7–43.

— Sulla cronologia della cultura di Canegrate. *Rivista di Scienze Preistoriche*, Vol. 12, 1957, pp. 99–103.

SÄFLUND, G. Bemerkungen zur Vorgeschichte Etruriens. *StEtr*, Vol. 12, 1938, pp. 17–55.

— *Le terremare*. Lund, 1939.

— Über den Ursprung der Etrusker. *Historia*, Vol. 6, 1957, pp. 10–22.

SCHACHERMEYR, F. *Etruskische Frühgeschichte*. Berlin, 1929.

SUNDWALL, J. *Die älteren italischen Fibeln*. Berlin, 1943.

SZILÁGYI, J. Zur Frage der früheisenzeitichen Beziehungen zwischen Italien und dem vorderen Orient. *Acta Antiqua Academiae Scientiarum Hungaricae*, Vol. 7, 1959, pp. 69–83.

TAYLOUR, LORD WILLIAM *Mycenaean Pottery in Italy*. Cambridge and New York, 1958.

TRUMP, D.H. The Apennine Culture of Italy. *ProcPS*, Vol. 24, 1958, pp. 165–200.

— *Central and Southern Italy before Rome*. London, 1966.

VACANO, O.W. VON *The Etruscans in the Ancient World*. London, 1960; Indiana, 1965.

VIGHI, R. Caere II:Il Sepulcreto arcaico del Sorbo. *Mon.Ant.*, Vol. 42, 1953, pp. 260–200.

WARD PERKINS, J. B. Etruscan and Roman Roads in Southern Etruria. *JRS*, Vol. 47, 1957, pp, 139–143.

— Excavations beside the Northwest Gate at Veii, 1957–58. *Papers of the British School at Rome*, Vol. 27, 1959, pp. 38–79.

— The Problem of Etruscan Origins. *Harvard Studies in Classical Philology*, Vol. 64, 1959, pp. 1–26.

— Veii: the Historical Topography of an Ancient City. *Papers of the British School at Rome*, Vol. 39, 1961, pp. 1–123.

Central and Eastern Europe

BERCIU, D. *Arheologia preistorică a Olteniei*. Craiova, 1939.

— Neue Forschungsergebnisse zur Vorgeschichte Rumäniens. *Antiquitas*, Reihe 2, vol. 4, 1966.

BERCIU, D. AND COMŞA, E. Săpăturile Arheologice de la Balta Verde şi Gogusu. *Materiale şi Cercetări Arheologice*, Vol. 2, 1956, pp. 251–489.

DUMITRESCU, V. Quelques observations au sujet des civilisations danubiennes des champs d'urnes de l'âge du bronze. *Nouvelles études d'Histoire publiées à l'occasion du XIe Congrès des Sciences Historiques*, Stockholm, 1960, pp. 19–30.

— Necropola de incinerație din epoca bronzului de la Cîrna. *Biblioteca de Arheologie*, Vol. 4, 1961.

KOSSACK, G. Studien zum Symbolgut der Urnenfelder- und Hallstatt-zeit Mitteleuropas. *Römisch-Germanische Forschungen*, Vol. 20, 1954.

MERHART, G. VON Zu den ersten Metallhelmen Europas. 30. *BRG Komm*, 1941.

— Donauländische Beziehungen der früheisenzeitlichen Kulturen Mittelitaliens. *BonnJbb*, no. 147, 1942, pp. 1–90.

— Studien über einige Gattungen von Bronzegefässen. *Festschrift des Römisch-Germanischen Zentralmuseums in Mainz*, Vol. 2, 1952, pp. 1–71.

THOMAS, H. Near Eastern, Mediterranean and European Chronology, *Studies in Mediterranean Archaeology*, vol. 17, 1967.

VULIĆ, N. AND GRBIĆ, M. *CVA*. Yougoslavie, fasc. 3. Belgrad. Undated.

ZAHARIA, E. Remarques sur le Hallstatt ancien de Transylvanie. Trouvailles de Mediaş. *Dacia* N. S., Vol. 9, 1965, pp. 83–104.

The Aegaean and the Eastern Mediterranean

ALBRIGHT, W.F. *Cambridge Ancient History*, revised edition, Vol. 2, Chapter 33, Syria, the Philistines and Phoenicia, Cambridge, 1966.

ÅLIN, P. Das ende der mykenischen Fundstätten auf dem griechischen Festland. *Studies in Mediterranean Archaeology*, Vol. 1, 1962.

BARNETT, R.D. *Cambridge Ancient History*, revised edition. Vol. 2, Chapter 30, Phrygia and the Peoples of Anatolia in the Iron Age, Cambridge, 1967.

BRONEER, O. The Cyclopean Wall on the Isthmus of Corinth. *Hesperia*, vol. 35, 1966, pp. 346–62.

DESBOROUGH, V.R.D'A. *The Last Mycenaeans and their Successors*. Oxford and New York, 1964.

DESBOROUGH, V.R.D'A. AND HAMMOND, N.G.L. *Cambridge Ancient History*, Vol. 2, Chapter 36. The End of Mycenaean Civilization and the Dark Age, 1962.

HARDEN, D.B. *The Phoenicians*. London and New York, 1962.

JEFFERY, L.H. *The Local Scripts of Archaic Greece*. Oxford and New York, 1961.

MYRES, Sir J.L. A History of the Pelasgian Theory. *JHS*, Vol. 27, part 2, 1907, pp. 170–225.
NELSON, H.H. The Naval Battle Pictured at Medinet Habu. *JNES*, Vol. 2, 1943, pp. 40–55.
POPHAM, M.R. AND SACKETT, L.H. Excavations in Euboea. *Illustrated London News*, June 5, 1965, p. 31.

Language

DE VOTO, G. *Gli antichi italici.* 2nd Edition, Florence, 1951.
GEORGIEV, V. La toponymie ancienne de la péninsule balkanique et la thèse méditerranéene. *Linguistique Balkanique*, Vol. 3, Fasc. 1, 1961.
— Hethitisch und Etruskisch. Die Hethitische Herkunft der Etruskischen Sprache. *Linguistique Balkanique*, Vol. 5, Fasc. 1, 1962.
KRETSCHMER, P. Die vorgriechische Sprache- und Volkschichten. *Glotta*, Vol. 28, 1940, p. 231; Vol, 30, 1943, p. 84.
PALLOTTINO, M. *The Etruscans.* Harmondsworth, 1955, part 3, The Problem of the Language.
— *Etruscologia.* Milan, 4th Ed., 1957. Parte III, Il problema della lingua.
PULGRAM, E. *The Tongues of Italy.* Cambridge, Mass., 1958.
STOLTENBERG, H.L. *Etruskische Gottnamen.* Leverkusen, 1957.
— *Etruskische Namen für Personen und Gruppen.* Leverkusen, 1958.
— *Etruskische Namen für Seinsformen und Sachen.* Leverkusen, 1959.
WHATMOUGH, J. *The Foundations of Roman Italy.* London, 1937.

Sources of Illustrations

Most of the illustrations in this book have already appeared in my monograph, Tarquinia Villanovans and Early Etruscans, *Bulletin* 23, *American School of Prehistoric Research*, a publication of the Peabody Museum of Harvard University, and are reproduced here by permission of the President and Fellows of Harvard College. I am also indebted to the University of Chicago (Copyright 1943) for Fig. 43, c (H. H. Nelson, *Journal of Near Eastern Studies*, vol. 2, Fig. 4.)

The following text figures are from the publications of the Deutsches Archäologisches Institut: Figs. 39, 42 and 43a.

The following text figures are from the publications of the Römisch-Germanisches Zentralmuseum, Mainz: 40, 41.

Plates 1, 2 and 47 are by the Soprintendenza alle Antichitá, Florence; 139–41 are after Å.Åkerström; 142, 145 after D.Berciu. Plate 144 is by Fotofast; 146 by Z. Vinsky. Plate 147 is by the British Museum and is published here by permission of the Trustees. Plate 157 is after M. Pallottino. Plate 156 is by the Staatliche Museen zu Berlin; 165 by the Soprintendenza alle Antichitá dell'Etruria Meridionale, Rome; 172 by Alinari.

All other photos were taken for the author by Johannes Felbermeyer, Rome.

The sources of text figures derived from the work of others are acknowledged in the captions.

THE PLATES

1
2

3
4
5

6
7

8
9
10
11
12

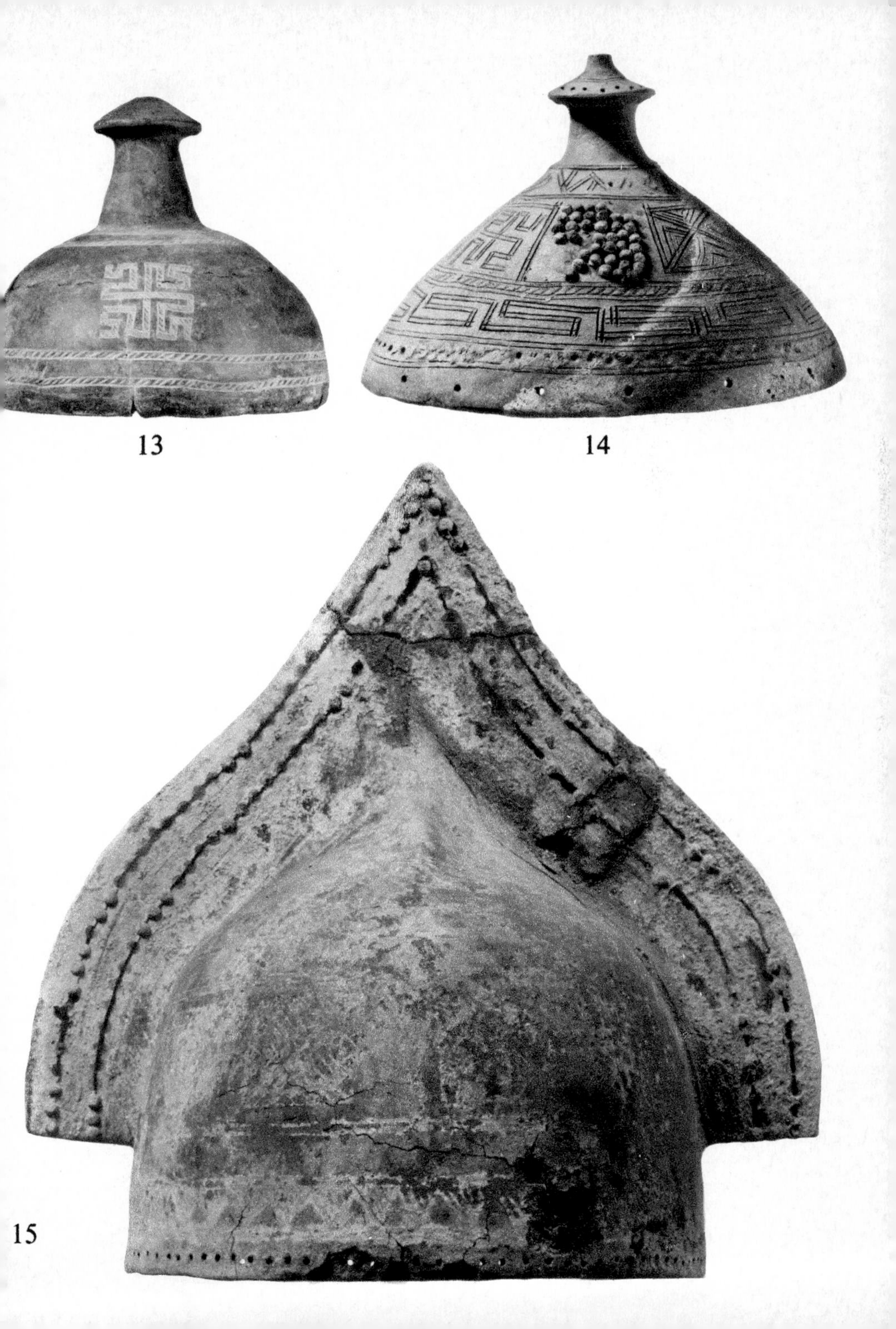

13

14

15

16

20

17

18

19

21
22
23
24
25
26

27
28
29

30
31
32
33
34

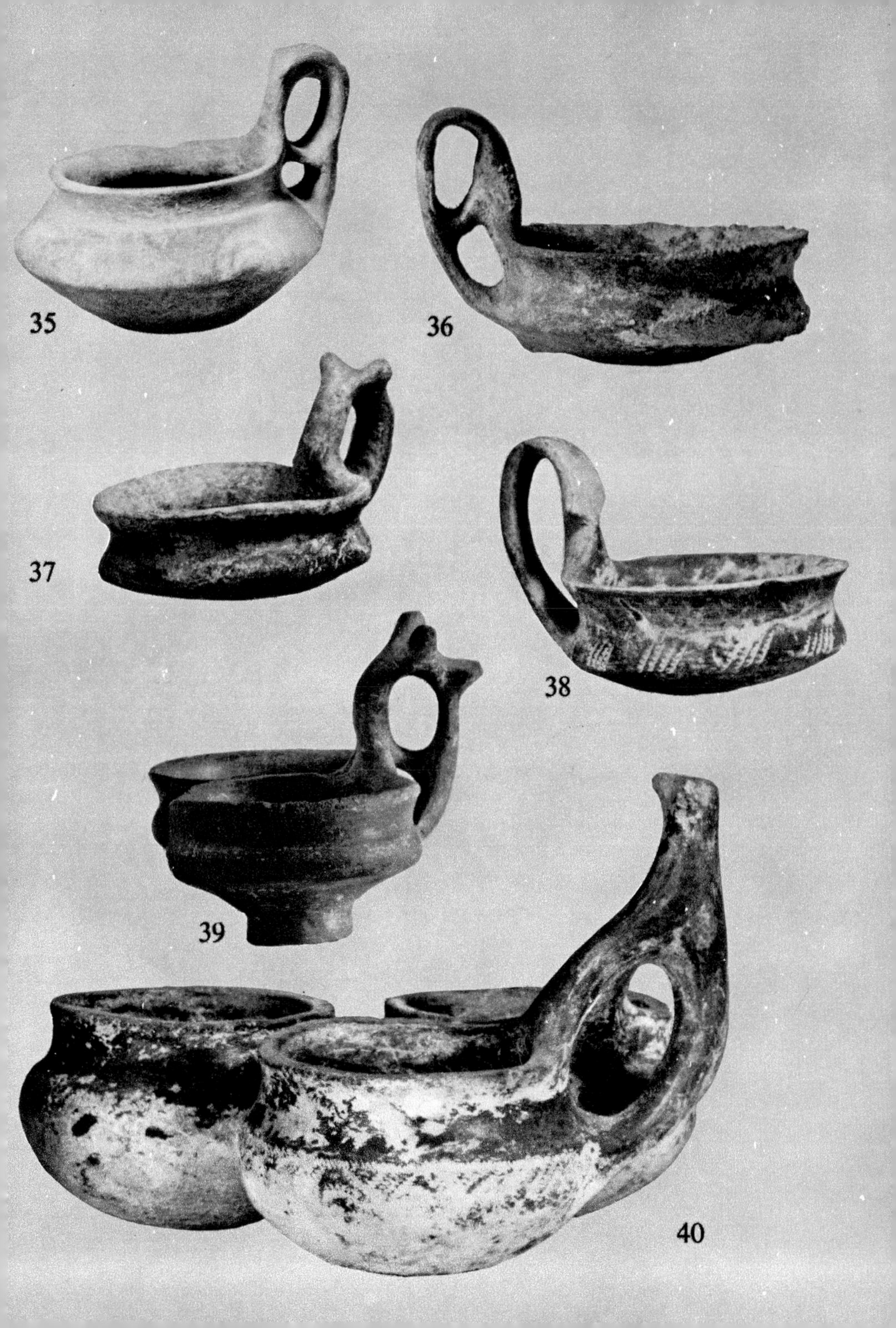
35
36
37
38
39
40

41
42
43
44
45
46

47
48
49

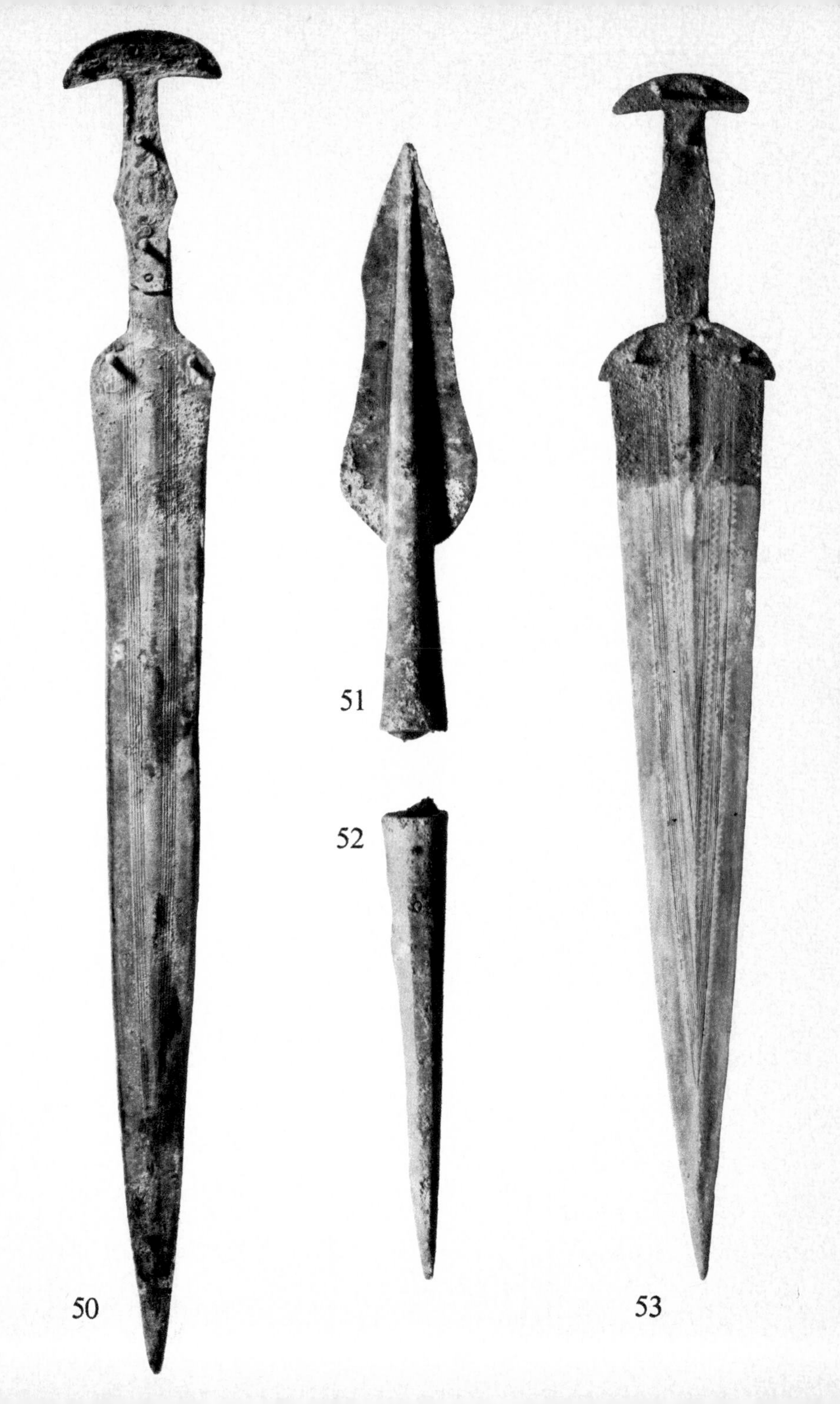
50
51
52
53

54
55
56
57
58

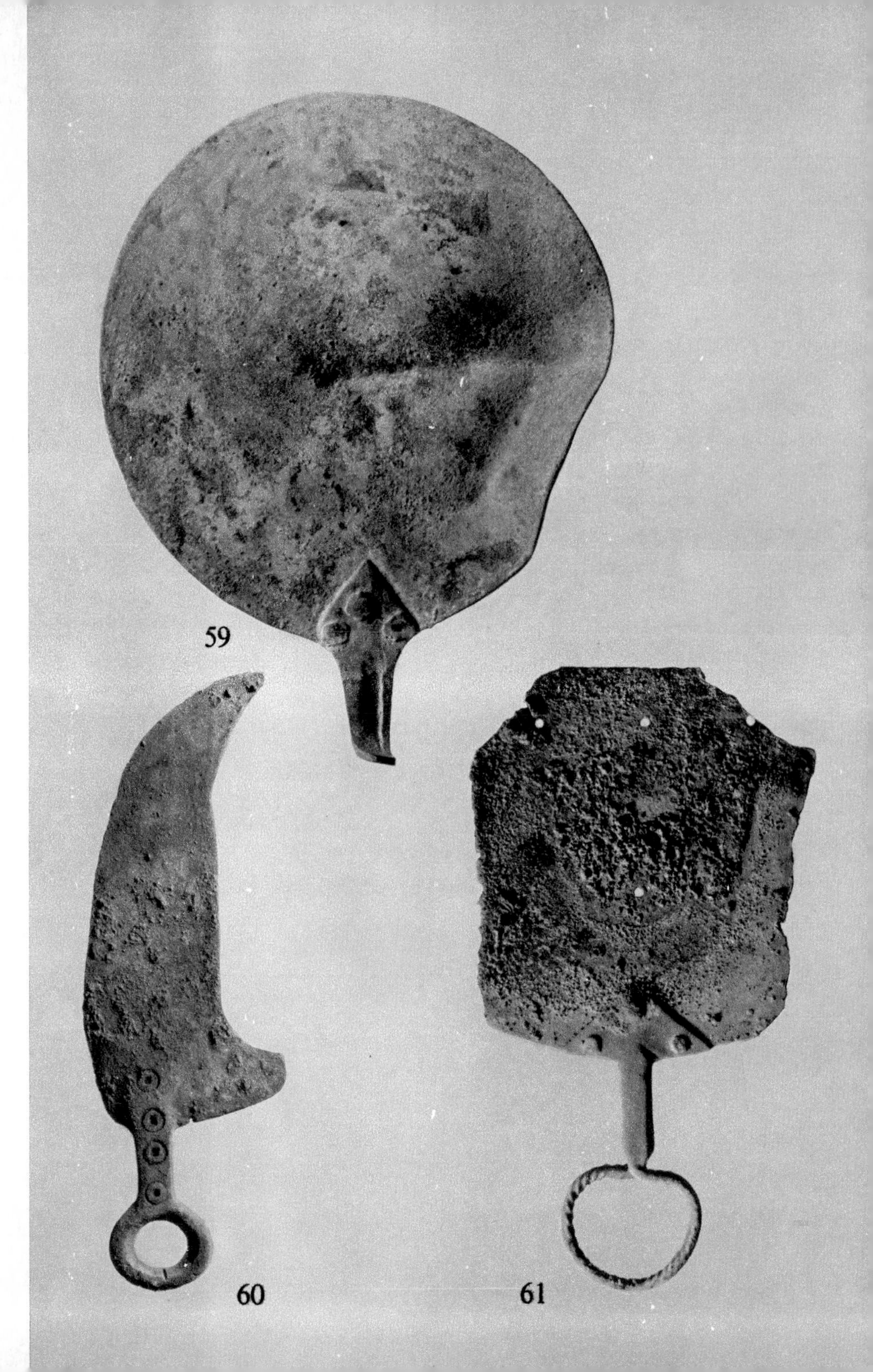
59
60
61

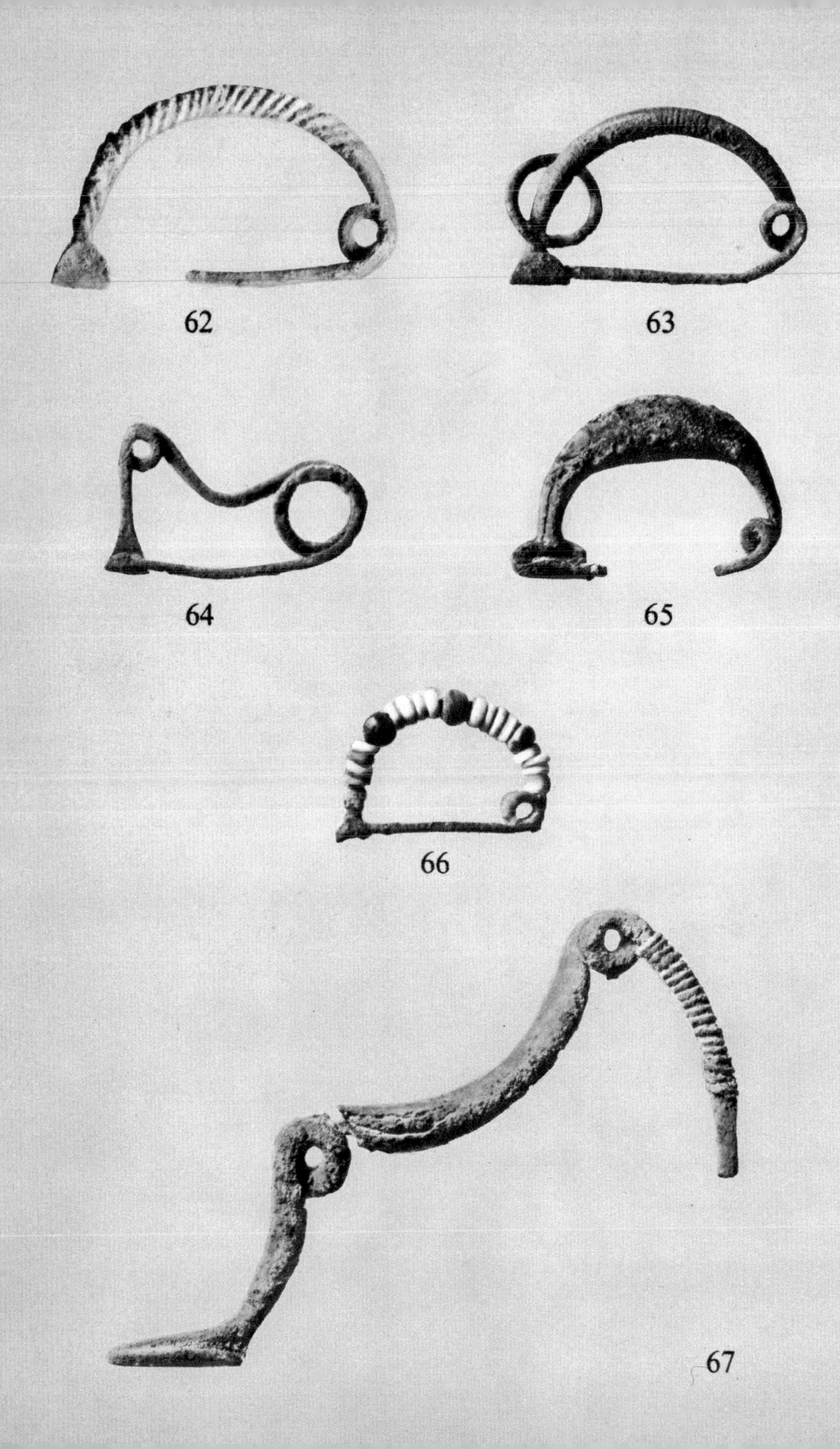
62
63
64
65
66
67

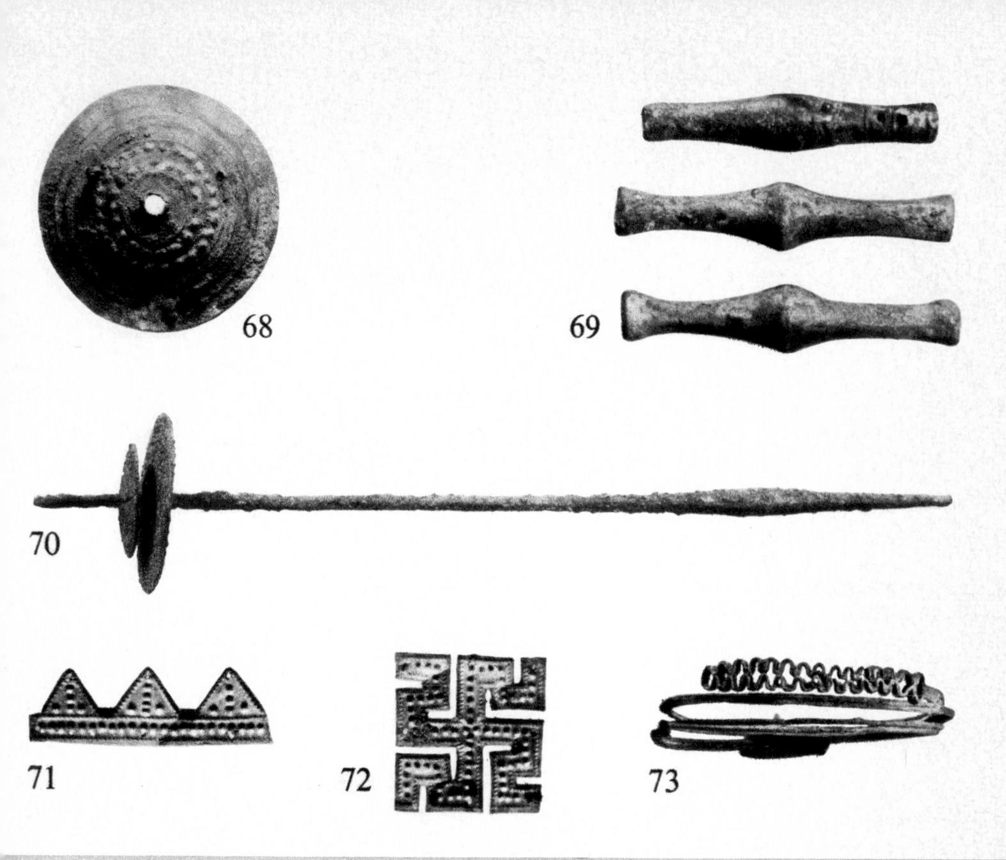
68
69
70
71
72
73

74

75

76
77
78

79

80 81

82

83

84

85

86

87

90

88 89

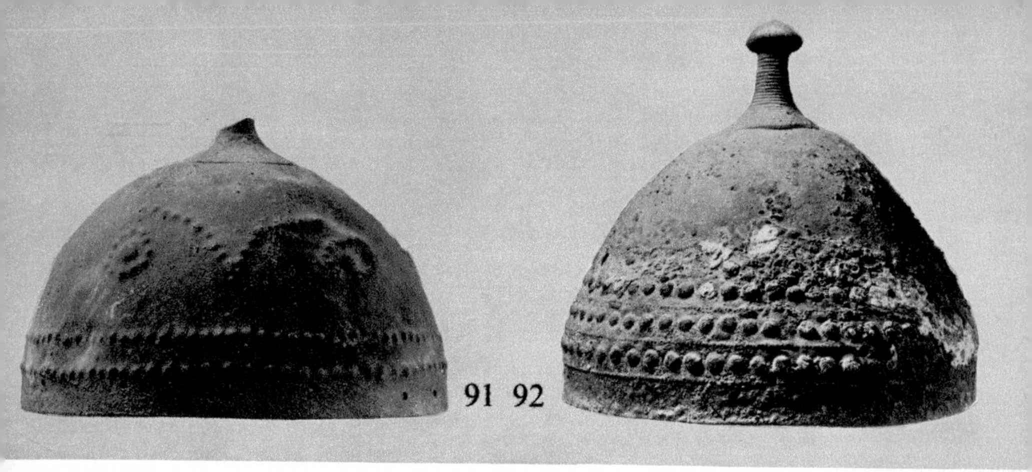

91 92

93

94

95

96
97
98

99
100

101

102
103

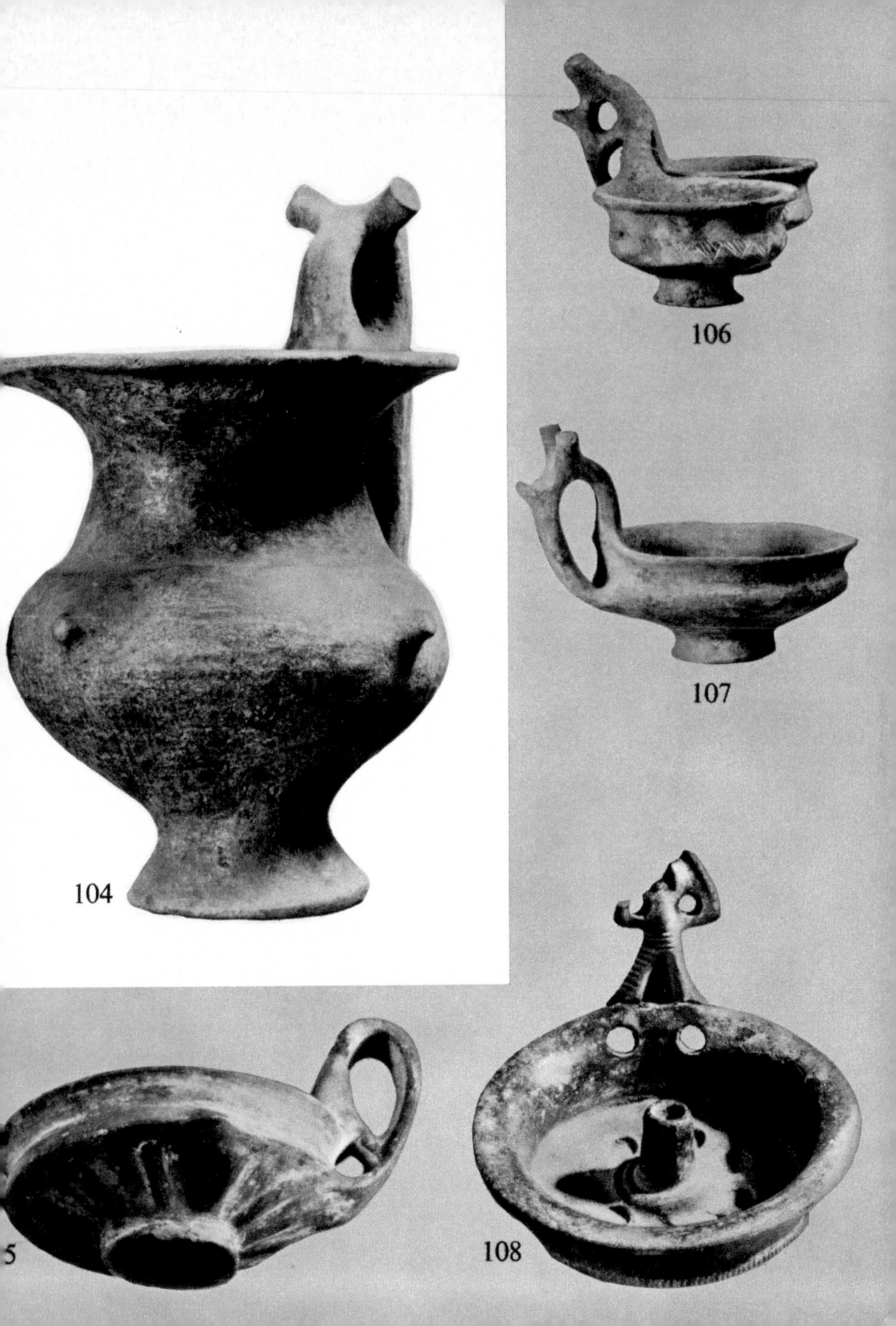

106

107

104

5

108

109

110

111
112
113
114
115

116

117

118

119

120

121

122

123

124

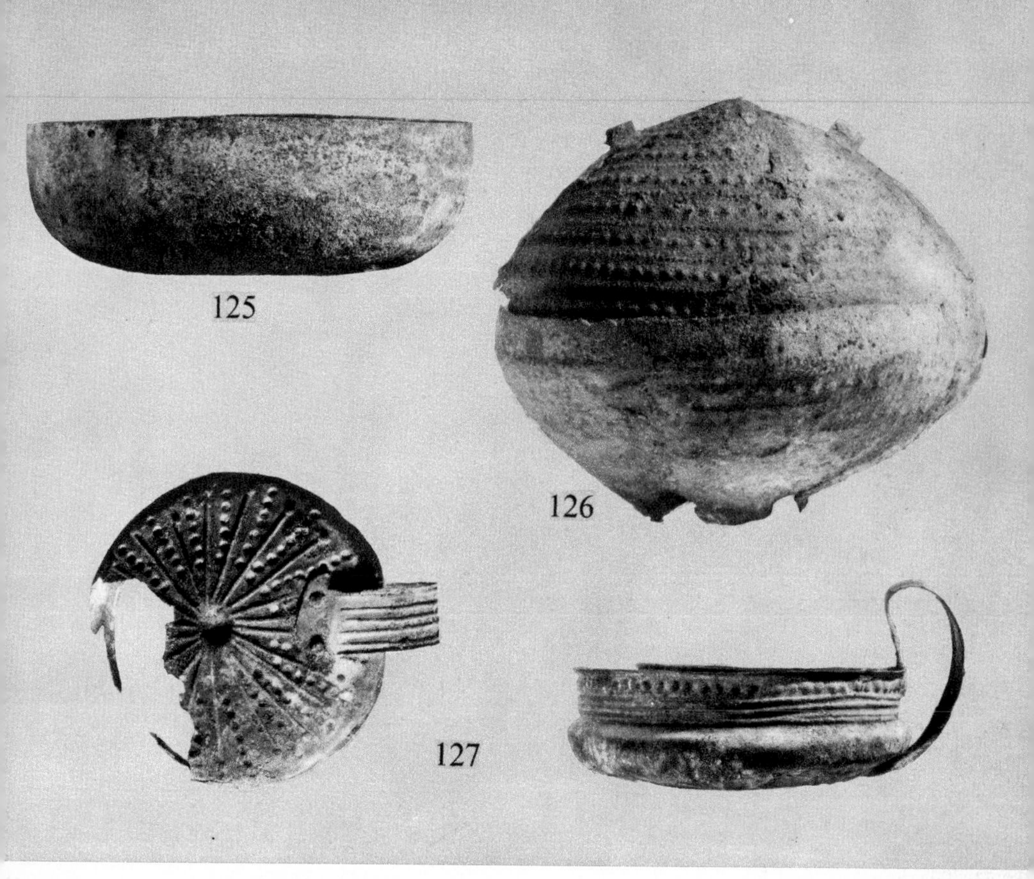
125
126
127

128

129

130

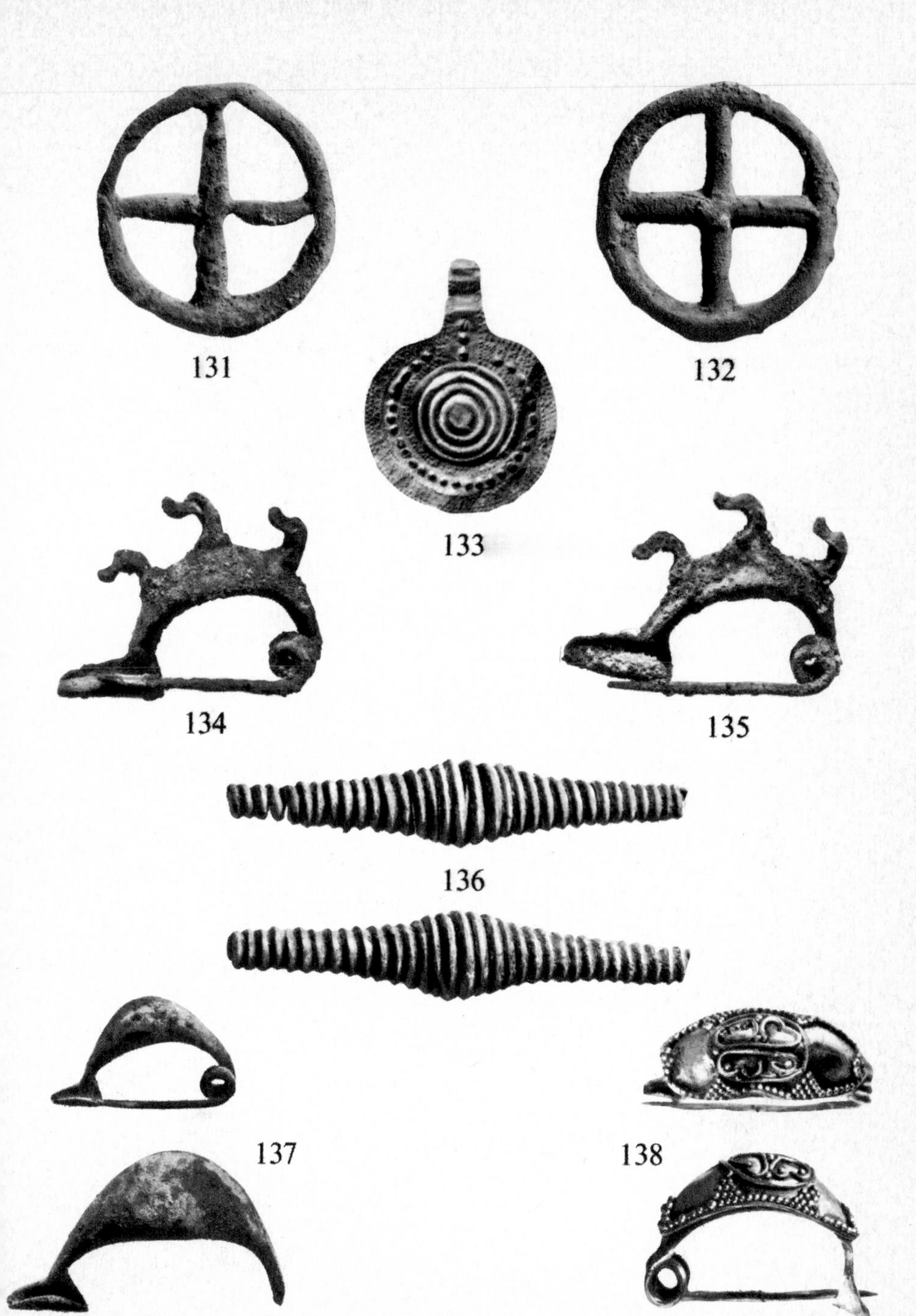
131
132
133
134
135
136
137
138

139

140

141

142

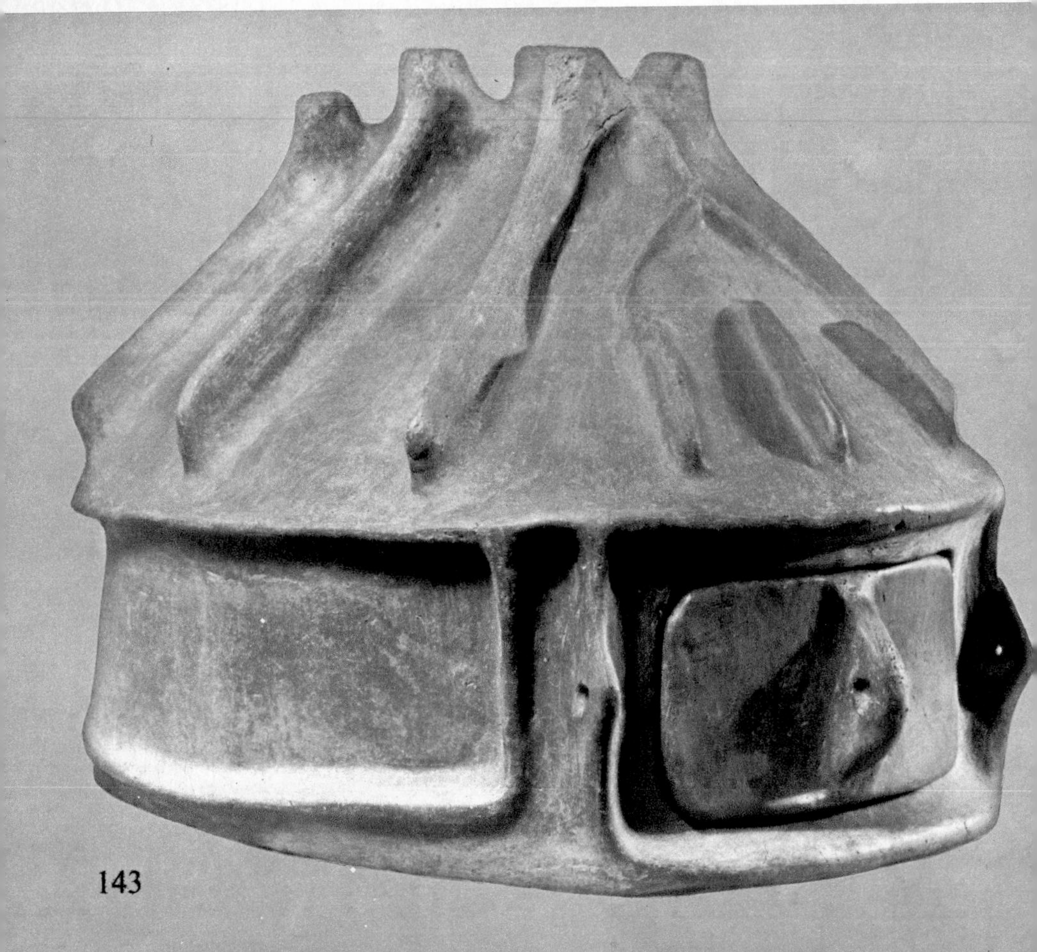

143

144

145

146

147

148

150

149

151
152
153

154

155

157

158

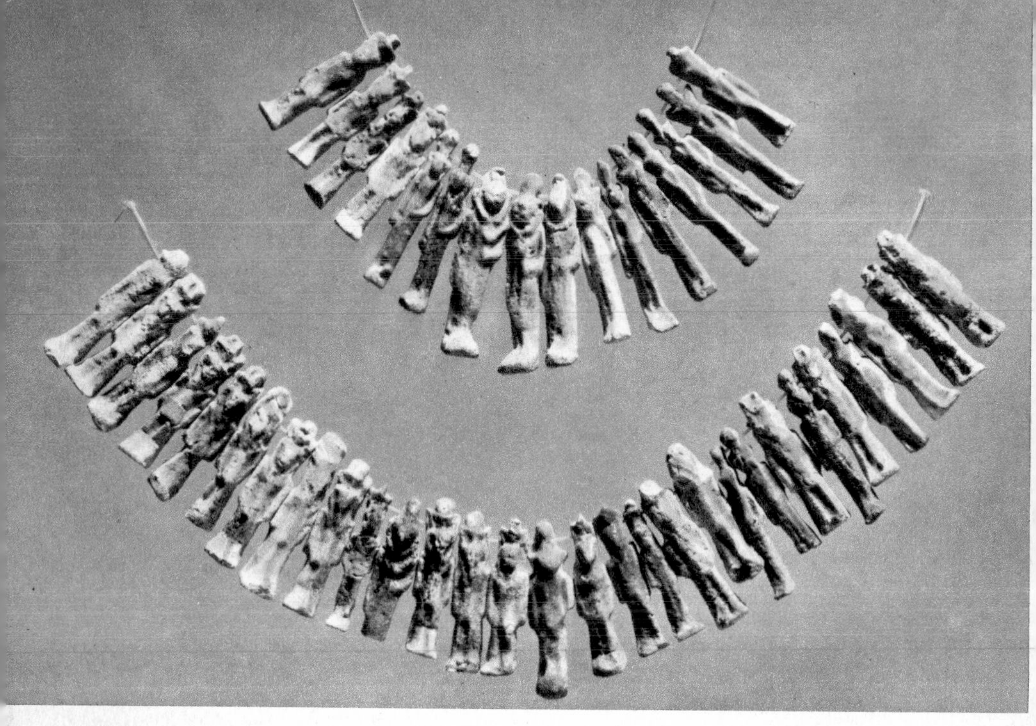

159

160

161 162

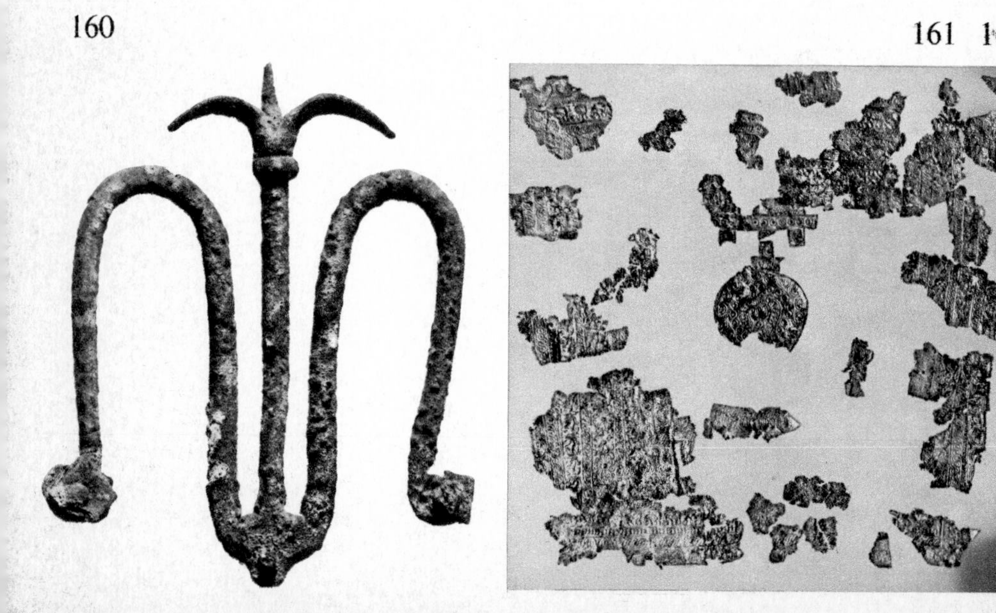

163

164

165

166

167

168

169

170

171
172
173

Notes on the Plates

1 Stone grave-marker shaped like the knob of a pottery bell helmet. No scale. Museo Archeologico, Florence.

2 Stone grave-marker shaped like the roof of a house-urn. No scale. Museo Archeologico, Florence.

3 Urn of Villanovan I, with two seated figures with upraised arms over the handle, a complex pattern of two seated figures on the body and a plain pattern of two seated figures at the base of the neck (see Fig. 6). 1:4. Museo Archeologico, Florence.

4 Urn of Villanovan I, with a large seated figure talking to a small one over the handle. At the base of the neck is a plain pattern of two seated figures and on the body a complex pattern of two seated figures (see Fig. 6). 1:4. Museo Archeologico, Florence.

5 Urn of Villanovan I, with two seated figures with outstretched arms over the handle and on the body a careless rendering of the complex pattern of two seated figures. 1:4. Museo Archeologico, Florence.

6 Villanovan urn with two seated figures with their hands on their knees over the handle. 1:4. Museo Archeologico, Florence.

7 Villanovan urn with two seated figures back to back over the handle. 1:4. Museo Archeologico, Florence.

8 House urn from Monterozzi of early Villanovan I, with double birds on the roof. 1:4. Museo di Villa Giulia, Rome.

9 Cover-bowl for an urn. Villanovan I. 1:4. Museo Archeologico, Florence.

10 Cover-bowl for an urn. Villanovan I. The horned handle is a survival from the Apennine Bronze Age. 1:4. Museo Archeologico, Florence.

11 Cover-bowl for an urn. Villanovan I. 1:4. Museo Archeologico, Florence.

12 Cover-bowl on a high foot. Villanovan I. 1:4. Museo Archeologico, Florence.

13 Pottery bell helmet placed in the grave as a substitute for a valuable bronze original. Villanovan I. 1:4. Museo Archeologico, Florence.

14 Pottery bell helmet decorated with bronze studs, of mid Villanovan I, placed in the grave as a substitute for a valuable bronze original. 1:4. Museo Archeologico, Florence.

15 Pottery crested helmet decorated on the crest with bronze studs, placed in the grave as a substitute for a valuable bronze original. Villanovan I. Ht: 32 cm. Museo Archeologico, Florence.

16 Jug with binocular handle. Early Villanovan I. Ht: 15 cm. Museo Archeologico, Florence.

17–20 Jars with wide bodies, flaring rims and narrow feet. Late Villanovan I. That in Plate 19 has four long horns rising from the shoulder. 1:4 Museo Archeologico, Florence.

21 Jug. Villanovan I. The angular pattern above the shoulder is a survival from the Apennine Bronze Age. Ht: 22 cm. Museo Archeologico, Florence.

22 Jug of Villanovan I, with false cord ornament. Ht: 14 cm. Museo Archeologico, Florence.

23–25 Spheroid jars. Late Villanovan I. Ht: 23, 16 cm. 24, 19 cm. 25, 15 cm. Museo Archeologico, Florence.

26 Spheroid jar on a foot. Late Villanovan I. Ht. 13 cm. Museo Archeologico, Florence.

27 Jug. Villanovan I. 1:2. Museo Archeologico, Florence.

28 Jug. Villanovan I. The ornament may have originally been made of little lead plates. 1:2. Museo Archeologico, Florence.

29 Jug in the shape of a Villanovan urn. Villanovan I. 1:2. Museo Archeologico, Florence.

30 Double Jug. Villanovan I. 1 : 3 Museo Archeologico, Florence.

31 Jug with a neck and one handle. Late Villanovan I. 1 : 3 Museo Archeologico, Florence.

32, 33 Bottle-shaped jugs with handles surmounted by heads of animals. Late Villanovan I. The head in Plate 32 is that of a ram, while that in Plate 33 is that of a horned animal with one horn broken off. Animal-headed handles are an inheritance from the Apennine Bronze Age. 1:3. Museo Archeologico, Florence.

34 Bottle-shaped jug of late Villanovan I, with false cord ornament and a broken handle. 1:3. Museo Archeologico, Florence.

35–38 Cups of Villanovan I, with angular profiles recalling forms of the Apennine Bronze Age. Plate 37 also has a pair of horns on the handle, another Apennine feature. Plates 35 and 36 have binocular handles in which the lower hole is fairly large in contrast to those of Villanovan II when the lower is much smaller as in Plate 105. 1:2. Museo Archeologico Florence.

39 Double cup of late Villanovan I, with an animal's head on the handle recalling the Apennine Bronze Age. 1:2. Museo Archeologico, Florence.

40 Triple cup of Villanovan I, with a human or animal handle. 2:3. Museo Archeologico, Florence.

41 Pottery boat of early Villanovan I, perhaps representing the ship of the deceased, much too large and valuable to be put in a pozzo grave. 1:4. Museo Archeologico, Florence.

42, 43 Spindle-whorl and spool of pottery. Villanovan I. These are among the objects denoting women's graves. 1:2. Museo Archeologico, Florence.

44 Amphora of a type commoner in the Trench Grave Culture of southern Italy and indicating southern influence among the Villanovans. Late Villanovan I. 1:4. Museo Archeologico, Florence.

45 Pottery boat with a foot like the stand in Plate 46 and having a little cup at one end. Evidence available since the preparation of my larger work on this subject (*Bulletin of the American School of Prehistoric Research*, vol. 23) allows this to be placed in early Villanovan I. 1:2. Museo Archeologico, Florence.

46 Stand, possibly really a lamp. Villanovan I. 1:2. Museo Archeologico, Florence.

47 Bird-shaped askos with a basket handle of early Villanovan I. It recalls such vases in the Aegean world and Cyprus but is locally made. 1:3. Museo Archeologico, Florence.

48 Ring-shaped askos with a basket handle recalling ring-shaped askoi in the Aegean and Cyprus, but this is a local product. Villanovan I. 1:3 Museo Archeologico, Florence.

49 Askos with a basket handle recalling the animal askoi of the Aegean and Cyprus, but this is a local product and represents the Dunubian horned animal-bird with a plump bird-like body and a bovine head. It had four stumpy legs of which the forelegs are replaced here by a piece of plasticene. Mid Villanovan I. 1:3. Museo Archeologico, Florence.

50 Sword of early Villanovan I, bronze with iron rivets in the hilt. This type occurs in the Modica hoard in Sicily in Pantalica II, about eleventh and tenth centuries BC. Length: 45 cm. Museo Archeologico, Florence.

51, 52 Spear and spear-butt. Late Villanovan I. Length: spear, 18 cm. spear-butt, 17 cm. Museo Archeologico, Florence.

53 Sword of late Villanovan I, with more elaborate decoration on the blade. Length: 40 cm. Museo Archeologico, Florence.

54 Crested helmet. Mid Villanovan I. 1:4. Museo Archeologico, Florence.

55, 56 Bit and cheek piece from a bridle. Villanovan I. The cheek-piece is in the form of the central European boat with a bird's head at either end with the 'sun-disc' (much corroded) in the middle. 55, 1:2; 56, 2:5. Museo Archeologico, Florence.

57 Bronze cup of central European derivation though made in Italy. Late Villanovan I. 1:2. Museo Archeologico, Florence.

58 Cylindrical bronze container surmounted by a double bird. Late Villanovan I. 1:2. Museo Archeologico, Florence.

59 Bronze mirror based on a Mycenaean type known in Sicily in Pantalica I about the twelfth to eleventh centuries BC. Early Villanovan I. Ht: 15 cm. Museo Archeologico, Florence.

60 Elongated lunate razor. Early Villanovan I. Length: 14 cm. Museo Archeologico, Florence.

61 Rectangular razor. Early Villanovan I. Ht: 14 cm. Museo Archeologico, Florence.

62 Arc fibula with a twisted bow. Early Villanovan I. Similar fibulae but with thinner bows are found in Greece between about the eleventh and ninth centuries BC. Actual size. Museo Archeologico, Florence.

63 Arc fibula with a striated bow. Early Villanovan I. Analogous fibulae occur in Sicily in Pantalica II, about eleventh and tenth centuries BC. Actual size. Museo Archeologico, Florence.

64 Serpentine fibula with a straight pin. Early Villanovan I. This type occurs in Sicily in Pantalica II, about eleventh to tenth centuries BC. Actual size. Museo Archeologico, Florence.

65 Leech-shaped fibula. Early Villanovan I. This shape reflects a Greek fashion in fibulae from the eleventh century BC and later. Actual size. Museo Archeologico, Florence.

66 Arc fibula with glass beads on the bow. Early Villanovan I. Actual size. Museo Archeologico, Florence.

67 Serpentine fibula with a curved pin of early Villanovan I, a type found in Sicily in Pantalica III, about tenth to eighth centuries BC. Actual size. Museo Archeologico, Florence.

68 Hollow bronze object of mid Villanovan I, perhaps for attaching to a rod. Villanovan I. Diam: 10 cm. Museo Archeologico, Florence.

69 Spindle-shaped beads. Late Villanovan I. Length: 7 cm. Museo Archeologico, Florence.

70 Bronze spindle of early Villanovan I, indicating a woman's grave. 1:2. Museo Archeologico, Florence.

71, 72 Gold-plated ornaments including a swastika. Late Villanovan I. Length: 71,5 cm.; 72,3 cm. Museo Archeologico, Florence.

73 Spiral with undulating ends. This type begins in mid Villanovan I. Length: 6.5 cm. Museo Archeologico, Florence.

74 Bronze tripod. Early Villanovan I. This is the metal counterpart of a pottery type from the Roman Forum of about the eleventh to tenth centuries BC, which in turn is derived from a Greek type of the eleventh century (Fig. 35, c, d). Ht: 20 cm. Museo Nazionale, Tarquinia.

75 Six-mouthed pot from Monterozzi, Villanovan. Ht: 15 cm. Museo di Villa Giulia, Rome.

76, 77 Pottery boats with bird's heads on the bow, probably respresenting the owner's ship, too large and valuable to be placed in a pozzo grave. Villanovan. 1:3. Museo di Villa Giulia, Rome.

78 Bird-shaped askos which probably had a basket handle. It recalls such vases in the Aegean world and Cyprus but is locally made. Villanovan. 1:2. Museo Archeologico, Florence.

79 Candalabrum from Monterozzi with Cretan analogies of the ninth and eighth centuries BC. 1:3. Museo Nazionale, Tarquinia.

80 Askos of a type common in Vetulonia and Sardinia and distantly recalling those of Cyrpus and Asia Minor. Villanovan. 1:3. Museo Archeologico, Florence.

81 Pottery bell helmet, a substitute for a bronze original too costly to be placed in the grave. 1:3. Villanovan. Museo Archeologico, Florence.

82 Three pots shaped like miniature Villanovan urns joined together and with a handle in the shape of a woman whose breasts and long hair are indicated. The three pots are connected by holes so that liquid could flow between them. Perhaps Villanovan I. 1:3. Museo di Villa Giulia, Rome.

83 Dish with seated figures, A with arms upraised, B with arms upraised and seated on chairs. Villanovan. 1:3. Museo Archeologico, Florence.

84 Pottery tripod, the counterpart of the bronze one in Plate 74. Villanovan. 1:3. Museo Nazionale, Tarquinia.

85 Pottery tripod, the counterpart of the bronze one in Plate 74. Villanovan. 1:3. Museo Archeologico, Florence.

86 Horned animal-bird of bronze of Danubian derivation from Monterozzi. Villanovan. 1:2. Museo Nazionale, Tarquinia.

87 Two pottery wheels and a pair of pottery horses, probably representing the dead man's chariot, too valuable and also too large to be put in Villanovan pozzo grave. Length: 18.5 cm. Villanovan. Museo Archeologico, Florence.

88 Iron sword, the counterpart of the bronze swords in Plates 50 and 53. Villanovan. 2:3. Museo Archeologico, Florence.

89 Iron spear. Villanovan. 1:2. Museo Archeologico, Florence.

90 Bronze cap helmet from Monterozzi with a tubular knob intended to hold a plume. This is attached by rivets. Villanovan. Ht: 20 cm. Museo Nazionale, Tarquinia.

91 Bronze cap helmet from Monterozzi decorated with eyes and eyebrows and with a tubular socket now broken attached by casting on. Villanovan, Ht: 15.2 cm. Museo Nazionale, Tarquinia.

92 Bronze bell helmet which differs from the cap helmet only in being more conical. From Monterozzi. It has a tubular socket for a plume attached by casting on. See Fig. 18. Villanovan. Ht: 21 cm. Museo Nazionale, Tarquinia.

93 Crested helmet from Monterozzi. The central feature of its design is a late version of the Danubian boat with a bird's head at either end and carrying the 'sun disc'. For this design see Fig. 19. Perhaps Villanovan I. 1:3. Museo Nazionale, Tarquinia.

94 Urn of Villanovan II, with two seated figures shaking hands. 1:4. Museo Archeologico, Florence.

95 Urn of Villanovan II, with two seated figures bowing to each other with outstretched arms. 1:4. Museo Archeologico, Florence.

96, 98 Urns of Villanovan II, in the Angular Style. 1:4. Museo Archeologico, Florence.

97 Pear-shaped urn. Villanovan II. 1:4. Museo Archeologico, Florence.

99 Rounded bowl of Villanovan II, with a ram's head on the handle. Such animal-headed handles represent a survival of Apennine Bronze Age tradition. 1:2. Museo Archeologico, Florence.

100 Rounded bowl of Villanovan II, with a horned handle. Such horned handles represent a survival of Apennine Bronze Age tradition. 1:2. Museo Archeologico, Florence.

101 Jar with a wide body, flaring rim, and narrow foot. Villanovan II. 1:3. Museo Archeologico, Florence.

102 Cover-bowl of Villanovan II, with two little points on the handle recalling the Apennine tradition of horned handles. 1:4. Museo Archeologico, Florence.

103 Cover-bowl of Villanovan II, with a little cup attached to the handle. Such little cups attached to pots are survivals from Villanovan I. 1:4. Museo Archeologico, Florence.

104 Jar with wide body, flaring rim, and narrow foot, and with a binocular handle surmounted by horns. Such horns on handles are a survival of Apennine Bronze Age tradition. 1:2. Museo Archeologico, Florence.

105 Cup of Villanovan II, with binocular handle with a very small lower hole and ribbing on its underside. Both these features are characteristic of Villanovan II. 1:2. Museo Archeologico, Florence.

106 Double cup of Villanovan II, with a binocular handle surmounted by a horned animal head. Such animal heads on handles are a survival of Apennine Bronze Age tradition. 1:3. Museo Archeologico, Florence.

107 Cup of Villanovan II, with a handle surmounted by a horned animal-head. Such animal-heads on handles are a survival of Apennine Bronze Age tradition. 1:3. Museo Archeologico, Florence.

108 Cup with a pottery tube in the middle and a ring of little depressions around it. From Monterozzi. This recalls the lids of Apennine milk boilers (Fig. 32, b) with an opening in the middle and a row of little holes around it. Diam: 9 cm. Museo Nazionale, Tarquinia.

109 Askos with a basket handle from Monterozzi, recalling the askoi of the Aegean and Cyprus. The basket handle is flanked by two human figures. Despite its basically eastern form, it is a local product, and it represents the Danubian horned animal-bird, here with a plump bird-like body and a bovine head. Its four legs are missing. Villanovan II. Length: 18 cm. Museo di Villa Giulia, Rome.

110 Pottery bell helmet of Villanovan II, decorated with little metal strips. 1:3. Museo Archeologico, Florence.

111 Bird-shaped askos, head and basket handle broken. Villanovan II. 1:2 Museo Archeologico, Florence.

112 Bottle-shaped jug. Villanovan II. The horned handle represents a survival of Apennine Bronze Age tradition. 1:2. Museo Archeologico, Florence.

113 Jug with a binocular handle with the very small lower hole characteristic of Villanovan II. The animal-head on the handle is a survival of Apennine Bronze Age tradition. 1:2. Museo Archeologico, Florence.

114 Bottle-shaped jug of Villanovan II. 1:2. Museo Archeologico, Florence.

115 Amphora of a type commoner in Latium and Campania and indicating southern influence among the Villanovans. Villanovan II. 1:2. Museo Archeologico, Florence.

116 Bowl of light-coloured and refined clay, whose horizontal reddish lines recall the pottery of Corinth in the second half of the eighth century BC. It covered the hydria in Plate 118. Though this vase contains Greek elements, the shape is not Greek, and it must be a local product. Villanovan II. 1:4. Museo Archeologico, Florence.

117 Spheroid jar of red ware on a foot inherited from late Villanovan I and decorated with white paint in the Villanovan manner. Its shape recalls Greek Geometric kraters. Villanovan II. 1:4. Museo Archeologico, Florence.

118 Hydria of Late Geometric type painted with water birds, but made in Etruria. It served as an urn in a grave of Villanovan II, and as with two-handled Villanovan urns, one of its handles is broken off. 1:4. Museo Archeologico, Florence.

119 Cup with a water-bird of Late Geometric type but probably a local product. Villanovan II. 1:4. Museo Archeologico, Florence.

120 Cup of Late Geometric type but probably a local product. Villanovan II. 1:4. Museo Archeologico, Florence.

121 Cap helmet from Monterozzi, with birds' heads all facing the same way and degenerate 'sun discs'. Villanovan II. Ht: 15 cm. Museo Nazionale, Tarquinia.

122 Cap helmet with a stylized human face and on the sides panels with the boat with two birds' heads carrying the 'sun disc.' For this design see Fig. 23. Villanovan II. Ht: 16 cm. Museo Archeologico, Florence.

123 Long-necked bronze amphora from Monterozzi. Villanovan II. 1:4. Museo Nazionale, Tarquinia.

124 Bronze amphora from Monterozzi, resembling a two-handled Villanovan urn. One of its handles has been broken off. Villanovan II. It has the same pattern of bird-boat and 'sun disc' as in Fig. 19. 1:4. Museo Nazionale, Tarquinia.

125 Bronze bowl perhaps of eastern Mediterranean derivation. Villanovan II. 1:4. Museo Archeologico, Florence.

126 Bronze censer. Villanovan II. 1:2. Museo Archeologico, Florence.

127 Cup of local manufacture with pendulum ornament on its base derived from central Europe or the southern Baltic area. Villanovan II. 1:3. Museo Nazionale, Tarquinia.

128 Bridle bit with horse-shaped cheek pieces from Monterozzi. This type is probably derived from Luristan, but the horses have a Greek Geometric

quality while at the same time having bird-like beaks, an odd combination respresenting Villanovan taste. Villanovan II. 1:2. Museo Nazionale, Tarquinia.

129 Bronze pectoral of Villanovan II from Monterozzi. It is a simpler version of the gold example from the Warrior's Tomb in Fig. 31, f. Ht: 15 cm. Museo Nazionale, Tarquinia.

130 Bronze girdle from Monterozzi. On the left is a double bird and on the right a 'sun disc' with two birds' heads on long necks attached to it. This forms one half of a double bird-boat as illustrated in Fig. 42, e. Villanovan II. 2:3. Museo Nazionale, Tarquinia.

131, 132 Wheel pendants, perhaps another form of the central European 'sun disc'. Villanovan II. Diam: 5.5 cm. Museo Archeologico, Florence.

133 Gold disc-pendant from Monterozzi. Villanovan II. Diam: 4 cm. Museo Nazionale, Tarquinia.

134, 135 Leech-shaped fibulae with somewhat lengthened catches and birds' heads from Monterozzi. Villanovan II. Length: 6 cm. Museo Nazionale, Tarquinia.

136 Two spindle-shaped beads of spiral wire. Villanovan II. Length: 10 cm. Museo Archeologico, Florence.

137 Leech-shaped fibulae with slightly lengthened catches, the larger of which has a bow of the exaggerated leech type. Villanovan II. Length: 6 and 4 cm. Museo Archeologico, Florence.

138 Electrum leech-shaped fibula from Monterozzi with granulation and filigree on the bow. These forms of ornament were eastern but were also taken up by the Greeks Length: 2.5 cm. Museo Nazionale, Tarquinia.

139 Warrior's Tomb, Monterozzi. Oinochoe of local make, but its rounded body and long conical neck suggests derivation from a type of Cypriot metal jug found in Italy; compare Plate 153. Villanovan II. No scale. After Åkerström. Staatliche Museen, Berlin.

140 Warrior's Tomb, Monterozzi. Askos in the shape of a bird with a horse's head and a row of drooping-tailed birds painted along it. This kind of zoomorphic askos with a basket handle could be inspired from Crete or Cyprus, but it is probably locally made. Villanovan II. No scale. After Åkerström. Staatliche Museen, Berlin.

141 Warrior's Tomb, Monterozzi. Skyphos of Greek type painted with drooping-tailed birds but probably locally made. Villanovan II. No scale. After Åkerström. Staatliche Museen, Berlin.

142 Pottery from Plopsor and Vîrtop, Romania. Left to right: an urn, a double cup, another urn, a tripod and a fruit stand. No scale. After Berciu. Craiova Museum.

143 Previllanovan house-urn from the vicinity of Tarquinia and of the same Latian type as those found in the Roman Forum and the Alban Hills. 1 : 3. Palazzo delle Science, Rome.

144 Askos in the shape of a horned animal-bird with four stumpy legs with a birdlike body and neck and a bovine head. From Bologna. No scale. Museo Civico, Bologna.

145 Horned bird of pottery, Ostrovul Mare, Romania. No scale. Muzeul Regiunii Portşilor de Fier, Turnu-Severin.

146 Horned bird, bronze, from Beravci, Slavonia. No scale. Arheološki Muzej, Zagreb.

147 Horned bird, bronze, from Isis Tomb, Vulci. No scale. British Museum.

148–50 Crested pottery helmet of Villanovan type, Villanovan urn and an Italo-Protocorinthian oinochoe all from Romanelli's Tomb 66, a pozzo grave on Monterozzi. Early Period III. Ht: 148, 31 cm.; 149, 41 cm.; 150, 26 cm. The helmet is in the Museo di Villa Giulia, Rome, and the urn and oinochoe are in the Museo Nazionale, Tarquinia.

151 Ring-shaped bull askos from a trench grave on Monterozzi. It combines the old Aegean or Cypriot ideas of an animal askos and a ring-shaped

askos, but it is of red ware of Villanovan descent. Period III. 1:3. Museo di Villa Giulia, Rome.

152 Spheroid jar of red ware on a foot from the same trench grave on Monterozzi that contained the oinochoe in Plate 153. The shape and the ware are of Villanovan descent, but the ribbing is new. Early Period III. 1:3. Museo Nazionale, Tarquinia.

153 Oinochoe from the same trench grave on Monterozzi that yielded the jar in Plate 152. The ornament is derived from the Late Geometric of Greece, but the rounded body and long conical neck resemble a type of Cypriot metal jug found in Italy. Compare Plate 141. Period III. 1:3. Museo Nazionale, Tarquinia.

154 Bottle-shaped jug from the Chamber Tomb of the Madonna del Pianto, Monterozzi. The shape of the jug, its ware and the handle in the shape of a horned animal are all features of Villanovan descent. Period III. No scale. Museo di Villa Giulia, Roma.

155 Large cup of dark polished ware perhaps from the Bocchoris Tomb on Monterozzi. The white paint visible on the foot is of Villanovan descent and the ware is also transitional between Villanovan dark polished ware and Etruscan bucchero, but the shape is new. Period III. 1:3. Museo Nazionale, Tarquinia.

156 Shield probably from the Avvolta Tomb of later Period III on Monterozzi. The concentric framework of the decoration is like that of the shield from the Warrior's Tomb of Villanovan II and the ornament on some of the bronze vessels of Villanovan II (see Fig. 22, a; 24, b, c; 27, f). But the following new elements are to be seen (beginning with the outer edge): a guilloche of oriental origin, a band of stylized lotus buds also oriental, a band of prancing horses, two bands of human figures, evidently women, and an innermost band of animals. No scale. Staatliche Museen, Berlin.

157 Ribbed jar on a foot probably from the Avvolta Tomb, Monterozzi. It is a further development in later Period III of the ribbed jar on a foot of

early Period III in Plate 152, but the high foot also recalls the pottery stand from the Bocchoris Tomb in Plate 158. The griffins' heads on the lid are of oriental origin but also occur in Greece. No scale. Staatliche Museen, Berlin.

158 Stand made of red ware inherited from Villanovan. From the Bocchoris Tomb of early Period III on Monterozzi. It was to support a large pot. Such stands and pots are the ceramic counterparts of oriental bronze stands and their cauldrons which are also known from Etruria. 1:5. Museo Nazionale, Tarquinia.

159 Figurines of Egyptian type but probably of Phoenician manufacture from the Bocchoris Tomb of early Period III on Monterozzi. Average height of figures 3 cm. Museo Nazionale, Tarquinia.

160 Handle of a bronze amphora from the Bocchoris Tomb of early Period III on Monterozzi. Its terminal in in the shape of a stylized oriental lotus bud. Ht: 17 cm. Museo Nazionale, Tarquinia.

161, 162 Gold pectoral probably from a chamber tomb of Period III on Monterozzi but not the Bocchoris Tomb. Its ornament is mainly oriental and (starting from the outside edge where best preserved) shows: Phoenician palmettes, guilloche, 'lions' looking backwards, guilloche, rosettes, guilloche, 'lions'?, guilloche, Phoenician palmettes. The only traces of Villanovan ornament are the rows of bosses surrounded by circles in the centre. 161, 1:4; 162, no scale. Museo Nazionale, Tarquinia.

163 Fibula from the Bocchoris Tomb of early Period III on Monterozzi. It is horse-shaped, continuing the idea of the animal fibula of Villanovan II (Fig. 31, b), but it also has a relationship to Greek Geometric horses, though the ape or monkey riding it may be due to Phoenician influence. Twice actual size. Museo Nazionale, Tarquinia.

164 Amphora of dark polished ware from the Bocchoris Tomb of early Period III found on Monterozzi. Its dark polished ware is of Villanovan origin but tending toward the later Etruscan bucchero. The shape is probably derived from Villanovan amphorae (Plates 44, 115), but above

the double spiral in the Phoenician palmette. 1:3. Museo Nazionale, Tarquinia.

165 The Bocchoris vase that gives its name to the Bocchoris Tomb of early Period III found on Monterozzi. The vase was evidently made in Egypt in the late eighth century. 1:2. Museo Nazionale, Tarquinia.

166 Skyphos from the Bocchoris Tomb of early Period III on Monterozzi. It is Italo-Protocorinthian and from the same workshop as the oinochoe in Plate 150. 1:3. Museo Nazionale, Tarquinia.

167, 168 Two oinochoai from the Chamber Tomb with Fish Oinochoai of Period III on Monterozzi. These have friezes of fish and recall vases from the Greek colony of Cumae near Naples, though that in Plate 169 is exceptional in having palm trees as well. 1:4. Museo Nazionale, Tarquinia.

169, 170 Two Italo-Corinthian olpai from a trench grave of the advanced sixth century on Monterozzi. 1:3. Museo Nazionale, Tarquinia.

171 Geometric figurine from a trench grave of Period III on Poggio Gallinaro. Actual size. Museo Archeologico, Florence.

172 Bucchero cup with a pair of lions with a common head on the handle. This is an ultimately Persian form or ornament. No scale. Museo Nazionale, Tarquinia.

173 Pot from a chamber tomb at Tarquinia with a very archaic form of the Etruscan alphabet. Period III. 2:3. Museo Nazionale, Tarquinia.

Index